OFF THE BEATEN PATH® SERIES

NINTH EDITION

OFF THE BEATEN PATH® CONNECTICUT ➡

A GUIDE TO UNIQUE PLACES

CINDI D. PIETRZYK

travel

Guilford, Connecticut

All the information in this guidebook is subject to change. We recommend that you call ahead to obtain current information before traveling.

Editor: Kevin Sirois
Project Editor: Lauren Brancato
Layout: Joanna Beyer
Text Design: Linda R. Loiewski
Maps by Equator Graphics © Morris Book Publishing, LLC

ISSN 1539-8641
ISBN 978-0-7627-8637-4

Printed in the United States of America
10 9 8 7 6 5 4 3 2 1

To Charley, Samantha, and Kailey—the brightest stars in my sky.

Contents

Acknowledgments

Authors always say that a book can't be written without the help of many people, but I'm not sure readers always appreciate just how true that statement is. Trust me, it's true! When I agreed to write this edition, my first thought was, "How will I find places to include?" My second thought was, "How am I going to fit all of this into one book?!" Connecticut is one of those little spaces that packs a whole lot of punch. There are so many hidden gems that uncovering them all would be impossible for one person. In that vein, I'd like to thank all those people who gave me suggestions, sent me in the right directions, visited places for me, and answered my questions.

Specifically, I'd like to thank Stephen Wood of CTMuseumQuest.com for his invaluable assistance in learning about our state's roadside rock art, especially his part in connecting me with Marge Wilson, who so willingly shared her story of Monster Rock in West Cornwall. Check out Steve's blog and follow his ramblings around the state.

Thank you to Ray Bendici for the information on DamnedCT.com and his willingness to share it.

A huge thank-you goes out to all the grassroots community groups who pulled together and saved so many historic sights for us to discover today. Without them, there just might not be a Connecticut off the beaten path.

Thanks always goes to my editor, Kevin Sirois, for having enough faith in me to trust me to do this edition, and for putting up with all my questions and neurosis. To Lauren Brancato, I'm so glad our paths have crossed again! Thanks to all the people at GPP who do what they do so well!

And finally I need to thank my husband, Steve, and my daughters once again for putting up with my hours away from them, the missed birthday parties, and the frantic scrambles to meet my deadlines, but most of all for accompanying me on our many journeys into the unknown. I am so glad we had the chance to discover our beautiful state together. May we have many more adventures.

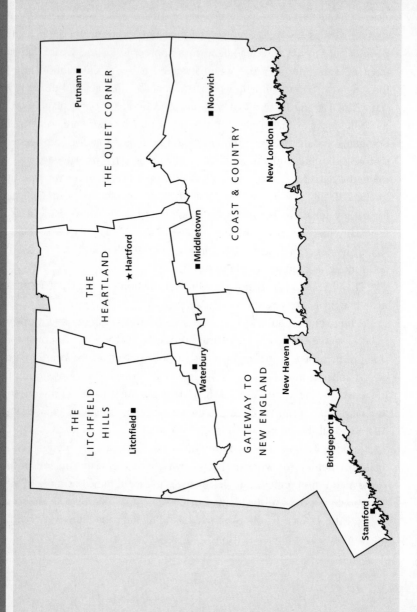

CONNECTICUT

THE LITCHFIELD HILLS

Litchfield ■

THE HEARTLAND

★ Hartford

Waterbury ■

GATEWAY TO NEW ENGLAND

New Haven ■

Bridgeport ■

Stamford ■

Putnam ■

THE QUIET CORNER

Norwich ■

Middletown ■

COAST & COUNTRY

New London ■

Introduction

"Twenty years from now you will be more disappointed by the things you didn't do than by the ones
you did do. So throw off the bowlines, sail away
from the safe harbor. Catch the trade winds in your
sails. Explore. Dream. Discover."   —Mark Twain

Nestled between the much larger states of New York and Massachusetts,
Connecticut should not be overlooked. While this little state occupies only
a bit more than 5,000 square miles along the coast of Long Island Sound, it
packs a punch. The third-smallest state in the Union, Connecticut has more
to offer than you might think. Nowhere in America can the traveler find so
representative a history, so rich a culture, and so great a physical diversity
packed into so small an area.

Connecticut's history is rich and varied. The Native Americans who
lived in the region for millennia before the arrival of the first Europeans
called it Quinnehtukqut ("Beside the Long Tidal River" or "Long River").
About 20,000 Native Americans lived in the area when the Dutch discovered the Connecticut River in 1614. As settlers and natives clashed, many of
the tribes were forced to work together, and tribal lines were blurred. Many
Native peoples who live today have
a mixed heritage from more than one
of these tribes.

English Puritans from Massachusetts began to move into Connecticut in 1633, and in 1638–1639, the
towns of Hartford, Windsor, and
Wethersfield adopted the Fundamental Orders of Connecticut, setting up
a government for the new Connecticut Colony. About the same time, the
colony of New Haven was founded farther west along the coast of Long
Island Sound. The two colonies were joined in 1662, and the state gained—
roughly—its current outline.

constitutionstate

Connecticut is called the "Constitution State" because the
Fundamental Orders, a govern-
ing principle based on the will of
the people, is considered one of
the first written constitutions of a
democratic government.

Since then the history of Connecticut has largely marched with that of America. During the past 350 years, the state has played a vital role in American experiences, such as the settlement of the frontier, the winning of the Revolutionary War, the adoption of the Constitution, the Union victory in the Civil War, and that vast upheaval known as the Industrial Revolution.

Connecticut's part in the American pageant has left a lasting mark on the state. Its towns have been ravaged by America's wars. Its language and culture have been molded by the nation's immigration patterns. Its geography has been altered by the spread of industrialization. Its economy has been shaped by the growth—and demise—of such industries as whaling, railroading, shipbuilding, and textile manufacturing. It has been, in many ways, a microcosm of America.

Sometimes known as the "Land of Steady Habits," Connecticut has taken as its official designation the title "Constitution State." George Washington called it the "Provision State" because it fed his army during the darkest days of the American Revolution.

Connecticut River

The Connecticut River is one of 14 waterways designated American Heritage Rivers by former vice president Al Gore.

The Connecticut River is 410 miles long—about 5,551 football fields.

Today's Connecticut River came into being between 10,000 and 13,000 years ago, after the Wisconsin Glacier receded from the New England area.

Connecticut developed about 220 million years ago in the late Triassic period.

The ecosystem of the Connecticut River watershed contains 10 endangered or threatened species:

- Three birds: the piping plover, the peregrine falcon, and the American bald eagle.

- One fish: the shortnose sturgeon

- One insect: the Puritan tiger beetle

- One mollusk: the dwarf wedge mussel

- Two plants: the Jesup's milk-vetch and small whorled pogonia

It is also called the "Nutmeg State," a sobriquet just as common as the official designation and perhaps more representative of Connecticut's history and culture; the name "Nutmegger" was often applied by the residents of neighboring states to Connecticut peddlers, who were famous for selling bogus nutmegs carved from local wood in place of the imported (and more expensive) real thing.

Whatever you call it, Connecticut is a land of odd contrasts and strange delights that have accumulated over centuries. Modern Connecticut has something to excite the whim and tickle the fancy of almost every traveler. Its diverse geography runs the gamut from the sandy beaches and teeming marshlands of its coastal plains and the fertile meadows of its central lowlands to the forested hills of the eastern and western uplands and the craggy granite cliffs that characterize its northwestern reaches. The many eras of its history are enshrined not only in countless museums, galleries, and restorations but in numerous historical structures that are still part of the everyday lives of its people; this is, in fact, one of the few places in America where you can find real Cape Cod saltboxes, Victorian gothic mansions, and Art Deco roadside palaces of the early automotive era all happily residing cheek by jowl.

In fact, residents of Connecticut take their history very seriously. Again and again strong Yankee ingenuity has been put into action, as dedicated Nutmeggers work to save historical property after historical property. Many times over, community action has resulted in the wonderful museums and galleries or historic neighborhoods you'll have the honor of exploring as you traverse this great state.

The densely populated cities along Connecticut's southwestern coast and the navigable portions of its major rivers are home to 90 percent of the state's inhabitants and give the state an urban flavor that stands in stark contrast to its rural uplands. This clustering of settlement along coasts and rivers explains why, even though Connecticut is the sixth–most densely populated state in the US (with an overall density of almost 740 persons per square mile), roughly 60 percent of the state is forest land. Most of the trees in these forests are northern hardwoods about 60 to 100 years old, and they are purely glorious in fall. In addition, approximately 11.5 percent of Connecticut is farmland.

In terms of amenities for the traveler, Connecticut has few equals. Though modern accommodations abound, this area, like most of New

England, is famous for its quaint inns and bed-and-breakfasts (or B&Bs), many of which are housed in buildings that have been around longer than the state. The eclectic cuisine, both cosmopolitan and casual, reflects the cultural and gustatory gifts brought to the state by succeeding waves of immigrants. Its great wealth and emphasis on tourism make Connecticut a shopping paradise; establishments range from some of America's largest and most attractive malls, to mom-and-pop operations offering only-in-Connecticut crafts, to factory outlets that fairly shout "bargains."

For the traveler who likes to venture off the beaten path, Connecticut is an especially satisfying venue; one constantly discovers the odd, the interesting, and the truly bizarre tucked away in the most unexpected places. Whether it be a mere whimsy, such as a roadside rock painted to look like a startlingly realistic giant frog, a truly spine-chilling gothic mystery, such as the deserted village of Bara-Heck Settlement, or something just plain nutty, such as the weird and wonderful United House Wrecking, you can never be entirely sure what you will find around the next bend.

We like to think of Connecticut as representing all the best of America in vest-pocket size: gilded beaches that would be the envy of California; rolling hills better than any in Virginia; pastoral farmland that makes you think you're in Indiana; downtown chic that rivals New York; and some of the friendliest people on earth. A truly dedicated traveler (and if you're reading this book, you probably fall into that category) could experience the full diversity of the state in one day. You could jump-start your day with an espresso in West Hartford, drive down to the shore for a few hours of sun and sand capped by a lunch of fried clams or lobster at the shore, and take an afternoon jaunt up into Litchfield County to browse the antiques shops before driving over to the Quiet Corner for a hayride through its fields and glens.

Geography isn't the only source of variety in Connecticut. Its northerly location and long coastline conspire to produce a multiplicity of seasonal variations in the weather. Each season brings its own wonders and offers its own characteristic activities. Winter means Old Wethersfield, all dressed up in the spare elegance of a colonial Christmas, pure white candles glowing in many-paned windows, and the faint sound of Christmas carols wafting across the green. Spring is the season for strolling along one of eastern Connecticut's back roads, watching farmers plow rolling farmlands, listening to the first few notes of birdsong, and sniffing the green tang of growing things in the air. Summer is a time for the shore; for golden beaches, the hiss of the waves, the crunch of fried seafood, and the sugary-sweet smell of cotton candy. Fall means Litchfield's amber and cinnabar hills, quintessentially New England white clapboard churches poised against the fiery reds of nearby sugar maples, the rush of the Housatonic, and the sweet taste of fresh-pressed cider and cider-glazed doughnuts.

Regardless of the season, traveling in Connecticut is easy, although traffic congestion has become an increasingly prevalent problem, especially during the summer, so you should build in extra time if you are planning to attend an event that has a specific starting time. Interstate highways crisscross the state, with I-95 (the Connecticut Turnpike) running the length of its shore, I-91 bisecting the state from north to south, I-395 winding along its eastern border, and I-84 running from Danbury through Waterbury to Hartford and then through the northeastern counties to the Massachusetts Turnpike. The interstate highway system is complemented by an excellent system of state highways. More often than not, this book takes you off the interstates and puts you on the smaller roads that evolved with our state's history from Indian trails to two-lane paved roads. Some of these back roads may seem awfully isolated. But never fear; no matter how far into the outback it feels, you're never more than half an hour from a major highway that will quickly return you to more populated areas.

Clearly, no one book can do justice to Connecticut's 350 years of history or to the diverse delights packed into this one small state. Just as an example, we're pretty certain that there's not a township in the state that doesn't have at least one museum located in a restored 17th- or 18th-century house and furnished with antiques and artifacts culled from local attics. We could, with some encouragement, write an entire book just on restored buildings.

We have, however, endeavored to include many stops on **_Connecticut's Freedom Trail_**, which includes locations that were important in the battle to end slavery, even if some are just a mere mention. For a complete listing of sites, go to ctfreedomtrail.org. We need to add a caution here, though, about these stops. While some are public museums, many are privately owned and are pointed out for informational purposes only and to give you the chance to see them if you're driving by. Please respect the property owners' privacy and view these properties only from the road.

As in most of life, some judicious editing is necessary. Thus, you won't find herein detailed descriptions of the well-known delights of Mystic or the popular casinos at Foxwoods or Mohegan Sun. Nor do we devote much space to the major attractions in the state's larger cities. These items are well documented in a host of travel books and brochures, many of which are available through Connecticut's tourism division. That office has divided the state into five tourism districts, each with a local office that can provide you with maps and information about the area. For further information on popular attractions and tourism in general, call or visit the **Connecticut Commission on Culture & Tourism** (860-256-2800; cultureandtourism.org).

This book does not pretend to compete with the State of Connecticut in offering general travel information or describing nationally famous attractions. Instead, we offer a directory of out-of-the-way places that you might not know to look for if you're not native to the area. Where can you get the best pizza or ice cream or chili dog in the state? Where will you find the most interesting pottery or the neatest antiques or the strangest stores? Where can you experience the uniquely Connecticut and the perfectly New England without having to fight the crowds? We may miss some of the major attractions, but if it's funky, funny, little known, or out of the way, you'll probably find it here.

For the purposes of this book, we've divided the state into five chapters, matching Connecticut's major geographic, historical, and cultural divisions. Within those chapters are smaller sections to help keep things organized. However, we have not laid things out, necessarily, in travel order. For example, it may make more sense for you to visit an attraction in western East Haddam and then move west to Haddam before visiting an attraction on the eastern side of East Haddam, but we have included all the East Haddam attractions in one section. Then we list the Haddam attractions, and so on. We suggest that when planning a trip, you pull out a Connecticut state map and look at all the surrounding towns. Decide where you'd like to go, then use a nifty route planner, in which you plug in street addresses (all of which we have provided for you), and the computer maps your route for you. You can see at a glance the best way to see everything on your list and how much time it will take.

In today's world, social media sites are invaluable for up-to-the-minute news on all your favorite places. We strongly suggest you "like," "follow," and "subscribe" to places you plan to visit. This way you'll know about special events, pricing, and closings ahead of time.

Tourism Information

The Connecticut Commission on Culture & Tourism annually publishes the *Connecticut Vacation Guide* and other publications of interest to visitors. These items are available for free by calling (888) 288-4748. The commission's web address is ctvisit.com.

Five regional tourism districts around the state provide information, guides, and special event listings targeted to their regions. Please note that these divisions do not necessarily match those in our book.

Here's how to contact the tourism districts:

Greater Hartford Convention & Visitors Bureau
31 Pratt St., 4th Floor
Hartford, CT 06103
(800) 446-7811
enjoyhartford.com

Central Regional Tourism District
1 Constitution Plaza, 2nd Floor
Hartford, CT 06103
visitctriver.com
This includes parts of Coast & Country and the Heartland.

Western Connecticut Convention & Visitors Bureau
PO Box 968
Litchfield, CT 06759

(860) 567-4506
litchfieldhills.com
This includes coastal Fairfield area.

Greater New Haven
127 Washington Ave., 4th Floor West
North Haven, CT 06473
(203) 777-8550
visitnewhaven.com

Mystic Country
27 Coogan Blvd., Building 3A
Mystic, CT 06355
(860) 536-8822
mystic.org
This includes the Quiet Corner area.

A bed-and-breakfast reservation service will help you find the inn that's right for you: bbonline.com/ct.

Fall Foliage

In most of Connecticut, fall foliage hits its peak around Columbus Day. Areas in the north, northwest, and northeast see peak color a little earlier. Starting in late September, you can get a daily fall foliage update by visiting

The following state agencies can provide other information on travel in Connecticut:

Department of Economic & Community Development Offices of Culture and Tourism
One Constitution Plaza, 2nd Floor
Hartford, CT 06106
(860) 256-2800
ct.gov/cct/site/default.asp

Museum of Connecticut History
231 Capitol Ave.
Hartford, CT 06106
(860) 757-6535
museumofcthistory.org

Department of Energy & Environmental Protection
79 Elm St.
Hartford, CT 06106-5127
(860) 424-3000
ct.gov/deep/site/default.asp

ct.gov/deep/site/default.asp and clicking on the Fall Foliage link; you can even sign up for text and/or e-mail updates.

Food in Connecticut

Here in Connecticut, our cuisine is an amalgam of rugged colonial dishes leavened with ethnic foods, the heritage of the immigrants who helped transform our state. It all makes for a diverse and heady cuisine. Try to sample some of these emphatically Connecticut foods when you visit.

Chowder. The origins of its name, *chaudière* (large kettle), may be French, but this hearty soup is all New England. You won't find as many fish chowders in Connecticut as in other parts of New England, but we make stellar clam chowders.

- **New England clam chowder** is a milk- or cream-based soup full of potatoes, onions, whole clams, and salt pork and seasoned with thyme. It's probably the version you think of when someone mentions clam chowder.

- **Rhode Island clam chowder** is New England clam chowder lightened with just enough pureed tomatoes to turn the soup a rosy pink.

- **Southern New England clam chowder** is a bracing, briny broth loaded with clams, potatoes, and onions—no milk or cream.

- **Manhattan clam chowder** is a tomato-based veggie soup with a few clams.

Check out the clam chowder offerings at Abbott's Lobster in the Rough in Noank or Lenny and Joe's Fish Tale Restaurants in Westbrook and Madison.

Lobster roll. In some New England states, a lobster roll is lobster salad (cold lobster, mayonnaise, seasonings) served on a toasted hot dog bun. But in Connecticut, a lobster roll is a spiritual experience: fresh, hot lobster meat, dripping with melted butter, served on a sesame-seed hamburger bun or toasted hot dog bun. Be sure to try one, and don't forget the extra napkins for wiping butter-drenched chins and fingers.

Grape-Nuts pudding. Baked custard served in a sweet shell of Grape-Nuts cereal; one version features a swirl of Grape-Nuts throughout the pudding. Much better than it sounds. Check out Zip's Dining Car in Dayville for Zip's recipe for Grape-Nuts pudding.

Indian pudding. A robust dessert dating back to colonial times, it's a mix of cornmeal, molasses, and warm spices cooked for hours at a low temperature until thick and amber-colored. Some heretics add raisins or apples. Served with vanilla ice cream or a rivulet of heavy cream. The Griswold Inn in Essex usually has Indian pudding on its fall and winter dessert menu.

Pizza. New Haven is the pizza capital of Connecticut, maybe of the US. New Haven pizza has a thin and crunchy crust and doesn't wallow in toppings. Pepe's and Sally's are the traditional top choices among New Haven pizza palaces. In Hartford County, the pizza at Harry's in West Hartford Center is glorious.

Famous Nutmeggers

- **Bill Blass,** designer

- **George W. Bush,** 43rd US president

- **David Bushnell,** inventor of the submarine

- **Glenn Close,** actress

- **Samuel Colt,** popularized the revolver

- **Plácido Domingo,** opera singer

- **Dominick Dunne,** author

- **Michael J. Fox and Tracey Pollan,** actors

- **Charles Goodyear,** inventor of vulcanized rubber

- **Katharine Hepburn,** actress

- **Dustin Hoffman,** actor

- **Elias Howe,** sewing machine inventor

- **Henry Kissinger,** diplomat

- **Larry Kramer,** AIDS activist and author

- **Edwin P. Land,** Polaroid camera inventor

- **Frank McCourt,** author

- **Arthur Miller,** playwright

- **Paul Newman and Joanne Woodward,** actors

- **Jacques Pépin,** chef and author

- **Keith Richards,** musician and rock star

- **Philip Roth,** novelist

- **Meg Ryan,** actress

- **Maurice Sendak,** author and illustrator

- **Igor Sikorsky,** inventor of the helicopter

- **Benjamin Spock,** pediatrician

- **William Styron,** author

- **Diane von Furstenberg,** designer

- **Horace Wells,** pioneered the use of nitrous oxide anesthesia

- **Eli Whitney,** cotton gin inventor

State Symbols

- **Official designation:** Constitution State

- **Indian name:** Quinnehtukqut—"Beside the Long Tidal River"

- **State motto:** He who was transplanted still sustains

- **State flower:** mountain laurel

- **State bird:** robin

- **State tree:** white oak

- **State animal:** sperm whale

- **State insect:** praying mantis

- **State mineral:** garnet

- **State song:** "Yankee Doodle"

- **State ship:** USS *Nautilus*

- **State shellfish:** eastern oyster

- **State composer:** Charles Edward Ives

- **State poet laureate:** Dick Allen

- **State fossil:** *Eubrontes giganteus,* an 18-foot-long carnivore

- **State hero:** Nathan Hale

- **State heroine:** Prudence Crandall

Connecticut Firsts & Notables

1639: Connecticut adopts the country's first written constitution, the Fundamental Orders of Connecticut.

1647: Hartford hangs the first witch in the colonies at what is now the corner of Albany Avenue and Garden Street.

1656: New Haven creates the first public library from a gift of books from Theophilus Eaton.

1660: Hopkins Grammar School is established, the first private secondary school.

1737: Samuel Higley of Simsbury produces the first copper coinage in America.

1740: The Pattison brothers (Edward and William) of Berlin make tinware, which they sell door to door. This enterprise inaugurates the tradition of the "Yankee peddler," that slippery Connecticut character responsible for relieving countless residents of neighboring colonies of their excess cash.

1761: Jupiter Hammond of Hartford becomes the first African-American poet to be published.

1764: Publication of the *Connecticut Courant* (now the *Hartford Courant*), the nation's oldest continuously published newspaper, begins.

1771: The colony forms the Governor's Foot Guard, the oldest military unit in America.

1775: David Bushnell launches the first submarine, the *American Turtle*.

1776: Nathan Hale, a Nutmegger and the country's first martyr, is executed in Manhattan.

1777: The first trimmed and illuminated Christmas tree in America is erected in Windsor Locks.

1780: Benedict Arnold of Norwalk becomes the new nation's most famous traitor.

1783: Noah Webster's blue-backed speller is printed in Hartford by Hudson & Goodwin.

1784: America's first law school—Tapping Reeve—is established in Litchfield.

1796: Hartford's Amelia Simmons, who styled herself "an American Orphan," publishes America's first cookbook, *American Cookery*.

1801: A Mrs. Prout of South Windsor makes America's first cigars, the Long Nines.

1803: Salisbury establishes the first children's library.

1806: Noah Webster publishes America's first dictionary.

1809: Mary Kies receives a patent for weaving silk with straw or thread. She is the first American woman to receive a patent.

1814: Eli Terry patents the first shelf clock in Thomaston.

1817: The first school for the hearing impaired—the American School for the Deaf—is founded in Hartford.

1844: Charles Goodyear of New Haven receives a patent for vulcanization of rubber.

1854: Hartford votes to create Bushnell Park, America's first municipal park.

1873: The first football game is played at Yale University.

1878: The world's first telephone exchange opens for business in New Haven, and publishes the first telephone directory, which contained only 50 names.

1881: P. T. Barnum introduces the three-ring circus.

1889: Stamford's George C. Blickensderfer invents the first portable typewriter.

1891: William Gray of Hartford invents the world's first coin-operated pay telephone.

1897: The automobile industry is born when Albert Pope and Hiram Maxim show off their electric car.

1904: The first submarine base is established at Groton.

1906: Hartford's Alfred C. Fuller makes the housewife's life a little easier when he starts selling door to door the first twisted-in wire house brush.

1909: Hiram P. Maxim invents the gun silencer.

1917: John Browning invents the automatic pistol, Browning machine gun, and Browning automatic rifle, all for Hartford's Colt Firearms.

1919: Homogenized milk is first sold in Torrington.

1920: Stamford's Pitney Bowes introduces the first US postage meter.

1931: The first electric shaver is made in Stamford.

1934: Consumer advocate Ralph Nader is born in Winsted.

1937: Margaret Rudkin puts on her apron and bakes the first loaf of Pepperidge Farm bread in Fairfield.

1937: Connecticut becomes the first state to issue permanent license plates for cars.

1939: Igor Sikorsky builds the first helicopter in Stratford.

1949: James Wright of New Haven invents Silly Putty, delighting kids and frustrating moms everywhere who find the stuff impossible to remove from the family dog's fur.

1954: First nuclear submarine—the *Nautilus*—is launched in Groton.

1960: The world's first two-sided building, also known as the Boat Building, is erected in Hartford. It is the headquarters of the Phoenix Mutual Insurance Company.

1965: Connecticut becomes the first state to require cities with populations of more than 20,000 to use fluoride in municipal drinking water.

1975: Ella T. Grasso is the first woman in America to assume the office of governor without inheriting it from her husband.

1982: Dr. Robert K. Jarvik, a Stamford native, invents the world's first artificial heart.

1994: Nancy Wyman becomes the first woman to be elected Connecticut state comptroller.

1994: Jodi Rell becomes the first female Republican to hold the office of Connecticut lieutenant governor.

1998: Denise Nappier is the first African-American woman in the US to be elected state treasurer, the first woman (of any color) to be elected to that position in Connecticut.

1998: The Women's Health Research program is founded at Yale by Carolyn M. Mazure.

1998: Moira K. Lyons becomes the first woman to serve as Speaker of Connecticut's House of Representatives.

2000: Torrington native Susan Cogswell becomes the first woman to be Connecticut's insurance commissioner.

2007: The *Amistad,* located at Mystic Seaport, gains its first female captain, Eliza Garfield.

2009: University of Connecticut alum Rebecca Lobo is inducted into the Basketball Hall of Fame, becoming the state's first inductee.

2010: Dr. Susan Herbst becomes UConn's first female president, *and* the women's basketball team sets an NCAA record by winning 90 consecutive games.

2011: Groton's US naval base accepts its first class of female officers.

2012: Alice Bruno becomes the Connecticut's Bar Association's first female executive director.

Places to Stay & Places to Eat Price Codes

At the end of each chapter are area accommodations and restaurants you'll want to check out.

The rating scale for accommodations is based on double occupancy and is as follows:

Inexpensive: Less than $100 per night
Moderate: $100 to $200 per night
Expensive: More than $200 per night

The rating scale for restaurants is based on the price of an entree without beverages, desserts, tax, or tip, and is as follows:

Inexpensive: Less than $10
Moderate: $10 to $20
Expensive: More than $20

Please remember, these are rough guidelines and should not be considered actual rates. Always call ahead to confirm.

THE HEARTLAND

The upper Connecticut River Valley is a broad, fertile meadowland ideal for farming and grazing, and the state's Puritan settlers were naturally drawn to it. It was the first part of Connecticut to be colonized, and those original settlements thrived and expanded until they finally merged to form what is today Greater Hartford, a vibrant metropolitan area of almost 900,000 people.

Bounding Hartford County's urban and suburban core on the north and west are the rural Tobacco and Farmington Valleys. To the east is pastoral Tolland County, and to the south are New Haven County and Connecticut's Coast & Country areas. Within these rural boundaries is Connecticut's heartland, the seat of its government and one of its most important commercial centers. As you might suspect, the majority of the attractions in this area are historical and cultural; in addition, you can find the commercial activities and entertainments of a large metropolitan area.

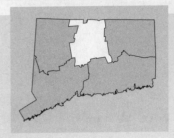

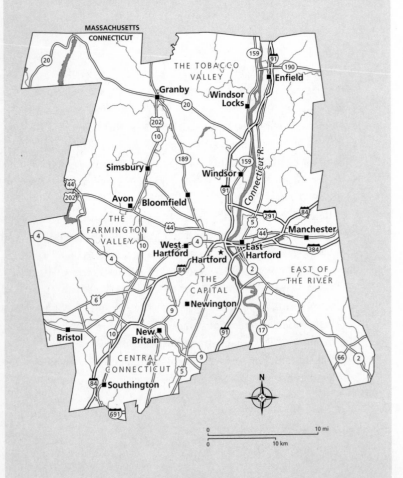

MASSACHUSETTS
CONNECTICUT

THE TOBACCO VALLEY

20

159
91
190

Granby

Windsor Locks

Enfield

20

202
10

189

159

Simsbury

Windsor

91

44
202

Avon

Bloomfield

Connecticut R.

THE FARMINGTON VALLEY

44

4

291

84

10

5

44

Manchester

4

West Hartford

4

East Hartford

384

Hartford ★

6

THE CAPITAL

2

EAST OF THE RIVER

9

Newington

Bristol

10

New Britain

91

17

9

66

2

CENTRAL CONNECTICUT

5

84

Southington

N

691

0   10 mi

0   10 km

The Capital

Hartford

Officially settled in 1635, **Hartford** was important in the 19th century as a center of the abolitionist movement and the tobacco industry. A hub of activity, Hartford played an integral part in shaping our nation's history. Merchants traded molasses, spices, coffee, and rum along with the tobacco from warehouses throughout the city. The Colt Firearms Factory, maker of the Colt Revolver, "the gun that won the West," called Hartford home.

Many Connecticut residents fought for freedom on more than one front. Many men went to battlegrounds throughout the region and fought on the front lines, but many stayed home and fought for freedom on a different level—a secret, underground level. Many places throughout the state saw the desperate fight for freedom through slaves' eyes, and many of our residents went above and beyond to help them. A tribute to these freedom fighters is on display in the **Museum of Connecticut History** (231 Capitol Ave.; 860-757-6535; museumofcthistory.org) in the form of the Connecticut Freedom Trail Quilt Project. Each square in these quilts represents one part of the story of our state's Freedom Trail. They are but one of the great exhibits throughout this not-to-be-missed public museum. The best part? Admission is free. Open Mon through Fri 9 a.m. to 4 p.m., Sat 9 a.m. to 2 p.m. Closed on state holidays and on Sat when a holiday observance falls on a Fri or Mon. Call ahead to be sure.

In more recent times the city has grown tamer and gained the moniker the "Insurance City," as Hartford is where insurance was born. Dating back to the city's thriving merchant district, from which many ships set sail to England and other far-off ports, the need for protection from pirates, storms, and accidents was prevalent. In 1810 the Hartford Fire Insurance Group was created, and it still operates today. Other insurance entrepreneurs followed suit. By 1898 the first automobile insurance policy, at the staggering cost of two cents, had been issued by Travelers Insurance Company, and the rest, as they say, is history. Today, even with consolidation and downsizing, Connecticut's capital city is still the place to be if you want to live long and prosper with insured security.

A testament to that industry is a pyramid-topped edifice completed in neoclassical style in 1919 by Donn Barber, an architect from New

connecticut
freedomtrail

Churches regularly played a very important part in our state's civil history, as they continue to do today. When people need a place to contemplate, grieve, come together as a community, or just question or affirm life in general, our churches offer sanctuary. Three such churches on Hartford's Main Street have served that purpose for many years and were especially important in the lives of our African-American civil libertists. All these churches are listed on the National Register of Historic Places. If you'd like to stop, sit, and contemplate for a spell, they are the *Metropolitan A.M.E. Zion Church* (2051 Main St.), the *Union Baptist Church* (1921 Main St.), and the *Faith Congregational Church* (2030 Main St.).

York who also designed the Hartford Times building, the Connecticut State Library, and the Connecticut Supreme Court Building, the *Travelers Tower.* In all its pink granite glory, the tower looms 527 feet over Hartford for visual prominence—including after nightfall, when its beacon shines. The tower was the seventh-tallest building in America when it was built, and stood for a long time as New England's tallest building and prominent home to Travelers Property & Casualty. In 2004 Travelers merged with another company and became St. Paul Travelers and is now based in St. Paul, Minnesota. The tower, however, continues to delight visitors and residents alike; in fact, certain visitors liked it so much they decided to call it home. No, we're not talking human visitors, but a peregrine falcon family that made its home there first in 2000. Here in Connecticut we take the protection of endangered species seriously, and our Department of Energy and Environmental Protection (DEEP) went so far as to install a "falconcam" at the sight. For years, people have been able to watch falcons nest, lay eggs, and care for their young ones. Unfortunately, the nest has since been relocated to nearby Travelers Tower and the cameras temporarily taken down due to building maintenance. The nest is being monitored closely, and you can check out future updates and past history, including pictures of the generations of baby falcons, at falconcam.travelers.com.

If you're in the city and have time, be sure to stop at the tower and ride the elevator (for free!) to the 24th floor, then climb a 72-step spiral staircase to the 27th-floor observation deck, where you can enjoy spectacular, falconlike views of the city. Open Mon through Fri from 10 a.m. to 3 p.m., mid-May until the last week of Oct. Call (860) 277-4208. Viewing spaces are both inside and on an outdoor deck.

Once you're ready, head into the center of the city to the traditional starting point for a tour of Hartford. The **Old State House** (800 Main St.; 860-522-6766; ctoldstatehouse.org) has a long and interesting history. Construction on the building began in 1792 but was not completed until 1796 due to various financial obstacles. Since then, the magnificent building has seen many improvements and changes as well as a wealth of history. It has faced the wrecking ball many times, but each time Nutmeggers rallied and saved this important part of their history. In 1961 the Old State House was named a National Historic Landmark. In the late 1970s, the Old State House Association set forth to turn the building into the museum you see today. Currently it houses a number of exhibits—some inspiring, including hands-on children's activities, and others just wonderfully silly. It all adds up to great fun in the least stuffy historical site/museum you're likely to come across. For travelers off the beaten path, the big draw is a re-creation of Joseph Steward's Curiosity Room with its conglomeration of "natural and other curiosities." The wide-ranging diversity from near and far includes "A Calf with Two Complete Heads," African tribal masks, sharks' jaws, a stuffed cobra, giant tortoise shells, artfully impaled tropical insects, a wing-spread bat under glass, a crocodile's head, and drawers full of birds' eggs. For the more serious-minded, there are various historical displays and a famous portrait of George Washington by Gilbert Stuart. There's also a gift shop and a fairly extensive tourist information center. The latter is a good place to start a tour of downtown Hartford; you'll find directions to enough museums, homesteads, galleries, and such to keep you busy for at least a week.

What looks vaguely like a National Guard armory as you do some sightseeing on Main Street is actually one of Hartford's most distinguished

AUTHOR'S FAVORITES

Dinosaur State Park

Elizabeth Park Rose Gardens

First Company of the Governor's Horse Guards

New Britain Museum of American Art

High Victoriana in Hartford

Its 8-sided gilded cupola gleaming in sunlight, Connecticut's **State Capitol** greets your eyes when you come into Hartford by way of I-84. Designed by Richard M. Upjohn, primarily a cathedral architect, this high Victorian gothic–style colossus — completed on its hilltop site in 1878 — is a marble-and-granite riot of pinnacles, turrets, columns, bas reliefs, statues, heraldic emblems, arches, and porticoes. In addition to state executive offices and legislative chambers, the capitol building offers a variety of historic exhibits, including bullet-riddled battle flags, vintage weaponry, the Marquis de Lafayette's canvas camp bed, and Israel Putnam's tombstone. Visitors can take a 1-hour guided tour of the premises between 9:15 a.m. and 1:15 p.m. on weekdays year-round (to 2:15 p.m. in July and Aug). The Capitol and Legislative Office buildings are closed on weekends. If you're in the area and want to visit, go to the League of Women Voters information desk on the 1st floor by the west entrance (210 Capitol Ave.). If time allows, though, it's best to call ahead and schedule a tour. For more information, visit cga.ct.gov or call (860) 240-0222. If you prefer, you can certainly take a self-guided tour. Be sure to ask for a free, fully detailed booklet before you embark.

cultural institutions: the **Wadsworth Atheneum** (600 Main St.; 860-278-2670; thewadsworth.org). Founded in 1842 by Daniel Wadsworth, the Atheneum is our nation's oldest public art museum The mock-gothic "armory appearance" constitutes the central part of an architectural grouping of the museum's 5 buildings that includes Renaissance revival and Tudor-style add-ons. The Wadsworth Atheneum's holdings now exceed 50,000 works, with the strongest emphasis on all periods of American and European art. Head upstairs to view a couple of world-class attractions—the Nutting collection of early American furniture and idyllic 19th-century landscapes painted by such Hudson River School exponents as Frederic Edwin Church, Thomas Cole, Albert Bierstadt, and Sanford Gifford. A gallery devoted to decorative arts includes 18th- and

hartfordtrivia

In the mid-1700s the men who lived along the Connecticut River and accumulated vast wealth from the West Indies trade were known as River Gods. You can see a re-creation of a formal parlor belonging to one of the River Gods at the Atheneum. For the 1700s those River God boys lived very well indeed.

Amistad Center for Art & Culture

Housed in the Wadsworth Atheneum, the Amistad Center for Art & Culture offers thousands of pieces of history that evidence the important role African Americans played in our history. You'll find posters, photos, books, and various changing exhibits throughout the year.

19th-century china crafted in half a dozen countries. And save time to admire large-scale American colonial canvases turned out by John Trumbull, born in Lebanon, Connecticut, and the son of an early state governor. The museum is closed Mon and Tues, otherwise open 11 a.m. to 5 p.m. Wed through Fri, with extended hours to 8 p.m. on the first Thurs of every month; and 10 a.m. to 5 p.m., Sat and Sun. The museum offers free admission on the second Saturday of the month if you arrive before 1 p.m. Many local libraries also offer free passes. Be sure to check the museum's website for an ongoing list of special events and exhibits.

Art lovers should make a point of seeing two famous pieces of art in the downtown area. Connecticut's own Alexander Calder's **Stegosaurus** is a huge, red steel construction that towers over the Alfred E. Burr Memorial Mall, a pocket park between the Wadsworth Atheneum and Hartford City Hall. This Hartford treasure stands 50 feet tall and has stood its ground since 1973. As you continue north, turn left onto Gold Street and watch for Carl Andre's **Stone Field** sculpture. Not that you can miss it. This $87,000 sculpture has always been a subject of conversation in Hartford. It consists of 36 large rocks arranged in rows on a slope of lawn. Some critics consider it a statement of minimalist art; some witty citizens call it Hartford's Meadow Muffins. You decide what it really is.

hartfordtrivia

Founded in 1764, the *Hartford Courant* (once the *Connecticut Courant*) is our country's oldest continuously published newspaper. The *Courant* has been around long enough to report the Boston Tea Party as breaking news. In 1796 a Virginia farmer named George Washington advertised in its real estate section.

After you check out *Stone Field,* walk over to the **Ancient Burying Ground** (corner of Gold and Main Streets near Center Church; 860-280-4145; theancientburyingground.org). This cemetery was created in 1640 and holds the bones of some of Hartford's most prominent citizens, including Thomas Hooker. It's also the site of the **African-American Memorial** that honors the unmarked graves of more than 300 African Americans, including five governors, who are buried here. If you're a fan of early American art, the tombstones are a treasure trove of colonial death imagery and epitaphs. The cemetery is open Apr 1 through Nov 30, Mon through Fri 8:30 a.m. to 4:30 p.m., Sat 9 a.m. to 5 p.m.

While strolling through the downtown area, look up at the architecture. Hartford has many buildings with some lovely gothic ornamentation that

Connecticut Freedom Trail Cemeteries

Old North Cemetery (N. Main Street at Mather Street) contains the graves of numerous African-American Civil War soldiers. Some served in the state's all-black 29th Regiment, some were from the 31st Regiment US Colored Troops, and some came from other units. Many of the headstones have since gone missing, but at one time there were almost 30 military-issued headstones here. Take notice of headstones that are generally made of marble (or granite) and have a rounded top; these are usually military issue. The soldier's name typically will appear at the top with his company, regiment, date of death, and age.

Also located in Old North Cemetery is the grave of Mary Townsend Seymour, a civil activist and leader in Hartford. She is credited with cofounding the city's chapter of the National Association for the Advancement of Colored People (NAACP), fighting for women's rights, and being active in local and state politics. In fact, she was the first black woman to run for a state office. Seymour fought tirelessly throughout her life and in 2006 was inducted into the Connecticut Women's Hall of Fame. You'll find her family plot on the left side of the drive if you enter the cemetery from Main Street and walk toward the back gate.

Since you're in the area, be sure to stop and explore *Spring Grove Cemetery* (2035 Main St.). Here you'll find the final resting place of William Henry Jacklyn, Hartford's first African-American firefighter, along with that of Laurent Clerc, American School for the Deaf founder.

Both cemeteries are open from dawn to dusk.

are certainly worthy of a second look. If you're a fan of gargoyles, grotesques, greenmen, and chimeras, you won't be disappointed. Be sure to check out the gargoyles protecting **Christ Church Cathedral** (45 Church St.; 860-527-7231; cccathedral.org), and the wolf and salamander gargoyle ornamenting the Richardson Building (942 Main St.), formerly the G. Fox building and now a hotel, office building, and rehearsal area for the Hartford Stage Company.

Next to the State Capitol building on Jewell Street is **Bushnell Park** (166 Capitol Ave.; bushnellpark.org), the oldest publicly funded park in the country, and one of the first plots of land in America acquired through eminent domain for use as a park. The vision of Rev. Horace Bushnell, the park was first known as City Park and was designed not by Fredrick Olmstead as many think, but by Jacob Weidenmann, a Swiss-born architect. Olmstead was busy on New York's Central Park when Reverend Bushnell asked him to work on the project, and he recommended Weidenmann instead. Now, more than a hundred years later, the renamed Bushnell Park continues to be "a place of life and motion," as its creators intended. Fun activities usually are taking place somewhere in the park, but there are also plenty of places to sit quietly and enjoy the beauty. Whatever your plans, definitely take the time to explore this park's hidden treasures, including the 1914 **Bushnell Carousel** (860-585-5411; thecarouselmuseum.org), whose 48 antique Stein and Goldstein horses revolve beneath 800 twinkling lights. The band organ is a refurbished 1925 Wurlitzer, and yes, you really can try to catch a brass ring. The park is open year-round, but the carousel operates only mid-May through mid-Oct. It is run by the New England Carousel Museum. Hours can be erratic, so it's best to check ahead. There's a small charge to ride, but it's well worth it.

Visitors will also want to stop and appreciate the history behind the monuments within Bushnell Park—the Soldiers & Sailors Memorial Arch (1886), Corning Fountain (1899), the bronze monument to Israel Putnam (1874), the statue of Horace Wells

hartfordtrivia

According to *Yankee* magazine, Bushnell Park is the proud possessor of the largest turkey oak (*Quercus cerris*) in New England. Its trunk is nearly 17 feet around. The tree gets its moniker from the crinkled edges of its leaves, which remind some of a tom turkey's tail feathers.

(1874), and the Spanish American War Memorial. Horticulturists may find the half-hour guided "Tree Tours of Bushnell Park" of interest, and the Pumphouse Gallery is worth a visit as well. Various volunteer-led tours are available throughout the year for some of the park's attractions. Be sure to wear good, sturdy walking shoes! If you prefer to go it alone, self-guided "Tree Walk" touring brochures are available from the League of Women Voters desk at the entrance to the Legislative Office building on Capitol Avenue, and there is a wealth of historic information on the website.

If you're done exploring the park and want to get out of the elements for a bit, head south to Summit Street and the campus of *Trinity College.* One don't-miss is the college's chapel. Completed in 1932, the *Trinity College Chapel* boasts stained-glass windows, a cloister, arches, and carved pews in keeping with the best medieval tradition. The chapel's most interesting elements are 78 hand-carved oak pews that face each other across the nave. It took more than 30 years to complete all the carvings. Most of the pews were the work of Gregory Wiggins of Pomfret, who taught Latin, Greek, and German before he decided to become a full-time wood carver. The Charter Oak Pew shows Captain Joseph Wadsworth hiding the Connecticut Colony's royal charter in an ancient oak tree to prevent its recall by Royal Governor Edmund Andros (not a beloved figure in Connecticut history).

The *Connecticut Department of Energy & Environmental Protection Bookstore* (79 Elm St.; 860-424-3555; ctdeepstore.com) is a bonanza for hikers, fishers, and armchair geologists. Connecticut's DEEP has produced more than 1,300 publications about the state and its environment, including some dynamite maps for hikers, naturalists, and birders and some publications from not-for-profit and private presses. It's open 9 a.m. to 3:30 p.m. Mon through Fri.

hartfordtrivia

The Phoenix Mutual Life building in downtown Hartford is popularly known as the "Boat Building" because it reminds many locals of a graceful, green glass boat.

For a taste of Hartford's signature food, head to Franklin Avenue. This is Hartford's Little Italy, and practically any place you wander into will have something to delight your palate. *Mozzicato de Pasquale's Bakery and Pastry Shop* (329 Franklin Ave.; 860-296-0426; mozzicatobakery.com) is a legend in the area, as they churn out rich pastries and beautiful, traditional Italian cakes, tortes, and cookies. Open every day from 7 a.m. to 9 p.m. They also have a second location in Plainville (125 New Britain Ave.; 860-793-2253).

Apparently we would be remiss if we didn't suggest you visit what has been called "Hartford's worst-kept secret." Unassuming, but a true hidden treasure, the **Polish National Home** (60 Charter Oak Ave.; 860-247-1784) offers some of the best Polish (and American) food in the area. When you visit (and we assume you will), don't be intimidated by the brick fortress in which the restaurant is located; it was designed by Hartford architect Henry F. Ludorf and has a wonderful history. Also, don't be deterred by the usually locked front door to this building. You'll find the entrance at the back by the parking lot; there's a sign that reads Patron Entrance. Once inside, follow your nose. While you will find some familiar American dishes on the menu (fried chicken, turkey, and so forth), the real stars are the Polish dishes, such as the crunchy, toothsome *placki* (potato pancakes) and pierogi (half-moon-shaped little dumplings filled with meat, potato and cheese, sauerkraut and mushrooms, or blueberries). For a taste of Poland, try the "Polish plate," a mini-buffet including everything from pierogi to *golabki* (stuffed cabbage) to *bigos* (sauerkraut braised with kielbasa and pork). Do we have to mention portions are huge? Open 11 a.m. to early evening ("about 7 or 8," later if there's an event scheduled) Tues through Sat and 11 a.m. to 3 p.m. Sun.

Elizabeth Park Rose Gardens (Prospect Avenue; 860-722-6514; elizabethpark.org) was the first municipally owned rose garden in America and is now listed on the National Register of Historic Places. This is truly a beautiful place. More than 14,000 roses grace the park. There are also perennial gardens, greenhouses, nature walks, and a rock garden.

The park offers something special during every season, but it's late June and early July when the roses are at their peak. In those few brief weeks, Elizabeth Park is an experience that overwhelms the senses. The many varieties of roses come in all sizes and hues, and the mingled scents, from the sweetly scented traditional American hybrids to the elegantly fragrant damask roses, are indescribable. There are amazing gardens with flowers of all varieties, and plenty of walking trails. Be sure to check out the more than 100-year-old gazebo that feels like a gateway into another world. The Pond House on the premises contains a snack bar, lounge, and auditorium. Open daily, dawn to dusk.

Back in 1874 the great American humorist and novelist **Mark Twain** (aka Samuel Langhorne Clemens) began summering in Hartford in a rambling, three-story, 19-room Victorian mansion that he had built to his eccentric specifications. In 1881 he had the place redecorated in an even more eccentric style by Louis Comfort Tiffany. For the next quarter century, this was the Twain family summer home, which he often described as "part house, part steamboat." It was the place where Twain wrote some of his best works, including *The Adventures of Tom Sawyer, The Adventures of Huckleberry Finn, The Prince and the Pauper,* and *A Connecticut Yankee in King Arthur's Court.*

hartfordtrivia

The Rev. Thomas Hooker is honored as the founding father of Connecticut. These days Hartford celebrates his memory (and that of parade founder and former Hartford mayor Mike Peters) with its laid-back and fabulously flamboyant "Hooker Day" parade in October. Pretty much anything goes, with obvious safety precautions. For more information, visit hartford .com.

The restored **Mark Twain House** (351 Farmington Ave.; 860-247-0998; marktwainhouse.org) is now a museum and storehouse of Twain memorabilia. The unmistakable redbrick building, with its startling three-color slate roof, many gables, monumental chimneys (it has 18 fireplaces), and flamboyant exterior walls painted in red and black Chinese stripes and trimmed in dark red, looms over the Farmington Avenue commuter traffic, almost like a lingering sardonic comment from the famous humorist. Inside, each of the unique rooms has been restored as close to its 1881 condition as possible. About half of the original furnishings remain or have been acquired, including Twain's Venetian bed, whose ornate headboard so intrigued the author that he slept with his head at the foot of the bed so he could see the intricate carvings.

The museum features a welcome center, exhibition galleries, a theater, and classrooms. While the welcome center and exhibits are self-guided, admission to the Twain family home is by guided tour only. There are a variety to choose from, including holiday tours (highly recommended), the ghostly Graveyard Shift Tour (learn what *Ghost Hunters* investigators discovered . . . if you dare), and the Servants' Wing tour. Visit the website for more details. Open Mon through Sat 9:30 a.m. to 5:30 p.m. (last tour at 4:30 p.m.);

Sun noon to 5:30 p.m. (last tour at 4:30 p.m.). Closed Tues, Jan to Mar. Also closed on major holidays. Gift shop. Admission.

Across the lawn from the Mark Twain House is the home where Twain friend and famous author Harriet Beecher Stowe once lived. Today the **Harriet Beecher Stowe Center** (77 Forest St.; 860-522-9258; harrietbeecher stowe.org) comprises a museum and library, with the stated purpose of "inspiring visitors to embrace and emulate her commitment to social justice." The complex has a visitor center, a museum shop, beautiful gardens, and the **Katherine Seymour Day House,** which offers a vivid glimpse into the life of the woman who helped galvanize the abolitionist cause and contributed to the start of the Civil War with her novel *Uncle Tom's Cabin.*

The Day House has magnificent interiors, changing exhibits, a research center, and Victorian gardens. The center is on the Connecticut Freedom Trail and the Connecticut Women's Heritage Trail. It is open year-round 9:30 a.m. to 4:30 p.m. Tues through Fri; 9:30 a.m. to 5:30 p.m. Sat, and noon to 5:30 p.m. Sun. Open on some Mondays for major holidays (see website for details).

West Hartford

West Hartford also has a couple of those restored houses that are ubiquitous in Connecticut. The **Sarah Whitman Hooker Homestead** (1237 New Britain Ave.; 860-523-5887; sarahwhitmanhooker.com) is a lovely 1720 mansion named for a resident heroine of the American Revolution. Outside there's an herb garden and an

marktwaintrivia

Twain was fascinated by technology and incorporated many of the day's latest inventions in his home, including central heating and gas lighting fixtures. So it is fitting that the new museum center at the Mark Twain House was the first Leadership in Energy and Environmental Design (LEED)–certified museum in the country and the first LEED building in Connecticut. Among the many cutting-edge environmental features are the geothermal walls as the predominant cooling source.

Twain's ill-advised investment in a typesetting machine called the Paige Compositor resulted in such a devastating financial loss that he was forced to leave his Farmington Avenue home and move his family to Europe.

The Adventures of Tom Sawyer was the first novel in America to be written on a typewriter.

Four Connecticut Freedom Fighters

Throughout Hartford are four houses that have been added to the National Register of Historic Places due to previous occupants' important contributions to our nation's history. These houses are all still privately owned and not open to the public, but they are considered stops on the Connecticut Freedom Trail. If you're in the area and are interested, you can drive by and at least start a dialogue with the kids about these important Nutmeggers. Please be respectful of the current owners' privacy.

Frank T. Simpson House (27 Keney Ter.). Dr. Frank T. Simpson moved to Hartford in 1929, where he was active in social work. In 1944 he became the first employee of the Connecticut Inter-Racial Commission, the predecessor to today's Connecticut Commission on Human Rights and Opportunities. Dr. Simpson worked tirelessly to end discrimination in education, housing, unions, and employment. Simpson purchased the Keney Terrace house in 1952 and lived there until his death in 1974 at the age of 67.

Marietta Canty House (61 Mahl Ave.). Marietta Canty received critical acclaim for her performances in theater, radio, motion pictures, and television throughout the 1930s, '40s, and '50s, including *The Spoilers, Father of the Bride,* and *Rebel Without a Cause.* As was the time, though, Canty was often offered only roles portraying black domestic servants. Her acceptance of this fact and her dignified way in which she performed the parts helped pave the way for future African-American artists of radio, stage, and film. When she retired from show business, Canty didn't

trivia

In 1774, when he was 16 years old, Noah Webster attended Yale, Connecticut's only college at that time.

antique (heritage) rose garden. The museum is run by the Sarah Whitman Hooker Foundation, and hours and days are sporadic. It's best to call ahead or e-mail to arrange a tour.

The ***Noah Webster House*** (227 S. Main St.; 860-521-5362; noahwebster house.org) in West Hartford is the birthplace and childhood home of Noah Webster, author of the first American dictionary. The house is furnished much as it would have been when Webster lived there in the 18th century.

Through his dictionary, which he began when he was 43, Webster is credited with Americanizing the English language. He launched the project sit back and relax. Her political and social activism in the 1960s, '70s, and '80s further increased her status as a pioneer in advancing opportunities for women and minorities. Canty died in 1986 at the age of 81.

Wilfred X. Johnson House (206 Tower Ave.). Wilfred Xavier Johnson was the first black candidate endorsed by the Democratic Party anywhere in the state. Johnson successfully ran for election to the General Assembly in 1958 and served four terms as Connecticut's first black state representative. His wife, Gertrude Johnson, was also active in city politics and was one of the founders of Hartford's Project Concern, a program designed to correct racial imbalance in Connecticut's public schools. The family purchased this house in 1966. Mr. Johnson lived here until his death in 1972 at the age of 52. The house is still owned by the family.

Boce W. Barlow Jr. House (31 Canterbury St.). Boce W. Barlow Jr. was the first African American in the Connecticut judiciary and the first to be elected state senator (1966). As a lawyer, prosecutor, and judge, Barlow worked for equal justice and helped write Connecticut's pioneering civil rights laws. He attended Harvard Law School, where he was one of only four African-American students in a class of 600. In 1957 he was appointed judge of Hartford's municipal court, and later, hearing examiner for Connecticut's Civil Rights Commission. Throughout his life, he worked for social and political reform. Judge Barlow died in 2005 at the age of 90.

Visit ctfreedomtrail.org for more information.

because Americans in different parts of the country spelled, pronounced, and used words differently. Webster thought that all Americans should speak the same way and that Americans shouldn't speak and spell just like the English. So, for example, his dictionary uses "color" instead of "colour." He also added some distinctly American words, such as "skunk" and "squash." It took him more than 27 years to finish the dictionary, which contained 70,000 words.

The delightful thing about this house is that there's always a staff of "interpreters" on hand to answer questions. They dress in colonial garb, and they actually perform tasks such as baking in the kitchen fireplace; you may even get to taste the result. Guided tours are also available. Don't leave without checking out the gift shop on the property that sells locally created craft items. Open year-round Thurs through Mon 1 to 4 p.m., but there are exceptions, so please call ahead to confirm. Last tour leaves at 3 p.m. Admission.

West Hartford is also home to the **Quaker Diner** (319 Park Rd.; 860-232-5523), a fine little eatery out of another era. The special labor of love of Harry Bassilakis, whose grandfather built it in 1931, this diner has been carefully restored. Harry gave up a career with a local insurance company in 1987 to restore the place to its original state, and many of the fittings—the high-back wooden booths, the counter stools, and the black and white deco tile in the hall leading to the bathrooms—are carefully tended original appointments. Other furnishings are from Harry's personal collection of antiques.

Aside from being a fine restoration, the Quaker offers some of the best diner food in New England. Harry's mom, Agnes, does much of the cooking, including most of the specials and desserts. Just about everything is made from scratch, and some of the recipes, such as Agnes's justly famous meat loaf, are quite elaborate. The breakfasts are also first-rate. We especially like the Hole-in-One: french toast with the center cut out and replaced with a fried egg (the circular section of toast that was removed to make way for the egg goes back on as a hat).

The Quaker is open 6 a.m. to 2:30 p.m. Mon through Fri, and for breakfast only Sat, 6 a.m. to 1:30 p.m., and Sun, 7 a.m. to 1:30 p.m. Weekends are notoriously busy, so arrive early if you don't want to wait. Also, they don't accept credit cards, so be prepared, though you won't need much cash, as prices are reasonable.

The **Park Road area** is another neighborhood that's pleasant for walking and window shopping. You'll find a variety of stores and restaurants, along with special events planned throughout the year.

Not far from the Quaker, you'll find another equally delicious sampling of Connecticut's melting-pot cuisine. **Pho Tuong Lai** (355 New Park Ave.; 860-523-9134) is a simple, family-run storefront, but we think you'll find some of the best Vietnamese cooking in the state at bargain-basement prices. We're big fans of their *cha gio tom,* triangular, deep-fried shrimp rolls stuffed with shredded carrots, ground pork, and shrimp. Less adventurous palates will feel well fed and satisfied with any of the ginger dishes—for example, the chicken and ginger with steamed broccoli cooked in a tasty reduction of soy with lots of snappy ginger flavor. Meat and potatoes lovers can chow down on the *bo luc lac* or "shaken beef," which is stir-fried cubes of filet mignon and onion in a savory sauce, served on a bed of cold, crunchy watercress. The "house dish" is *pho,* the beef and noodle soup that's the national soup of Vietnam. What makes this dish special are the garnishes: lime wedges, bean sprouts, fresh basil, and chiles. Open daily from 9 a.m. to 8 p.m.

Another great place to stop in the area if you're hungry is **Harry's Pizza** (39 S. Main St.; 860-231-7166; harryspizza.net). Winner of numerous awards, Harry's serves up delicious thin-crust pies, fresh salads with their signature balsamic vinaigrette, and a complimentary Italian sorbet to cleanse your palate when you're done (if you still have room, that is). Open 4:30 to 9 p.m. Mon through Wed, 11:30 a.m. to 2 p.m. and 4:30 to 10 p.m. Thurs (till 10:30 p.m. Fri). On Sat and Sun, Harry's mixes it up and serves a weekend breakfast (8 a.m. to noon Sat, and 8 a.m. to 1 p.m. Sun), but don't worry, they are also open for their pizza: 12:30 to 10:30 p.m. Sat, and 1:30 to 9:30 p.m. Sun.

The **New Children's Museum** (950 Trout Brook Dr.; 860-231-2824; thechildrensmuseumct.org) in West Hartford is a great hands-on place to visit with the kids. They claim it's "where science and nature are fun," and they're right! Most kids we know like the giant walk-in kaleidoscope, but just as many love the giant, walk-in whale. Voted *Hartford Magazine*'s "Best

A Self-Made Man

He had only one name, but he was so much more. Born around 1731, Bristow was an African man who was sold into slavery. Brought to America with so many other slaves, Bristow was sold to Sarah Whitman and Thomas Hart Hooker, but eventually he was able to purchase his own freedom. He then led a rather successful life, gaining the respect of his neighbors for his knowledge of agriculture. Bristow died in 1814 and was buried in West Hartford's oldest cemetery. He was the only known African American of that time period to have a gravestone. This fact sparked a great deal of interest, and Bristow has become a well-known name throughout town, even having a middle school named after him. More information can be found at noahwebsterhouse.org. Bristow's grave is on the Connecticut Freedom Trail and can be found at **Old Center Burying Yard** (28 N. Main St., West Hartford; open dawn to dusk). The gravestone spells the name "Bristol."

A Walk in the Center

People who've developed an attachment to the diversity, energetic buzz, and everything-that's-needed convenience of a centrally situated place to live generally appreciate their urbanite advantages. At their whim, they can head out for some strolling-while-people-watching, entertainment, window-shopping, and museumgoing without having to traipse to a distant city or town. The charming all-American Main Streets of countless New England villages have comparable advantages, even though they exist on a smaller, more intimate scale.

Suburbanites—at least in some areas, and those places are increasing—needn't feel neglected. Which brings us to that upscale enclave called **West Hartford Center** and **Blue Back Square,** where Farmington Avenue and LaSalle Road intersect, about half an hour's driving (or by public transportation) time westward from the capital city's riverfront.

Many metro-Hartford insurance executives choose to raise their families in this privileged neighborhood, with brick sidewalks leading to some 140 shops (ritzy jewelry stores, salons, and a dozen designer-label fashion boutiques included), augmented by an abundance of restaurants, coffee shops, and chic cafes.

Although what residents simply refer to as "the Center" or "the Square" has become something of a yuppified Westport clone in recent years, it still offers welcome relief from cookie-cutter mega-malls. Here you'll find unique treasures in a community atmosphere while enjoying the outdoors as well. Throughout the year, merchants launch events such as a farmers' market (May through Oct), the Style Stroll (a ladies' night usually held in Sept), Halloween Stroll (yes, trick-or-treating is involved), and of course the Holiday Stroll (complete with horse and carriage rides). This area continues to be revitalized and enlarged with a large variety of stores and services. Here are just a few noteworthy neighborhood haunts:

Coffeehouses have proliferated along Farmington Avenue. So if you're hit with a caffeine yen, try **Cafe Sofia** (984 Farmington Ave.; 860-315-0844) or **Cosí** (970

Kid's Attraction," the center offers a space theater (the state's largest, in fact), a planetarium (separate admission required), a wildlife sanctuary (very cool with lots of neat animals to see), and an off-site nature center (located in Canton). There's a cool gift shop, too. Open Tues through Sat 9 a.m. to 4 p.m., and Sun 11 a.m. to 4 p.m. Closed major holidays. Admission for adults and children age 2 and older.

Farmington Ave.; 860-521-8495; getcosi.com) for a jolt. In the Square, check out **It's a Grind Coffee House** (51 Memorial Rd.; 860-761-3290; itsagrind.com). Or if you prefer tea, stop by **The Green Teahouse** (40 Isham Rd.; 860-232-6666; thegreenteahouse.com), where you can sample to your heart's content and then purchase some tea to bring home. The staff is super friendly and helpful here.

If you're looking for something more substantial to eat, you can't go wrong at **The Cheesecake Factory** (71 Isham Rd.; 860-233-5588; thecheesecakefactory.com) with their 21-page menu. This is one of only two in the state. The service is helpful and friendly and the food delicious.

If it's something cold and frothy you desire, check out **Pinkberry** (38 Isham Rd.; 860-232-1801; pinkberry.com) for frozen yogurt, fruit parfaits, fresh fruit bowls, and other delicious frozen delights.

Once you're full, keep strolling and visit some of the great shops. **Toast Wines** (984-B Farmington Ave.; 860-236-3515; toastwines.com) is an interesting shop that sells wines "by taste." Wines are organized by taste categories and all offer suggestions on what foods the wines complement—great for the wine newbie who needs help in selecting a bottle. Prices are reasonable.

Pfau's Hardware (982 Farmington Ave.; 860-523-4201) is an old-fashioned, wooden-floored hardware store with all types of cool stuff in every nook and cranny, and is an experience in itself. Kids love the place.

Charming Charlie (76 Memorial Rd.; 860-232-0708; charmingcharlie.com), a relative newcomer to our state, offers a wide variety of women's accessories all organized by color. Now, these are not high-end, jeweler-quality accessories, but if you're looking for inexpensive and fun items, this is your place. It's huge!

No doubt, you'll find something that pleases your eye or your taste buds at this wonderful collection of establishments.

Newington

If you have a ham-radio fan in your life (or even if you don't), don't miss a visit to the **American Radio Relay League** (225 Main St.; 860-594-0200; arrl.org) in nearby **Newington.** Founded in 1914, the ARRL is the largest group of radio amateurs in the US, with more than 150,000 members. It is not only a mecca for ham-radio operators but also the official voice of amateur radio. In these days of lightning-quick communication, you may think of ham radio as merely an interesting hobby. During natural disasters, however, ham radios provide vital information while our cell towers may be inoperable. Beside the administrative offices of the ARRL, you'll find **W1AW,** the league's amateur-radio station. Visitors can tour the station, listen to radio calls, try their hand at tapping out code, or view artifacts of the league's history. By the way, there's no one story as to why operators are called hams. Some people say it's because the radio gives operators a chance to "ham it up"; others say it comes from the ham-fisted way early operators pounded their code keys. The most likely story is that "ham" is derived from "am," an abbreviation for "amateur."

Wethersfield

South of Hartford is **Wethersfield,** once known as "Oniontown" because the crop, especially the red onion, grew so well within its confines and its scent permeated everything. In fact, the red onion still has a strong presence here. Wethersfield also boasts the motto of "ye most auncient towne in Connecticut." It was an important port on the Connecticut River until the river changed course and left Old Wethersfield behind. Today Old Wethersfield, the remnants of the original town, claims to be the state's largest historic district with more than 300 historic homes, some dating back to before the Revolution.

wethersfield trivia

Old Wethersfield was the setting for two amusing novels of gothic horror—*The Other* and *Harvest Home*—written by Wethersfield native Thomas Tryon.

A visit to the **Webb-Deane-Stevens Museum** (211 Main St.; 860-529-0612; webb-deane-stevens.org) will transport you back to the 18th century, where you will once again see the influences of Connecticut's River Gods. This museum is composed of 4 historic houses. The 1752 **Joseph Webb House** was a stopover for General George Washington in 1781; he and French general Comte de Rochambeau met there to plan the Yorktown campaign. The opulence of the house is contrasted by the attic quarters of the family's slaves—a true insight into our state's history. The 1776 **Silas Deane House** belonged to a member of the First Continental Congress (and America's first envoy to France). Silas Deane lived here with his wife,

Elizabeth Saltonstall Evards, until he left for France in 1776. She died a year later, and Silas then faced a challenging career full of betrayal and intrigue that eventually led to his demise in in 1789. The house then passed through myriad hands until it was finally bequeathed to the Colonial Dames in 1958 and underwent a careful restoration to how it would have appeared in 1776. The 1788 **Isaac Stevens House** is a testament to the changes the country was facing as it entered the Industrial Revolution. There is a great children's room that showcases wonderful textiles and well-loved dolls and toys. Not quite as opulent as its neighbors, the Stevens House would have been typical of a middle-class family in the early 19th century. Owned by Connecticut Land-marks, but within walking distance and maintained by the museum is the 1715 **Buttolph-Williams House,** the setting for the wonderful young adult book *The Witch of Blackbird Pond* by Elizabeth George Speare. Collectively, there are 5 acres of open grounds and wonderful period gardens. Oper-ated and maintained by the Colonial Dames, the museum is open 10 a.m. to 4 p.m. (last tour at 3:30 p.m.) daily except Tues from May through Oct; during the winter, open weekends only (Sat 10 a.m. to 4 p.m., Sun 1 to 4 p.m.; last tour 3:30 p.m.). There are special December and holiday hours, so be sure to check the website for details. Admission.

wethersfield trivia

If you're of an architectural bent or just love old houses, you'll love Wethersfield. Wandering through this area, you're sure to spot houses in architectural styles ranging from colonial saltbox to 1950s ranches and everything in between.

Also in the neighborhood is the **Captain James Francis House** (about 3 blocks away at 120 Hartford Ave.; 860-529-7656; wethhist.org). Although open by appointment only, the house is a true treasure. Privately owned until 1969, the house lovingly showcases time periods from the late 18th century to the 20th. The **Hurlbut-Dunham House** (212 Main St.; 860-529-7161; wethhist.org) is another historic jewel. Although also privately owned until 1970, the house has been extensively restored. Though it was built in the 1790s, the house now showcases its early 20th-century glory. Open 11 a.m. to 2 p.m. Sat and 1 to 4 p.m. Sun, mid-May to mid-Oct. Admission. Both of these homes are owned by the **Wethersfield Historical Society** (860-529-7656;

wethhist.org), whose offices are across the street from the Webb-Deane-Stevens Museum in the Old Academy building (150 Main St.). The society also manages *Keeney Memorial Cultural Center* (which has changing exhibits throughout the year), *Cove Warehouse* (located on the waterfront and featuring exhibits of the town's maritime glory), and the *Deming-Standish House* (a house with a very interesting history that includes a horse being ridden right through the front door; be sure to check out the society's website section on this property). Also across the street from the museum at 250 Main St. is the *First Church of Christ* and *The Meetinghouse* (860-529-1575; firstchurch.org), one of the oldest churches in our nation whose congregation of more than 2,000 still worships there each Sunday; you can view the interior with its original hand-carved pulpit on weekdays from 9 a.m. to 5 p.m. Behind The Meetinghouse is the *Ancient Burying Ground;* thousands of headstones dating from 1670 (although burials no doubt took place before this, since the cemetery was established in 1638) record the thoughts, philosophies, and attitudes of generations of local citizens. In 1799, one Quash Gomer was buried here when he died at the age of 68. Gomer was a slave who had purchased his freedom 30 years earlier for 25 pounds.

The *Wethersfield Historical Society* offers tours of the Ancient Burying Ground at certain times of the year. Admission. The society also sells a booklet for self-guided tours.

At 263 Main St. you'll find *Comstock, Ferre & Company* (860-571-6590; comstockferre.com), the oldest continuously operating seed company in the US. Since 1820, it's been a source for seeds and plants, and it still carries some of the seed varieties that founders Joseph and John Belden would have used in their own gardens 200 years ago. Facing closure in 2008, the business was saved when it was bought by Jere and Emilee Gettle, who have been working tirelessly to bring the company and all its surrounding historic buildings back to their former glory. Really a destination in itself, Comstock, Ferre & Company is worth the visit. Open 10 a.m. to 4 p.m. Sun through Fri; closed Sat.

Rocky Hill

Leaving the 19th century behind, we travel to nearby *Rocky Hill,* and to another time in our history.

In 1966, while clearing ground for the construction of a new state building in Rocky Hill, bulldozer operator Ed McCarthy uncovered some unusual rocks. They had strange markings and scorings on them. It turned out that these were the tracks of dinosaurs that prowled the area 185 million years ago. In those days this part of Connecticut was a mud flat on the shore of a huge lake, rich in fish and small crocodilians—good eating for a growing dinosaur.

After covering the initial excavation of 1,500 tracks to preserve them, the state excavated an additional 500 tracks, enclosed them in a geodesic dome, added an audiovisual facility that offers a neat presentation, and called the result *Dinosaur State Park* (West Street; 860-529-8423; dinosaurstatepark .org). Inside the dome you'll be greeted by a full-size reconstruction of a carnivorous dinosaur called dilophosaurus, but the big attraction is the amazing collection of tracks. Most of the impressions are three-toed, and they run up to 16 inches long.

The park also has 2 miles of nature trails and picnic tables, and a place where you can make your own dinosaur casts out of plaster (check the website; you'll need to bring your own supplies). The Exhibit Center is open 9 a.m. to 4:30 p.m. Tues through Sun. The grounds are open daily 9 a.m. to 4:30 p.m. Admission.

When you're in Rocky Hill, you're very close to Cromwell and the site of a family-friendly animal sanctuary, *Amy's Udder Joy Exotic Animal Farm Park* (27 North Rd.; 860-635-3924). Amy's takes in injured, abused, and endangered and native animals that cannot be released into the wild again. You'll find more than 50 indoor and outdoor exhibits here. Self-guided. Admission. Open Tues through Sun 11 a.m. to 4 p.m.

East of the River

Glastonbury

The *Rocky Hill–Glastonbury Ferry* (860-443-3856), spanning the Connecticut River and linking one part of Route 160 (Ferry Lane) to the other, has been in operation since 1655. That makes it the oldest continuously operating ferry in America. It's also a good place to cross the river if you want to avoid the usually heavy traffic around Hartford's bridges. Service is provided by a tug called the *Cumberland,* which tows a three-car barge called the *Hollister.*

In 2011 the ferry, along with the Hadlyme–Chester Ferry, was almost shut down by the state in an effort to reduce the ever-present deficit. Nutmeggers again rallied—politicians were motivated, grassroots groups sprung up, and, yes, Larry the Cable Guy was even called. Voices were heard, and the decision was reversed, for now. Local groups continue to work with the state Department of Transportation on long-term solutions to make the ferries more self-sufficient and less costly to the state. The Rocky Hill–Glastonbury ferry operates daily (weather permitting) 10:30 a.m. to 5 p.m. May 1 to Oct 31. Prices are almost insignificant (but this could change with those long-term plans).

When Senator John Quincy Adams received a petition signed by 40 women in **Glastonbury,** he probably had no idea what he was dealing with. The petition was circulated by sisters Julia and Abby Smith and their mother, Hannah, to protest slavery. But the women didn't stop there. They, along with the other members of the Smith family, used their home, known as **Kimberly Mansion** (1625 Main St.), as a base of operations for their work for freedom, including hosting antislavery lectures and abolition-ist meetings, and distributing literature throughout the area. In 1994 the Glastonbury family was inducted into the Connecticut Women's Hall of Fame to honor their tireless work. You can drive by the home, but please respect the present owners' privacy, as the home is privately held and not open to the public, although it is a National Historic Landmark.

East Hartford

Any Connecticut guidebook will tell you that the **Makens Bemont House** (307 Burnside Ave.; 860-568-5188) in **East Hartford**'s Martin Park is an excellent example of a restored colonial house. They'll talk about the gam-brel roof and the vaulted dormer windows. What they won't tell you is that the house has ghosts, albeit friendly ones. When the house was moved in 1971 from its original location on Tolland Street to the park, workers started reporting seeing the ghost of a lady in a blue dress. Then, as construction to restore and anchor the house to its new site began, work was frequently disrupted by the loud sounds of crashing, knocking, and hammering, even when the house was empty.

The occurrences became so regular, workers dubbed the haunt "Benny," and the foreman made out a daily work list for the ghost. Some believe the ghost or ghosts are the original residents of the house, Edmund and Abigail Bemont. Edmund built the house for his wife and son, Makens, in 1761. Descendants lived there into the 19th century, so who knows who haunts the residence now. The house was donated to the Historical Society of East Hartford in the late 1960s, and they now offer limited tours. Hours

easthartford trivia

In 1687 Governor Edmund Andros, appointed by the British Crown to oversee Connecticut, demanded colonists return the royal charter that made Connecticut a separate colony. Hartford colonists hid the charter in a towering oak tree, since called the Charter Oak. When the Charter Oak finally toppled in 1856, it was 1,000 years old.

are varied, so it's best to call ahead. The society is run completely by volunteers, so be patient and give yourself enough time to wait for a call back. Maybe you'll get lucky and have the chance to meet the spirits who roam the rooms and go bump in the night.

Manchester

New England's population has swelled from numerous waves of immigrants over the years, and as each ethnic group has assimilated, it has left behind a host of bakeries, restaurants, and similar establishments. **Manchester** is no different, and its residents work hard to preserve that history.

Dedicated to preserving the artifacts of the fireman's life, the **Fire Museum** (230 Pine St.; 860-647-9436; thefiremuseum.org) has everything relating to firefighting, from old leather fire buckets and ornate marching hats to wooden water mains and a rare 18th-century fire warden's staff. There's even a collection of old prints and lithographs of fires, from the pre-photographic era when the artist and lithographer were as important as the reporter to the process of communicating the news. It's all displayed inside a big old firehouse that was built in 1901 to protect the Cheney Brothers silk mills, at the time the main industry of this "Silk City."

There's a good deal of large equipment on display, with the emphasis on the hand-operated and horse-drawn. Some of the hand pumpers needed as many as 30 men to operate them. There's also a horse-drawn hose wagon, a steam-operated pumper, and an ornate, hand-pulled, four-wheel hose reel designed mainly for use in parades, a reminder of an age when the local firehouse was a center of social and political activity. The museum is open mid-Apr through mid-Nov, noon to 4 p.m. Fri and Sat. Other dates and times may be available by appointment only. Suggested donation.

Also in Manchester, you'll find ***Shady Glen*** (840 E. Middle Turnpike; 860-649-4245), one of those places that make you think you've walked into a filming of *Happy Days*. It's been around since 1948 and once sold the milk and ice cream produced on John and Bernice Reig's dairy farm. Today it's a popular eatery and old-fashioned soda fountain. Besides soaking up the old-time atmosphere, you'll want to try the cheeseburgers. Topped with crispy slabs of fried cheese, they look a little like UFOs. Cheese fanciers can get an order of fried cheese on the side. Then try the ice cream or a soda fountain creation, such as a sundae or soda. Every day there are about 25 ice cream flavors from which to choose. Popular flavors such as chocolate chip are always on the menu, while flavors such as mincemeat or cranberry sorbet rotate with the seasons. Things get really hectic and crowded at Shady Glen because it's something of a Manchester tradition, but the tables turn over quickly, so be patient and wait. Oh, and bring cash; they don't accept credit cards. Open 7 a.m. to 10 p.m. Mon through Thurs, 7 a.m. to 11 p.m. Fri and

Connecticut Freedom Trail

As long as you're driving around Manchester, take note of these two houses if you should pass them: The first is the ***Walter Bunce House*** (34 Bidwell St.), which was built by Alpheus Quicy, an African-American stonemason, and is the only such building of his that still stands today. Quicy, along with his father and brother, are credited with building important fieldstone homes and several dams in the Manchester area. The second home on the trail is the ***Hart Porter House*** and outbuilding (465 Porter St.), built sometime between 1840 and 1845 and believed to be a stop on the Underground Railroad due to a full basement in the outbuilding that is accessible only through a trapdoor. While skeptics may say that the Manchester area was not necessarily known to have abolitionist sympathies, there is evidence of Hart Porter's connections to the movement. Both homes are private and not open to the public.

Sat, and 10:30 a.m. to 10 p.m. Sun. There's a second Shady Glen at 360 W. Middle Turnpike (860-643-0511), if you just can't get enough.

If you visit Shady Glen with kids, why not let them run off their sugar high with a visit to the *Lutz Children's Museum* (247 S. Main St.; 860-643-0949; lutzmuseum.org). This place is scaled for and built for children. The emphasis here is on "please touch" science and natural history exhibits including live animals. The museum sponsors several excellent programs throughout the year. Open 9 a.m. to 5 p.m. Tues through Fri, noon to 5 p.m. Sat and Sun. Closed Mon. Admission.

The Tobacco Valley

East Windsor

The *Connecticut Trolley Museum* and the *Connecticut Fire Museum* (58 North Rd.; 860-627-6540 for Trolley Museum or 860-623-4732 for Fire Museum; ct-trolley.org) in *East Windsor* offer you the opportunity to visit two great museums for one price in one location. How can you beat that?

The Trolley Museum is run by the nonprofit Connecticut Electric Railway Association and has a collection of more than 70 pieces of rail equipment, some dating back to 1869. The collection includes freight and passenger cars, interurban cars, elevated railway cars, locomotives, and more.

Halloween Spooktacular

New England and Halloween go together hand and glove. Maybe it's the scudding clouds posed against a full harvest moon. Maybe it's the whirling wisps of ground fog whipped along by a shuddering wind. Maybe it's the weight of all those years of history. We're not sure what it is, but in New England we enjoy Halloween a lot.

The Connecticut Trolley Museum in East Windsor offers "Rails to the Darkside" Fri and Sat at 7 p.m. The rides take about 2½ hours and take you out on the rails when few dare to join you. According to trolley records, a cemetery was relocated due to the construction of the Hartford & Springfield line to Rockville. Perhaps some of the spirits are not so happy with their new homes. Will they choose to let you know about it? Visit ct-trolley.org/events/darkside.php for more details . . . if you dare.

While most of the trolleys are from New England and Canada, there are some from as far away as Illinois and Ohio and one from Rio de Janeiro. The museum offers a car-barn tour and a 3-mile trolley ride. Special events are held throughout the year including a wine and beer tasting in May and the annual Winterfest in December, which features leisurely rides along a 1 ½-mile route decorated with twinkling colored lights.

The Connecticut Fire Museum has a collection of about 20 fire trucks built between the early and late 20th century.

The museums are open Mon and Wed through Fri 10 a.m. to 3:30 p.m., Sat 10 a.m. to 4:30 p.m., and Sun noon to 4:30 p.m. Closed Tues.

Windsor

Once upon a time, every town had a **Bart's Drive-In** (55 Palisado Ave.; 860-688-9035; bartsdrivein.com). Today they are as scarce as hens' teeth. But you'll find one in **Windsor,** and once you find a place like Bart's, you become a customer for life—it's just that kind of place. Bart's started as a hot dog stand, eventually expanded to include an indoor dining area, and has now expanded even further to include the Beanery Bistro right next door. Whether you're craving a chili dog, fresh fish, or an ice cream cone, or maybe a gourmet coffee and a muffin, you'll find it here. Watch for Seafood Sunday, when all seafood is delivered and prepared fresh daily.

There are picnic tables that overlook the river, and you can usually spot anglers fishing from the shore or in boats, so after a meal it's fun to sit awhile and watch or stroll down the sidewalk that runs along the river. Bart's grill is open Mon through Thurs 7 a.m. to 8 p.m., Fri 7 a.m. to midnight, Sat 8 a.m. to 8 p.m., and Sun 11 a.m. to 4 p.m., while the deli is open Mon through Fri 7 a.m. to 8 p.m., Sat 8 a.m. to 3 p.m., and closed Sun.

windsortrivia

Settled on October 4, 1633, Windsor claims to be the "oldest English settlement in Connecticut," though Wethersfield disputes this claim.

In 1647 Alse Young of Windsor was the first person to be hanged for witchcraft in New England.

Windsor resident Amy Archer-Gilligan was the inspiration for the elderly poisoners in the play and movie *Arsenic and Old Lace.* She ran a boardinghouse on Prospect Street and poisoned some of her pensioner tenants with home-made wine.

Connecticut Freedom Trail

William Howard Best began his job as Windsor's first African-American police officer in 1951 at the age of 27. He served the town until 1969, when injury forced him into retirement. Not one to sit idle, Best opened a printing shop in town and spoke freely to anyone interested about his experiences as an African American in the turbulent '50s and '60s (and times beyond). He and his wife, Jean, were active members in Windsor's Historical Society. Mr. Best passed away at the age of 82. You can see his house at 377 Hayden Station Rd., which was constructed in 1953 but sits on land that had been in Best's family since 1873. The house is privately owned and not open to the public, but not far from the Best house is the *Archer Memorial A.M.E. Zion Church* (320 Hayden Station Rd.), which you can visit. This church was built by a community of African-American parishioners in the late 1800s. While that building no longer stands (the current one was built in 1982), the land on which it sits was the site of many community gatherings and camps held by Rev. Dennis Scott White throughout the 1880s and '90s.

Joseph Rainey was the first African American elected to the US House of Representatives. He served his home state of South Carolina from 1870 to 1879, introducing legislation to help guarantee full constitutional rights for everyone—no matter what color they were. At one point, he refused to leave the dining room of a Virginia hotel, causing the owners to forcibly remove him. In 1874 Rainey purchased a summer home in Windsor (299 Palisado Ave.). In 1876 he spoke at Windsor's American centennial celebration. Today you can drive by the home, but it is privately owned and not open to the public.

So often history is lost to us because records just weren't kept. Sometimes our cemeteries hold the tales of lives we would otherwise not know about. This is the case at *Palisado Cemetery* (Palisado Avenue), where Nancy Toney is buried along with Civil War veteran Virgil Simmons, who served with the Connecticut 29th. Toney was a slave of the Chaffee/Loomis family in Windsor. While she died in 1857, nine years after the Emancipation Proclamation, she stayed with the family she had served for years, most likely because of her advanced age. Palisado Cemetery is open sunrise to sunset.

Riverside Cemetery (East Street) south of Veteran's Memorial Cemetery is the final resting place of Francis Gillette, former Connecticut senator (1832–1838) whose Bloomfield home was a reputed stop on the Underground Railroad and is now a stop on the Freedom Trail. Also buried here is a man named Foone, who hailed from Mende, Africa.

Windsor is also home to the annual **Shad Derby Festival** (windsor shadderby.org). The Connecticut River shad is a fat but bony, blue-green-and-silver relative of the herring. Each spring the shad migrate to northern waters to spawn, and one of their favorite spawning grounds is in the Connecticut River near Windsor. This means Windsor gets the best of the shad world, both fish and roe.

As a comestible, shad has both its partisans and its detractors. Some natives feel spring isn't spring in Connecticut without a dish of broiled shad roe with bacon or shad baked on a plank. Others maintain that you should throw away the shad and eat the plank.

In Windsor they've been celebrating the shad as part of the town's annual rite of spring for more than four decades. The shad season lasts about six weeks, but most of the shad festivities happen during the first two weeks of May. That's when you'll find everything from the Shad Derby (biggest shad caught) to the crowning of the Shad Queen, with a golf tournament and road race thrown in just to make things interesting. On Derby Day, Windsor pretty much closes up shop to honor the shad with a town-wide festival on Broad Street, where you'll find many food booths featuring the shad and its roe.

If you want to immerse yourself in any New England town, one of the best places to visit is the historical society. Windsor is no exception. The **Windsor Historical Society** (96 Palisado Ave.; 860-688-3813; windsor historicalsociety.org) was founded in 1921 and continues to preserve the town's history and share it with all those who visit. The society operates a museum and library as well as a gift shop, learning center, and 2 additional historic houses. One admission gets you into all, where you can explore and discover myriad permanent and changing exhibits, including old journals and maps, an 1800 highway survey, and an original payroll list of the Windsor residents who answered the rebel alarm in Boston in spring 1775. The museum also contains a variety of Indian relics and a display of Americana.

Open Tues through Sat, 10 a.m. to 4 p.m. Closed Sun, Mon, and major holidays. Guided tours available. Admission.

Windsor Locks

For anyone interested in the history of aviation, the **New England Air Museum** (36 Perimeter Rd.; 860-623-3305; neam.org) in nearby **Windsor**

Visit a Few, Save a Few

If you are planning a visit to the New England Air Museum during July or August, perhaps take a detour to the *Connecticut Trolley Museum* as well. The two museums run a cross promotion during those months, so if you visit one and bring your ticket to the other, you will receive a discount off your admission for up to four people. Memberships to either museum also work together and get you in free. What a deal!

Locks is a must. The museum features an extensive collection of aircraft, memorabilia, and exhibits housed in 3 large display hangars. Some of the larger aircraft are kept outdoors. The oldest of its 75 aircraft, a beautiful wood-and-canvas Bleriot XI monoplane, dates from 1909. There is also an extensive collection of World War II fighters and bombers and quite a number of modern jet aircraft.

There are also numerous smaller items of interest, including a variety of engines, cockpit simulators, and a collection of flight memorabilia. Many of these smaller items were acquired from area aerospace companies and can't be seen anywhere else.

Guided tours are available for an extra cost, or you can download an app to your phone or iPod and do your own thing. Visit their website for details. Open daily 10 a.m. to 5 p.m., the museum also offers numerous special events throughout the year. Don't miss their Open Cockpit and Veterans Day programs; they are a family favorite. Gift shop. Admission.

Suffield

A few miles up Route 75 from the New England Air Museum is another museum commemorating a quite different era. The restored 1764 home on *Suffield*'s beautiful Main Street (Route 75) is the *King House Museum* (232 S. Main St.; 860-668-5256). The building's interesting architectural features include 7 original fireplaces (one with a beehive oven) and a unique shell-carved corner cupboard.

Among the period furnishings is a four-poster bed that formerly graced the Jonathan Trumbull house in Lebanon. Displays include an assortment of Bennington pottery, a tinware collection, and, appropriately enough for the

Tobacco Valley, a collection of cigar and tobacco memorabilia. The King House Museum is open Wed and Sat, May through Sept from 1 to 4 p.m. Admission is free, but donations are welcome.

Enfield

About 20 minutes east of Suffield is the town of *Enfield* and the site of Connecticut's only community of Shakers. This community thrived in Enfield from 1792 to 1917. Based on the premise of direct communication between man and God, Shakers did not believe in praying through a church, priests, or other men of cloth, but members would sit and meditate until they received a sign from God personally. At this point, they would begin to tremble or shake, hence the name "Shaking Quakers," which was eventually shortened to Shakers and adopted by the group. While it may have started off as a derogatory term, it came to symbolize quality and integrity.

Facing serious opposition in England, Shaker leader Ann Lee set sail for America with some of her supporters in 1774 and began spreading word of their religion on the shores of America. First visiting Enfield in 1781, Mother Ann, as she was known, was met with opposition and barely escaped being tarred and feathered. She risked a second visit the following year and again met with opposition that broke out in serious riots. Not to be deterred, however, Ann returned to Enfield in 1783. While this visit was much more peaceful than the previous two, Mother Ann would not live long enough to enjoy it. She died the following September at the age of 48. She had laid the seeds in this community, however, and in 1792 the first Shaker community was established in Enfield.

Throughout the years, the Enfield community grew to include five families who lived on nearly 3,000 acres in town. The group held true to its beliefs in feminism, pacifism, and freedom. It became an important stop for fugitive slaves in their quest for justice, as evidenced by a diary of a member that chronicles the visit of one Sojourner Truth. The community thrived through the first half of the 1800s, but then things started to decline. The stringent demands of the religion began to take their toll, and one by one the families disbanded or merged until only eight members were left. When they could no longer survive on their own, they moved to other established Shaker communities.

Connecticut Freedom Trail

At the height of his career, famous actor/athlete/singer **Paul Robeson** called Enfield his home. As an outspoken civil rights advocate, Robeson stepped on more than a few toes. In the 1950s, powers that be, namely Senator Joe McCarthy, revoked Robeson's passport, preventing him from performing abroad, which he had done for years as an accomplished entertainer. It took eight years for his passport to be reinstated, but time had taken its toll, and Robeson was not the man he used to be. In the mid-1960s, Robeson stepped out of the public eye and quietly retired to Philadelphia until his death in 1976 at the age of 78. The home Robeson owned in Enfield is included in Enfield's National Historic District, though it is privately owned and not open to the public.

Today only a few buildings built and owned by this Shaker community remain. Some are privately owned, and the rest, unfortunately, are not open to public access, as they are on the grounds of the state Department of Corrections facilities on Shaker Road in Enfield. Visitors can, however, learn more at Enfield Historical Society's **Old Town Hall Museum** (1294 Enfield St.; 860-745-1729) and the **Martha A. Parsons House Museum** (1387 Enfield St.; 860-745-6064) or by visiting enfieldhistoricalsociety.org.

Like every other successful business, Powder Hill Farm in Enfield was feeling the need to diversify to survive. For this working dairy farm, the 1990s brought falling milk prices and struggling times. Owners Jack and Mavis Collins decided to open the **Collins Creamery** (9 Powder Hill Rd.; 860-749-8663; thecollinscreamery.com) in 1997. The business took off and today is managed by Jack and Mavis's daughter and son-in-law, Tony and Michele Bellafronte, which is funny because Tony doesn't eat ice cream. They do just fine, however, by offering more than 20 flavors of the richest, creamiest ice cream we have ever tasted. For those of you who can't handle the high-test stuff, there is also frozen yogurt, fat- and sugar-free, and soft serve. While there is no indoor seating, you are welcome to stay and enjoy your frozen treat at the picnic tables among the beautiful farmland. Open Fri through Sun, noon to 9 p.m. Remember to bring cash; they don't do plastic here.

East Granby

Okay, so "copper mine" and "prison" are usually not two things one might link together, but such is the case with *Old New-Gate Prison & Copper Mine* (115 Newgate Rd.; 860-653-3563) in *East Granby.* Originally chartered as the first copper mine in America in the early 1700s, the mine didn't produce the results necessary to make it profitable, although not for lack of trying—50 years of trying, in fact! Work was finally abandoned in 1750. The mine, with all its holes and tunnels, sat empty for 20 more years or so until 1773, when it was decided by the General Assembly that the dark, dank environment might be just the place to deposit criminals. On December 22, 1773, New-Gate Prison (its notorious namesake being in London) welcomed its first prisoner—John Hinson. (Okay, so he escaped 18 days later, but he was still the first.) The prison operated as our nation's first state prison until 1827 and in that time proved to be a nasty, cruel, and horrible place, gaining a reputation as "the worst hell-hole in North America." While the prison did include a substantial complex of aboveground buildings, the prisoners were confined 50 feet belowground in the dank passageways of the old mine. Disease claimed many. Others committed suicide or went insane. In fact, some people say that spirits of the men and women who met their demises here still haunt the tunnels to this day.

The site is now a National Historic Landmark and a State Archaeological Preserve. Normally open to the public, the prison and copper mine is currently closed for restoration with an anticipated opening in May 2014. I guess those haunts will have a little downtime.

Granby

If you are a lover of attractions of the biggest, smallest, first, and oldest variety, take a minute in *Granby* to visit the 300-year-old *Granby Oak* on Day Street, off Route 20. It's shown prominently on Granby's town seal, which appears on everything from official stationery to town vehicles. It even has its own website (salmonbrookhistorical.org/granby.htm), which tells you all you will ever need to know about this beautiful tree that has seen so much. In the fall, the oak is especially attractive and worthy of a photograph, as numerous artists and photographers can attest.

Folks with a passion for antiques love to discover just the right store, shop, gallery, yard sale, barn, or auction house. One such place in Granby—**Salmon Brook Shops** (563 Salmon Brook St.; 860-653-6587; salmonbrookshops.sharepoint.com)—offers that kind of tough-to-find challenge. (Granby itself is what you'd have to politely call remote: a fair distance north of Hartford and close to the Massachusetts state line.) But getting there is definitely worth the drive. Salmon Brook Shops comprises 30 dealers who offer their wares throughout the building's 6 rooms. While you won't find 18th-century Newport desks, you will find lots of nice kitchen items and a plethora of ephemera (postcards, movie posters, and advertising art). The people who staff the place are as charming as the objects they sell. Open daily 10 a.m. to 5 p.m.

The Farmington Valley

Simsbury

Simsbury was settled in 1648 by a group of Windsor families who acquired the land from the Massacoe Indians. They called their new settlement Massacoh Plantation, a name that was eventually changed to Simsbury when the town was incorporated by the Connecticut General Court in 1670. In March 1676, when King Philip's War began to heat up, the entire village of about 40 dwellings was destroyed by Wampanoag Indians. The Wampanoag uprising was over by August, but it took two years for reconstruction to begin. Once it did, Simsbury quickly became an important factor in Connecticut's economy and politics. The first copper coins in America were struck here in 1737, and the first steel mill in America was built here in 1744. Hundreds of residents fought in the American Revolution, including Major General Noah Phelps, who as America's first spy (he was just a captain then) entered Fort Ticonderoga in disguise to gather information for Ethan Allen; Allen then proceeded to capture the fort. By the 1820s the town was a major stop on the Farmington Canal, which ran along the route of today's Hopmeadow Street (Route 10).

Abigail's Grill & Bar (4 Hartford Rd.; 860-264-1580; abigailsgrill.com), formerly Pettibone's Tavern, is housed in a colonial tavern that was originally built in 1780. It served as both private residences and a tavern through its more than 200-year history. Today it still serves travelers with a creative continental menu. The big draw, though, is the restaurant's resident ghost, who has been known to give diners a friendly pat or poke now and again.

Abigail's ghost is thought to be Abigail Pettibone herself, or perhaps a child. Whoever the ghost is, she appears to be friendly and has become a Farmington Valley tradition, with radio disk jockeys often spending All Hallows'

simsburytrivia

In 1737 Simsbury's Samuel Higley developed the first copper coinage in America. The Higley copper was worth two and sixpence (42 cents) in paper currency. The coin's motto was "I am good copper." The first safety fuse, used for mining and exploration, in America was made in Simsbury in 1836 by Richard Bacon. Bacon, who ran the mine at Newgate, entered into a partnership with the English firm of Bickford, Smith & Davey.

Eve at the restaurant reporting on ghostly doings. Open for lunch Mon through Fri 11:30 a.m. to 2 p.m.; for dinner Mon through Thurs 4:30 to 9:30 p.m., Fri and Sat 4:30 to 10 p.m. Sunday brunch is served from 11 a.m. to 2 p.m., with dinner from 3 to 8:30 p.m. The tavern is open Mon through Sat from 4 to 11 p.m. and Sun from 4 to 9 p.m.

The **Phelps Tavern Museum** (800 Hopmeadow St.; 860-658-2500) in historic Simsbury is housed in the original Phelps home. Today the museum consists of period rooms and interactive exhibition galleries, showing visitors what it was like to be a guest at the Captain Elisha Phelps House when it was an inn between 1786 and 1849. Three successive generations of Phelps tavernkeepers are chronicled, along with the social history of New England taverns. Back then, Connecticut towns were required by law to have at least one tavern to accommodate travelers, who arrived by horse, stagecoach, and canal boat.

The museum sits on a 2-acre complex commonly known as the Massacoh Plantation and operated by the **Simsbury Historical Society** (800 Hopmeadow St.; 860-658-2500; simsburyhistory.org). The grounds are home to more than a dozen buildings, including a one-room schoolhouse, Victorian carriage house, museum store, and research center, as well as award-winning period gardens. Open mid-Apr to mid-Oct, except holidays, Thurs through Sat from noon to 4 p.m. Guided tours at 12:15, 1:15, 2:15, and 3:15 p.m. Admission. Grounds are open year-round during daylight hours.

For much of Simsbury's early history, **Talcott Mountain** cut the region off from the meadowlands of the Connecticut River Valley to the east. This isolation ended when the Albany Turnpike was hacked across the mountain, but the state of mind engendered by that knife-edge of rock looming dramatically over the landscape remains. Though separated by only a mile from the towns of Hartford's meadowlands, Simsbury, Avon, and even Farmington, to the south, have far more in common with the small towns to their west than with the suburbs east of the mountain.

simsburytrivia

Simsbury's main avenue, Hopmeadow Street, gets its name from the fields of hops that once grew where the street runs today.

There has been a tower atop Talcott Mountain for most of the past 200 years. The first was built in 1810 and was the inspiration for John Greenleaf Whittier's poem "Monte Video." It was blown down in a windstorm in 1840.

Others followed until finally, in 1914, businessman Gilbert Heublein built a fourth tower atop the mountain, a grand white 165-foot-high edifice of steel and concrete anchored in the rock. For 20 years this so-called **Heublein Tower** was a summer home for the Heublein family. Today the mountain and its tower are all part of **Talcott Mountain State Park** (Route 185; 860-424-3200). Four states are visible from the top of the tower, but first you have to get there. The main public access route is off Route 185. A road leads partway up the mountain to a parking area, from which you can hike the 1¼-mile trail to the top. The early part of the climb is fairly steep, but there are benches for resting. Once you reach the tower, you'll have to make another climb up the stairs to the top; there are no elevators.

The park is open year-round from 8 a.m. to sunset. Heublein Tower is open Thurs through Sun, 10 a.m. to 5 p.m., late May through Aug, and daily, 10 a.m. to 5 p.m., Labor Day through Oct.

When leaving Talcott Mountain, turn left on Route 185 and drive west toward Route 10. A mile or so west of the access road, you'll come to an old iron bridge. On your right is a huge, bare, witchy-looking tree whose branches loom over the road like some spectral presence. Right before the bridge is the entrance to a very small park where the **Pinchot Sycamore,** reputedly the oldest tree in Connecticut, resides. Take the turn slowly, as it's a bit steep as you enter the park. You'll be in awe as you stand under the tree that sports a 23-foot-diameter trunk. You have to stop and wonder about all this beautiful sycamore has seen in its history.

Canton

Canton, like so many Connecticut towns, has a ghost. This one is supposedly in the shape of a Revolutionary War messenger who disappeared in the vicinity while conveying a payroll from Hartford patriots to French officers aiding the Americans. After a bleached skeleton was found under the Canton Tavern, where the man was last seen alive, stories began circulating that the innkeeper had murdered the hapless messenger and stolen the money. Shortly thereafter, people started seeing a headless horseman, presumed to be the ghost of the paymaster, riding west along the Albany Turnpike (US 44) toward Saratoga. They still do. So if you're down by the Canton Golf Course some dark and foggy night, and you notice that your headlights are shining through a ghostly horseman and his steed to illuminate the road beyond, don't pay it any mind. It's just the Headless Horseman of Canton on his perpetual journey.

The headless horseman isn't the only antique in Canton. In fact, from Canton west to the state line, the Albany Turnpike is dotted with antiques shops, flea markets, and just plain junk stores filled with antiques, collectibles, and vintage items. Some of the best are in Canton itself, including *Antiques at Canton Village* (220 Albany Turnpike; 860-693-2715) in the *Canton Village Shopping Center,* and *Balcony Antiques* (81 Albany Turnpike; 860-693-4478). Both are multidealer shops, and Balcony is the oldest such shop in the state.

One of the best ways to learn about antiques or to snap up some good furniture at bargain prices is to go to an auction. Two people who know auctions are Richard Wacht and Susan Wacht Goralski, co-owners of *Canton Barn Auction Gallery* (75 Old Canton Rd.; 860-693-0601). Richard is a second-generation auctioneer, and Susan helps in all other aspects of the business, which specializes in Victorian and colonial-era antiques, but occasionally has some other very cool items. You never know what you'll find. Auctions are conducted weekly on Sat at 7:30 p.m. (Check the website cantonbarn.com for special dates, though.) Doors open at 5 p.m. for advance viewing. The shop is also open Sun from 10 a.m. to 4 p.m. for pick-up, appraisals, and more advance viewing for the next week's auction. While this can be loads of fun, please note that children under the age of 16 are not allowed.

If you have teens, or you consider yourself young at heart, you may want to consider a stop at the *Trading Post* (233 Albany Turnpike; 860-693-4679;

tradingpostct.com) in Canton. Offering an eclectic collection of all things rock and roll, Trading Post is open Mon through Sat from 10 a.m. to 8 p.m., and Sun 11 a.m. to 7 p.m. Inside you will find a huge selection of band T-shirts, CDs, DVDs, jewelry, women's clothing and accessories, posters, the requisite lava lamps, and so much more. All we can say is, "Groovy, man."

OTHER ATTRACTIONS WORTH SEEING IN THE HEARTLAND

Antiq's LLC
(American and English furniture)
1839 New Britain Ave.
Farmington
(860) 676-2670
antiqs.com

Behind the Scenes at the Bushnell
166 Capitol Ave.
Hartford
(860) 987-6000
bushnell.org

Garden of Light
(natural food market)
395 W. Main St.
Avon
(860) 409-2196
gardenoflight.net

International Skating Center of Connecticut
1375 Hopmeadow St.
Simsbury
(860) 651-5400
isccskate.com

Luddy/Taylor Connecticut Valley Tobacco Museum
Northwest Park
135 Lang Rd.
Windsor
(860) 285-1888
tobaccohistoc.org

Rose's Berry Farm
295 Matson Hill Rd., South
Glastonbury
and 1200 Hebron Ave., Glastonbury
(860) 633-7467
rosesberryfarm.com

Tulmeadow Farm & Ice Cream
255 Farms Village Rd. (Route 309)
West Simsbury
(860) 658-1430
tulmeadowfarmstore.com

Vintage Radio & Communications Museum of Connecticut
115 Pierson Ln.
Windsor
(860) 683-2903
vrcmct.org

Vintage Shop
61 Arch St.
New Britain
(860) 224-8567

Water Gardens of Eating Greenhouse
(hydroponic greenhouse)
Hartford Farms
3 Fowler Place
Windsor
(860) 724-3700

In the southern part of Canton on Route 179 is the village of Collins-ville, formerly home of the **Collins Company,** an 18th- and 19th-century manufacturer of axes and machetes that were sold around the world, and now home to **Antiques on the Farmington** (10 Depot St.; 860-693-0615; antiquesonfarmington.com), a multidealer shop with furniture and appoint-ments displayed in room settings so you really feel as if you've walked back in time. Browse slowly and you may just find a bargain. Open daily 10 a.m. to 5 p.m.

The story of the Collins Company is recounted in a series of exhibits in the **Canton Historical Museum** (11 Front St.; 860-693-2793; canton museum.org). This small museum houses one of the largest collections of Victoriana in the US. There is also a striking 2,000-square-foot railway diorama accurately showing Collinsville and Canton as they appeared circa 1900. Open Apr through Nov, 1 to 4 p.m. Wed through Sun; Dec through Mar, 1 to 4 p.m. Sat and Sun. Admission.

If you're looking for something sweet, be sure to check out **Village Sweet Shoppe** (5 River St.; 860-693-3301; villagesweetshoppecollinsville .com), where you'll find quality chocolates and other candy that promise to "satisfy even the most discriminating sweet tooth." Village Sweet Shoppe also carries a large assortment of primitive decorations and seasonal good-ies. Located in one of the village's historic buildings, this one is another must-see.

Avon

Crossing into **Avon,** follow Town Farm Road to its end. If you turn left, you travel the narrow, winding roads past **Avon Old Farms School.** This private school for boys was designed by Theodate Pope Riddle of Hill-Stead Museum fame. The buildings are modeled after cottages in Great Britain's Cotswolds. There are no tours of the campus for the public, but you can drive through the school to look at the buildings. By the way, Old Farms Road can be tricky; it's full of sharp curves, twists, and narrow bridges, so drive carefully and obey the speed limits.

If you had turned right instead of left, you would have quickly hap-pened upon **Fisher Meadows Conservation Area,** a wonderful little park for hiking and walking. The green trail around Spring Lake measures a little over a mile and is a good, flat walk. For a more strenuous hike, take the

Talking Turkey

Gobble, gobble, gobble. You probably won't be watching the Horse Guards practice when the winter holidays roll around, so stick a bookmark here to remind you to seek out the farm next to the Horse Guards headquarters: **Miller Foods Inc.** (308 Arch St.; 860-673-3256; millerfoodsonline.com) in Avon grows some of the best gobblers in the region, but fresh birds are available only during the fall and winter holidays. At Thanksgiving Miller's pitches its "turkey tent," an outdoor bazaar full of special goodies for your holiday table. The turkeys sell like hotcakes, so call ahead to order. Outside the holiday season, Miller Foods sells other meats such as hams and smoked turkeys plus natural pet food.

2-plus-mile red trail, which follows the Farmington River. The red trail offers lots of up-and-down walking, so it's not a good walk for small kids or tots in strollers. In the spring and summer, both trails offer great opportunities to spot wildflowers, such as the Virginia waterleaf, a declining species that is protected in Connecticut. Feel free to bring Fido, but please be sure he stays on his leash; it's the rule.

About ¼ mile south on Route 10 (Waterville Road) from Avon Old Farms is the ***Avon Cider Mill*** (57 Waterville Rd.; 860-677-0343). Armando Lattizori built the mill back in 1919, and the present generation of Lattizoris still makes cider the old-fashioned way. When Armando opened his cider mill, he bought a used cider press; today that more-than-200-year-old press is still making cider. During cider season the press runs six or seven days a week and produces 35,000 to 60,000 gallons of cider. Avon Cider Mill also sells produce, lots of local apples, crafts, home-baked goods, jams, jellies, salad dressings, honey, pumpkins galore, and Christmas trees. Between Columbus Day and Christmas Eve, you can get hot fritters and doughnuts on weekends. The mill shuts down for Christmas and opens again in the spring to sell bedding plants. In season, open daily, 9 a.m. to 5 p.m.

If you continue west on US 44, you'll pass ***Old Avon Village*** (E. Main Street; 860-678-0469; oldavonvillage.com), where you'll see a huge Hitchcock-style rocking chair that is something of a local landmark. People give directions based on proximity to the rocker and rival high school students often "chair-nap" it to celebrate a football victory.

Old Avon Village boasts a pretty neat history of revitalization that started in the early 1960s when old houses were converted into retail shops. The craze caught on and over the next quarter century more homes, barns, and other buildings were converted until there was the thriving retail and commercial district you see today with 50 shops, businesses, and restaurants. Remember, stop at the chair, and enjoy!

Farther west on US 44, you'll find the **Avon Congregational Church** (6 W. Main St.; 860-678-0488; avon-church.org) at the intersection with Route 10. Completed in 1819, this classically New England church still holds services and church school every Sun at 10:30 a.m., and maintains a proud Yankee heritage of grit and determination.

This area of our state saw its first Congregational church organized in 1652. The **West Avon Congregational Church** (280 Country Club Rd.; 860-673-3996; westavonchurch.org), built in 1751, is the descendant of this congregation. But as the community began to grow and more settlers arrived, the population began to spread out, one such expansion including the area of Cider Brook in Avon. On a knoll near the end of Reverknolls Road, about a mile north of the Cider Brook Cemetery, there is a marker for the location of the "Lord's Barn," the meetinghouse of this second congregation. It was built in the mid-1700s when residents found the trip along the Farmington River from their homes to the village of Farmington to be too arduous and dangerous in the winter months. They were allowed to build their own church, to be known as the "Lord's Barn," which survived until it burned down in 1817. By that time, however, plans for a new meetinghouse to serve the growing community were already under way—if only residents could agree on a location. Unable to come to a decision, the two groups began to diverge. Changes occurred within the General Assembly that allowed additional congregations to form. The society on the east side of the river assumed the title of Third Church in Farmington and their church was built, with the help of none other than David Hoadley, the future builder of many New England churches at the intersection of what are now Routes 44 and 10. You can read more of the fascinating history on their website.

Heading north past Avon Old Farms along Nod Road, you'll eventually come to the **Pickin' Patch** (276 Nod Rd.; 860-677-9552; thepickinpatch .com). The land here has been farmed since 1666 and operates as a family-friendly farm stand and pick-your-own place. During strawberry season, the

Pickin' Patch looks like the Grand Central Station of strawberry patches. In addition to produce, raspberries, and blueberries, pumpkins, Christmas trees, wreaths, and holiday flowers are sold.

The farm stand opens when the pansies start to bloom and stays open until Christmas Eve; open 8 a.m. to 6 p.m. daily. On October weekends, you can take a free hayride to the pumpkin patch or book a group hayride during the week for a small price and receive a sugar pumpkin, cider and doughnut holes, and a souvenir cider sipper. Perfect for those gorgeous New England fall days.

Just west of the junction of Routes 44 and 10 north is Avon Park North, where you'll find the *Farmington Valley Arts Center* (25 Arts Center Ln.; 860-678-1867; artsfvac.org). Home to the Fisher Gallery and Shop and to about 20 artists' studios, this arts center represents pottery, basket weaving, printing, painting, leatherworking, and silversmithing. The center believes in promoting the arts and giving visitors the chance to experience the creative process from start to finish. What a wonderful way to inspire your inner artist! Studios are open the first Sat of every month from noon to 4 p.m., and at the discretion of the individual artists. The shop and gallery are open Wed through Sat (daily during Nov and Dec), noon to 4 p.m.; they are closed for major holidays.

The *First Company of the Governor's Horse Guards* (280 Arch Rd.; 860-673-3525; ctfirsthorse.org) is the oldest cavalry unit in continuous service in the US, tracing its lineage back to 1658, when the Connecticut

Peach Orchards

Connecticut orchards produce myriad varieties of peaches. You can buy them at roadside stands or pick your own at farms. A couple of the best places to PYO in the Heartland are: *Belltown Hill Orchards* (483 Matson Hill Rd.; 860-633-2789; belltownhillorchards.com), *Dondero Orchards* (529 Woodland St.; 860-659-0294; donderoochards.com), and *Scagllia Fruit Farm* (360 Matson Hill Rd.; 860-633-9055) in South Glastonbury; *Scott's Orchard and Nursery* (1838 New London Turnpike; 860-633-8681; scottsorchardandnursery.com) in Glastonbury; and *Easy Pickin's Orchard* (46 Bailey Rd.; 860-763-3276; easypickinsorchard .com) in Enfield. Best time to pick peaches? From mid-July for yellow peaches through Aug for the incredibly fragrant and sweet white peaches.

Colony founded a troop of mounted guards. In 1788 the Horse Guards were reformed as a company of Light Dragoons, modeled on the Royal Regiment of Horse Guards in England. When Connecticut joined the Revolution against the British Crown, the new state took over the Horse Guards. In those days the unit's main function was to escort and protect visiting dignitaries, and it acted as an honor guard to President George Washington when he visited Wethersfield in 1789.

The unit saw somewhat more dangerous service as a mounted unit in the War of 1812 and the Spanish-American War. In 1916 it patrolled the Mexican border during operations against Pancho Villa. Dismounted and reorganized as a machine-gun battalion, it served in seven major engagements in France during World War I. At the end of the war, the Horse Guards were remounted as the 122nd Cavalry Squadron of the Connecticut National Guard; four days after Pearl Harbor they became the 208th Coast Artillery and served as an antiaircraft unit in the South Pacific.

Today the Horse Guards' duties are once again mainly ceremonial. The company makes appearances at presidential and gubernatorial inaugurations. All horses are donated, and they include just about every breed except Clydesdales. On Thursday from 7 to 10 a.m., the public is invited to watch the unit practice its drills. These consist of intricate, beautifully

Pass the Doughnuts

Like countless other travelers, we enjoy stumbling upon a locale's lesser-known place that oozes true neighborly folksiness—which would aptly describe *Luke's Donut Shop* (395 W. Avon Rd.; 860-673-0622), an old-time, independent doughnut shop that has come under new ownership but still retains its community feel. Okay, so they now sell pizza, but that doesn't diminish the wonders they do with doughnuts. Luke's is one of the few places these days you can get a "cup of joe," no fancy flavorings, no special Seattle roast, just fresh-brewed all-American coffee.

Regulars have been coming to Luke's for years, and if you want the skinny on what's happening in Avon or what the hot-button issues are, just hop on a stool and listen awhile. Be careful where you sit, because, depending on the time of day, seating around the counter at Luke's is a hard-won privilege of the regulars. Open 6 a.m. to 8 p.m. daily. Be sure to bring cash, though; Luke's doesn't accept plastic.

choreographed precision maneuvers, often accompanied by music. The Horse Guards hosts an annual Open Horse Show in June as well as various community programs. The Second Company of the Governor's Horse Guards holds its summer practices in Newtown; see the Danbury entry in "Gateway to New England" for details.

Once a large dairy farm, **_Riverdale Farms Shopping_** (124 Simsbury Rd.; 860-677-6437; riverdalefarmsshopping.com) in Avon is now the site of one of the more interesting shopping centers in the area. This complex occupies several low hills under the eye of the Heublein Tower, atop Talcott Mountain to the north and east. Nineteen barn-like buildings, some original and renovated, some new, now house offices, stores, restaurants, and boutiques—and new ones are opening all the time. Most of the stores are crafts, gift, or fashion stores, but you'll also find a personal training studio, pet groomers and pet supply stores, dance studios, and so much more. Check out their website for a detailed list and a more in-depth history of this former farm.

Burlington

LaMothe's Sugar House (89 Stone Rd.; 860-675-5043; lamothesugarhouse .com) in **_Burlington_** is one of just a handful of real old-fashioned sugar houses left in Connecticut. Here, during February and March, visitors can tour a working house and see the whole process of "sugaring off." There's a big old sap boiler that cooks maple sap into syrup, which you can then see blended with cream and butter and poured into molds to make creamy shaped candies (like Santas or maple leaves), or mixed with other ingredients to make maple taffy. The sugar house sells syrup, maple candy, and maple fudge. Visitors always get a sample of some type of maple sweet. In Connecticut the peak season for sugaring off is late February or early March, but LaMothe's is open year-round, 10 a.m. to 6 p.m. Mon through Thurs, to 5 p.m. Fri and Sat, and noon to 5 p.m. Sun.

Farmington

Hill-Stead Museum (35 Mountain Rd.; 860-677-4787; hillstead.org) is so **_Farmington_** that it is almost impossible to imagine it existing anywhere else. Housed in a white clapboard 1901 replica of a neocolonial house built in an 18th-century English farm style is an amazing collection of French impressionist paintings, prints, antique furniture, porcelain, textiles, and clocks.

Hill-Stead was originally home to Cleveland iron mogul Alfred Atmore Pope. In keeping with his wealth and pretensions, Pope made sure that when it was time for daughter Theodate to go away to school, his child was entrusted to a proper eastern institution: Miss Porter's School in Farmington. Upon graduation Theodate persuaded Daddy to forsake the Buckeye State and move east to the Nutmeg State. She also talked him into springing for a new house designed by then-trendy architect Stanford White, with a sunken garden designed by landscape architect Beatrix Farrand. And since Theodate had an abiding interest in architecture, nothing would do but that the young lady should assist White in designing the new family manse. White was either a very good businessman or he was truly impressed with Theodate's work, because he cut his fee by $25,000 in appreciation of her help. Miss Pope went on to become the first woman licensed to practice architecture in the US.

Like so many American captains of industry, Pope was a collector. This was an age in which America's newly rich raided the homes and galleries of Europe for furnishings, often buying art and antiques in wholesale lots. The Popes were fairly typical in this regard, and their tastes were certainly eclectic. Chippendale furniture, fine porcelain, contemporary bronzes, and pre-Columbian statuary all jostled for space in the Pope home. On the walls hung a Degas, a Manet, a Cassatt, and no fewer than three Monets. The piano was a custom-designed Steinway.

It was all gloriously excessive. And it is all still there, just as it was when Theodate died, leaving behind 50 pages of instructions for the house to be turned into a museum and maintained just as she left it.

Hill-Stead Museum is open 10 a.m. to 4 p.m. Tues through Sun, with the last tour leaving at 3 p.m. each day. The grounds are open 7:30 a.m. to 5:30 p.m. Hill-Stead has a wonderful gift shop with prints of works exclusive to it, such as Monet's *Haystacks* and Degas's *Dancers in Pink.* Admission.

Just around the corner from the Hill-Stead Museum is the ***Stanley-Whitman House*** (37 High St.; 860-677-9222; stanleywhitman.org), a beautifully restored 1720 colonial homestead. The original house, built to a typical early 18th-century standard, has a central chimney flanked by 2 chambers on each of 2 floors; it was later expanded by the addition of a lean-to that gives it a saltbox shape. The wood-sided exterior was originally painted with a mixture of ox blood and buttermilk; the restoration has not gone to quite that extreme, but otherwise it seems authentic. Hinged access panels inside the house let you see details of the original construction and restoration. The house is filled with period furnishings and is surrounded by herb and flower gardens. The gift shop sells items of local historical interest. Tours are offered Wed through Sun, noon to 4 p.m., with the last one leaving at 3:15 p.m. The museum is open Wed through Fri 9 a.m. to 4 p.m., Sat and Sun noon to 4 p.m. Admission.

The neighborhood around the Stanley-Whitman House includes a large number of 18th-century (and some 19th-century) homes and buildings, all of them still in use by modern residents. These can be seen to best advantage from Route 10, where, in less than a mile, you can view a 1772 Congregational meetinghouse, a renovated 1650 gristmill, a colonial-era graveyard, and the remains of the Farmington Canal. Also on Route 10, a couple hundred yards from the intersection with Route 4, is Miss Porter's School, known for turning out graduate Jacqueline Bouvier Kennedy Onassis.

Should you be in Farmington over a weekend and find yourself with a little time on your hands, stay on Route 4 west through Farmington Center, cross the bridge over the Farmington River, and turn right onto Town Farm Road.

You'll pass a monster 45-hole golf course called ***Tunxis Plantation Country Club and Golf Course*** (87 Town Farm Rd.; 860-677-1367; tunxis golf.com). How Tunxis Plantation Country Club came into being is something of a local legend.

Denied membership in one of Farmington's snootier golf clubs, a local developer simply built his own. Golfers of our acquaintance highly recommend the place, especially for autumn golfing. Tunxis Plantation usually opens around Easter and closes mid-Nov. Open 7 a.m. to 7 p.m. weekdays, 6 a.m. to 7 p.m. weekends. The clubhouse serves food.

About 2 miles past Tunxis Plantation, you'll happen upon the ***Simmons Family Farm*** (199 Town Farm Rd.; 860-679-9388). This was one of the oldest family-run dairy farms in Connecticut, and they were not going to be done in when the economy turned sour. In 2011, owners Robin and Ronnie Simmons decided that producing milk was getting too expensive and they needed to find another way to turn a profit. They decided to get in the yogurt business, and the rest is a tasty history. Now sold all over the state and even in surrounding areas, Simmons Family Farm Lowfat Yogurt has won numerous awards and gained a loyal fan base. The farm has since expanded the herd, created new packaging, and is doing quite well. If you'd like to stop in and see where it all started, the family welcomes visitors Mon through Sat 10 a.m. to 5 p.m.

Minigolf in the Heartland

Big-time, headline-making tournament champions and weekend duffers will tell you with equal outspokenness that golf belongs in its lofty niche on the international sports scene. And think about the famous courses, from California to Scotland. But miniature golf, with all its goofy charm, is a different story. Statewide, Connecticut has plenty of teeny-weeny putt-putt layouts in settings ranging from pretty and pastoral to outright Disney-ish. Here is a random trio:

Riverfront Miniature Golf and Ice Cream (218 River Rd., Unionville; 860-675-4653) doesn't rely on kitsch, but rather has constructed a course with hazards and holes made up of rocks taken from the nearby Farmington River. It's one of the prettiest minigolf courses we've seen and one adult enough that older kids will enjoy it without thinking it's uncool. A word of warning: The course runs along the Farmington River, so keep an eagle eye on overeager youngsters, who might go on a bender by inventing their own rules involving throwing balls and golf clubs into the rushing stream. There's a cute ice cream shop attached to the golf course, where parched duffers and their families can refresh themselves. Birthday parties and other special occasions are a specialty. Hours can vary, so it's best to call ahead to check.

Safari Golf (2340 Berlin Turnpike, Berlin; 860-828-9800). Safari Golf is probably Connecticut's most famous minigolf course. In fact, the *Hartford Advocate* has voted it the best miniature golf course in the state. Playing it is a lot like taking a safari; you'll find lots of life-size jungle animals lying in wait for you, waterfalls to traverse, and lots of waving, ominous jungle-like landscaping. The replicas of lions, tigers, and other critters give the course a sense of wonderful silliness, and the water hazards make it difficult enough that older kids and adults won't get bored. Open daily in the summer from 10 a.m. to 10 p.m., always weather permitting, with shorter hours in fall and spring. The folks at Safari Golf know how to make kids' birthday parties an occasion.

Hidden Valley (2060 West St., Southington; 860-621-1630; hiddenvalleyof southington.com). Like Riverfront, Hidden Valley relies on pretty rather than cute. It's a challenging course for older kids and adults with lots of waterfalls and other traps. Batting cages and snack foods are available. Available for birthday parties and other special occasions. Open (weather permitting) Sun through Thurs 10 a.m. to 9 p.m., and Fri and Sat 10 a.m. to 10 p.m.

Back out on Route 4 west and back in Farmington, you'll encounter, tucked away in a converted trolley barn, a restaurant called **Apricots** (1593 Farmington Ave.; 860-673-5405; apricotsrestaurant.com) that serves an eclectic cuisine based on French, nouvelle American, and country cooking. The downstairs is a comfortable bar and lower-priced pub-style restaurant, popular, noisy, and crowded. Pub food is also served on the patio. Upstairs is an elegant, white-tablecloth eatery, occupying several rambling, windowed rooms overlooking the Farmington River.

The menu changes throughout the year, but there's always a pasta and chicken dish of the day, as well as several fish and seafood entrees. Full menus are listed on their website. The dining rooms are open daily for lunch from 11:30 a.m. to 2:30 p.m., with the pub staying open until 5 p.m. Both the dining rooms and the pub are open for dinner Mon through Sat 5 to 9:30 p.m. and until 9 on Sun.

Farmington played an important role in the antislavery movement. Many abolitionists called the area home and offered their houses as stops on the Underground Railroad. In fact, Farmington soon gained the moniker "Grand Central Station" of the railroad. Many of these places, and others that saw important history, have been preserved and are part of the Connecticut Freedom Trail. The **Farmington Historical Society** (138 Main St.; 860-678-1645; farmingtonhistoricalsociety-ct.org) offers tours of Farmington's portion of the trail. Those interested should call ahead and make reservations; if you'd like to see the places on your own, the society publishes a brochure with all the places listed. It can be downloaded off their website.

About 5 miles east of the center of Farmington along Route 4 is the **Unionville** section of Farmington. During the late 18th and early 19th centuries, this area was a minor industrial center. It made flints for Washington's army and guns for the War of 1812. It also manufactured the pikes that Torrington native John Brown took with him to Harpers Ferry (and that he intended to use to arm the Southern slaves he planned to induce to revolt). The **Unionville Museum** (15 School St.; 860-673-2231; unionvillemuseum .org) displays some of these locally made items. The museum is open 2 to 4 p.m. Wed, Sat, and Sun.

Central Connecticut

New Britain

New Britain got its manufacturing start making sleigh bells. From these modest beginnings the city gradually branched out in the early 1800s and into the manufacture of other hardware products, until it eventually came to be known as the "Hardware City." With the industrial age came waves of new immigrants seeking jobs in the tool works. The Irish came first, then the Germans and Swedes, then the Italians. The biggest waves, though, consisted of Eastern Europeans, including Lithuanians, Ukrainians, and Armenians. Probably the largest group in this wave was the Poles. Even after the hardware industry moved abroad, Polish immigrants continued to arrive in New Britain. Today the city's population of first- and second-generation Poles is greater than that of many cities in Poland. They have contributed their music, their language, and their food to the city.

The center of the Polish community is a Broad Street business district where Polish is spoken almost as freely as English.

You can taste the wonders of Polish food at ***Cracovia*** (60 Broad St.; 860-223-4443; cracoviarestaurantct.com). The food gets consistently high reviews, but be prepared as the restaurant is not fancy, not by a long shot, but it is homey, dominated by the Polish falcon and Polish-language announcements about upcoming community events. Thankfully, the menu is in English, and the waitresses are good at explaining menu choices to non-Poles. The food is Central and Eastern European, bounteous, and cheap. The pierogi are excellent; so are the *golabki* (tender, tasty cabbage rolls stuffed with beef and rice, braised in a slightly sweet tomato sauce). Most of the entrees are served with true mashed potatoes, with the happy little lumps that mark them as the real thing instead of the instant variety. The homemade soups are served in bathtub-size portions; the white borscht and the dill pickle soup get high marks. Open 8 a.m. to 8 p.m. daily.

To create some of the Polish specialties you enjoyed at Cracovia at home, stop at ***Podlasie*** (188 High St.; 860-224-8467). It's like visiting a marketplace in Eastern Europe. You'll find Polish mineral water; dark, dense bread; newspapers; ingredients for Polish cooking; and some very intriguing Polish chocolates on the shelves. The back of the store is given over to a dairy case (great country butter), a pastry case full of elegant-looking tortes and cakes, and a case for cheeses, herring, fresh meats, and cold cuts, many made in the store. Most of the shoppers are Polish, so Polish is the common tongue. There's usually at least one English speaker in the store who is happy to help you translate.

Open Mon through Sat at 9 a.m. Closing hours: 5 p.m. Mon and Sat, 6 p.m. Tues and Wed, 7 p.m. Thurs and Fri. (There is another Podlasie in Bridgeport at 2286 E. Main St.; 203-335-0321.)

The Hardware City is not all about industry, however. There is also a true appreciation of the arts, evidenced by the **New Britain Museum of American Art** (56 Lexington St.; 860-229-0257; nbmaa.org). Established in 1903, this museum is the oldest in the US devoted solely to American art. Its 3,000 holdings include portraits by Cassatt, Stuart, Copley, and Sargent and the western bronzes of Solon Borglum, as well as works by the likes of O'Keeffe, Noguchi, Benton, and Wyeth. Its collection of American impressionists is second to none.

There are landscapes by Hassam, Inness, Bierstadt, Church, and Cole (including *The Clove,* with its mysterious disappearing figures) among others. Graydon Parrish's *The Cycle of Terror and Tragedy: September 11, 2001* is a truly moving experience. The 77-inch-by-120-inch painting covers most of the length of one wall of the building, making it life-like in size. The museum provides benches in front of the painting for visitors to sit and reflect. The feeling in the room as people pay their respects is almost tangible. The experience may be too intense for younger patrons, so please use discretion if you have children with you.

The museum also sponsors temporary exhibits throughout the year. One such exhibit, Lisa Hoke's *The Gravity of Color* was an amazing kaleidoscope of color made almost entirely of plastic and paper cups. The 2-story design graced the LeWitt Staircase beginning in 2008, and was even featured on the cover of *Art New England.* We saw children absolutely awed by its beauty and uniqueness.

The museum is open 11 a.m. to 5 p.m. Tues, Wed, and Fri, 11 a.m. to 8 p.m. Thurs, 10 a.m. to 5 p.m. Sat, and noon to 5 p.m. Sun. Closed Mon. Gift shop. Admission is charged except Sat from 10 a.m. to noon. This free window is a great time to introduce the kids to the art of this wonderful place without breaking the bank.

ANNUAL EVENTS IN THE HEARTLAND

FEBRUARY

Connecticut Flower & Garden Show
Connecticut Expo Center, Hartford
(860) 844-8461
ctflowershow.com
Just when you think spring will never
come, this fabulous show reminds you
it's just around the corner.

MARCH

Connecticut Spring Antiques Show
Connecticut Expo Center
265 Reverend Moody Overpass
Hartford
(207) 767-3967
ctspringantiquesshow.com

APRIL

River Run 5k & 10k Races
Iron Horse Boulevard, Simsbury
(860) 651-5917

JUNE

Travelers Championship
Hartford
(860) 502-6800
travelerschampionship.com
One of the crown jewels on the PGA
tour. A great chance to see your
favorite links guys up close. The

pro-am contest before the actual
tournament offers wonderful chances
for photos and autographs.

JULY

Greater Hartford Festival of Jazz
Bushnell Park, Hartford
(860) 727-0050
hartfordjazzorg
Three days, two stages, 14 bands, and
tons of food and marketplace vendors.

Riverfest
Hartford and East Hartford
(860) 713-3131
riverfront.org
A celebration of the Fourth of July
and the Connecticut River with
show-stopping fireworks over the
Connecticut River.

SEPTEMBER

Mum Festival
Bristol
(860) 584-4718
bristolmumfestival.org
It's mum madness throughout the
town, late Sept to mid-Oct. Beauty
pageants, parades, arts and crafts,
antique car show, and of course,
mums for sale.

New Britain's ***Central Connecticut State University*** is home to the
small ***Copernican Observatory and Planetarium*** (1615 Stanley St.;
.860-832-3399; ccsu.edu/astronomy), which offers free programs on a first
come, first served basis, usually on Saturday around 8 p.m. This is not a
well-funded program, so times and dates are sketchy; it's best to check the
website or call ahead. There is, however, enthusiasm and an obvious love

OCTOBER

Open Cockpit Day
New England Air Museum
Just off Route 75, at Bradley
International Airport in Windsor Locks
(860) 623-3305
neam.org
Your chance to visit the museum and,
most important, climb into the cockpit
of some of its coolest planes. This is a
very popular event, so expect to spend
some time waiting in line.

ING Hartford Marathon & Half Marathon
Begins at Bushnell Park
(860) 652-8866
hartfordmarathon.com
Course through downtown Hartford
and along Connecticut River.

NOVEMBER

Festival of Lights
Bushnell Park, Hartford
Enjoy outdoor skating rink and other
family activities. Late November to
early January, lights go on at dusk.
Santa has been known to make an
appearance.

Manchester Road Race
Main Street, Manchester
(860) 649-6456
manchesterroadrace.com
A 4.75-mile race with 15,000 runners.
Second-oldest in the state.

DECEMBER

Stanley-Whitman House Tour
37 High St., Farmington
(860) 677-9222
You'll begin with a stroll along High
Street, decorated for the holiday
season, then enjoy a light supper of
soups, breads, and dessert. Afterward
you'll take a tour of this historic house,
led by costumed guides, enacting
mini-dramas connected with Christmas
and the history of Farmington.
Admission; reservations required.

of the subject matter by the presenters. It's a great way to gain an intro into all things astronomical. Did we mention it's free?

New Britain's moniker as the Hardware City is commemorated in the *New Britain Industrial Museum* (185 Main St.; 860-832-8654; nbim.org). It's a small but choice museum, put together by people who genuinely love New Britain and its industrial past. You can trace New Britain's past and see

newbritaintrivia

The Copernican Observatory and Planetarium at Central Connecticut State University in New Britain houses one of the largest publicly available telescopes in the US.

its future as you view the history of the companies that put New Britain on the map: Stanley Works, Fafnir Bearing, Landers, North & Judd, and American Hardware. Open 2 to 5 p.m. Mon, Tues, Thurs, and Fri, and noon to 5 p.m. Wed. Free.

Taking the family to see a major-league baseball game is expensive. But here in Connecticut, you can get all the authentic appeal of America's pastime without having to sell your Mickey Mantle rookie card. You can sit close to the action, and chances are good you'll be able to snag a foul ball or a player's autograph. Best of all, you might discover the next Barry Bonds or Derek Jeter before the rest of the world catches on. Check out the **New Britain Rock Cats** (New Britain Stadium, Willow Brook Park, 230 John Karbonic Way; 860-224-8383; milb.com/index.jsp?sid=t538). The Rock Cats are members of the Eastern League, AA affiliate of the Minnesota Twins. They play Apr through Sept and offer many kid-friendly activities, all at a fraction of the cost of a trip to New York or Boston.

Avery's Beverages (520 Corbin Ave.; 860-224-0830; averysoda.com) is another jewel in New Britain. In fact, it's the wonderful Aladdin's cave of jewel-colored soda and mysterious Rube Goldberg machinery some readers might remember from their childhoods. At Avery's they bottle soda the way it used to be done back in the day, wooden carrying cases and all. The family has been bottling soda in the same red barn since 1904. Sherman F. Avery used to deliver his soda all over New Britain and beyond in a horse-drawn wagon before he went modern in 1914 and purchased a delivery truck. Today they still make deliveries to nearby towns. Or you can visit their store to sample that high-quality soda pop made from only the finest quality ingredients, including real cane sugar (no sugar substitutes here!), and naturally pure well water. You can even try your hand at making your own, but beware—some results from that endeavor include bottles of Dog Drool Soda, Toxic Slime, and Monster Mucus. Um, yuck? Perhaps it's safer to stick to some of Avery's original recipes of cola, lemon-lime, ginger ale, and root and birch beer. Whatever your taste, you'll find it bottled in glass to preserve that old-fashioned flavor. Avery's has such a fascinating history, and if you have the time, call ahead to arrange a tour of the bottling works. You won't be disappointed.

As you drive down Route 9 between New Britain and Farmington, you'll pass a hauntingly familiar sculpture of some American marines raising a flag. This is the *Iwo Jima Survivors' Memorial Park and Monument.* It is dedicated to 6,821 Americans who, during World War II, gave their lives in the desperate fight for the Pacific island of Iwo Jima, the place where it was said that "uncommon valor" was a "common virtue." The monument's sculpture re-creates the famous flag-raising by American troops atop Mount Suribachi. On special days, such as Veterans Day, the monument is decorated with an avenue of American flags. Open 24 hours daily.

Southington

Saint's (1248 Queen St.; 860-747-0566; saintsct.com) in *Southington* has a simple philosophy: Serve high-quality food, price it right, and deliver it with pride. The philosophy works—the eatery's been dishing up its famous hot dogs to popular acclaim since 1967. Family-owned for three generations now, Saint's continues to serve up some of the best hot dogs, Philly cheese-steak sandwiches, and homemade mac and cheese in the area. *Yankee* magazine gave Saint's an honorable mention when it rated "Best Hot Dogs of New England," and some chili dog connoisseurs swear these are the best in the state. Saint's is something of a local hangout with an easy camaraderie shared between the customers and the staff. Open Mon through Sat 6 a.m. to 9 p.m., Sun 6 a.m. to 8 p.m.

Once you're full, hop on I-84 and head south to exit 30 and the Plants-ville section of Southington, where you'll find *Plantsville Station Antique Shops* (75 W. Main St.; 860-628-8918). This wonderful shop carries lots of nice old linens, oak furniture, and collectibles. Owners Robert and Kathleen Celentano are very friendly and helpful. One interesting tidbit is that the building in which the shop makes its home only looks like a train station. In previous incarnations it housed a machine shop and other light industry—never a train station. Even so, the Celentanos frequently field phone calls from people wanting a train schedule. Open Wed through Sat 10 a.m. to 4:30 p.m., and Sun from noon to 4:30 p.m.

If you have little ones with you, be sure to visit *Karabin Farms* (894 Andrew St.; 860-620-0194; karabinfarms.com). They've been in town since

1972, and what started out as a hobby for owners Michael and Diane Karabin has turned into a family-run, family fun place. They offer pick-your-own apples, peaches, pumpkins, and Christmas trees (they also offer pre-cut ones). There are hayrides to the fields, live animals to visit (including very funky-looking Highland cattle), snacks to be had at the snack barn, as well as an entire treasure chest of things to be discovered in the store. Throughout the year, along with the fresh fruit and vegetables, you can also find local honey, maple syrup, Crowley cheese, jams, specialty soap and candles, home-baked pies, and soup mixes. Seasonal flowers are also available, including a huge variety of poinsettias at Christmas. The farm is open daily 9 a.m. to 5 p.m.; pick-your-own hours are generally from 10 a.m. to 4 p.m.

Plainville

Back in the 18th century, Route 10 was the major thoroughfare passing through *Plainville.* It was down this road that Rochambeau's French army marched on its way to join Washington and travel to Yorktown, and then win the decisive battle of the American Revolution and head back to Boston. The location of one of the French campgrounds is marked by a small plaque at the intersection of Main Street (Route 10) and Hatters Lane (on the right if you're traveling north). French armies notwithstanding, the road was less traveled in that century, and trips had to be planned more carefully. To aid the traveler, the route was marked with milestones indicating the distance to Hartford. Today, at three places along the east side of Route 10 (at the corner of Betsy Road, at the junction of Route 372, and in front of Woodmore Village), you can still see the old milestones, but they are hard to find, and Route 10 is very busy, so please be careful!

Bristol

If you're looking for some great family fun, especially in the summer or in October, head east from Plainville to *Bristol*'s *Lake Compounce* (186 Enterprise Dr.; 860-583-3300; lakecompounce.com). Now the country's oldest amusement park, Lake Compounce has been serving up family fun and thrills since 1846 with its 427 acres, 20-acre lake, and more than 50 rides and attractions. There really is something for everyone, including a great portion of the park for the smaller children, with age-appropriate rides and shows. The more daring can choose from 3 coasters: the Zoomerang, Boulder Dash,

Going Up?

On your way to Lake Compounce, you may notice a very tall, interesting-looking building jutting out of the trees. It looks a little like a transplanted skyscraper from the city. It is actually an elevator test tower. Located on the grounds of the Bristol Research Center, the tower is used by the Otis Quality Assurance Center. Topping out at 383 feet, the test tower is the tallest in North America.

and Wildcat. If you're willing to get wet, there's Riptide Racer, Clipper Cove, Mammoth Falls, and much, much more, including Lights Out, which is a high-speed water slide in, you guessed it, the dark. Okay, not for us! For those of you who are with us on this, there are tamer options, including the beautiful old-fashioned carousel. You'll find horses carved by Looff, Carmel, and Stein & Goldstein. There are 49 horses (27 jumpers and 22 standers), a goat, and two chariots. The original Wurlitzer organ still grinds out tunes for riders. Like we said, something for everyone. Admission. Open daily noon to 7 p.m. Memorial Day through Labor Day and then sporadically from Labor Day until the end of Dec, during which the park offers some way-cool Halloween and holiday lights events. Be sure to check their website for details and admission costs.

If you're interested in antiques, shopping at **Dick's Antiques** (670 Lake Ave.; 860-584-2566; dicksantiques.com) in Bristol is a must. Proprietor Dick Blaschke will entertain you with yarns about his adventures in antiquing. You'll be impressed by the dazzling collection of Victorian, oak, and country furniture; vintage glass; china; clocks; lighting fixtures; and accessories. Dick and his partner, Rick Kuracz, are not only extremely likeable guys, they're also top experts in their field, so you can buy with confidence. Hours: 10 a.m. to 5 p.m. Mon through Fri; noon to 5 p.m. Sat; closed Tues and Sun; July and Aug: 10 a.m. to 5 p.m. Mon or by appointment. While they try to keep shop hours, Dick says it's always best to call ahead to be sure he'll be there when you arrive.

About the middle of the 19th century, Bristol was the center of clock- and watchmaking in the Northeast. At one time the town supported 280 clockmakers, and in 1860 they turned out a total of 200,000 clocks. Today the great clockworks are only a memory preserved in the town's *American*

Clock & Watch Museum (100 Maple St.; 860-583-6070; clockandwatch museum.org). Within the walls of the 1801 Miles Lewis House and 2 modern additions, the museum manages to display a collection of more than 1,500 clocks and watches, including many made locally. This vast assemblage is organized by type and eras, so that as you move from room to room, you can observe how the styles of clock cases changed to match furniture styles. Tours are entirely self-guided and take a suggested hour and a half; the exhibits are well marked. Among the more interesting items are some oak clock cases from the 1920s and 1930s, which are exhibited together with the metal rollers that pressed the intricate designs into the wood. There are also lovely "tall" clocks, including some made by Eli Terry. There's even one clock whose workings are carved entirely from wood. The American Clock & Watch Museum is open daily 10 a.m. to 5 p.m. through early Dec. Admission.

Clocks and watches aren't the only items collected in Bristol. Housed in a restored turn-of-the-20th-century factory building, the ***New England Carousel Museum*** (95 Riverside Ave.; 860-585-5411; thecarouselmuseum .org) contains some of the best examples of antique carousel art in existence, more than 300 pieces in all. Featured items include a collection of band organs, the entire carousel from Santa's Land in Putnam, Vermont, and a gorgeous pair of 1915 carved chariots, each encrusted with 1,500 glass jewels. The museum also has 2 art galleries and a fine history exhibit. This was the first museum of its kind on the East Coast, and many preservationists still consider it the best.

The main museum occupies the building's ground floor. Wood-carvers and painters perform restorations on the second floor, and if you happen to be there while they are working, you can go upstairs and watch. The second floor also contains the Museum of Fire History, which is worth a visit and is included in the admission price. Open Mar through Dec, 10 a.m. to 5 p.m. Tues through Sat, noon to 5 p.m. Sun. Closed major holidays, but usually open for local school holidays. You can also reserve the museum for special events year-round, with youth-group sleepovers (called Painted Pony Pajama Parties) and weddings being hot tickets in this part of the state. Admission.

One of the best attractions in Bristol is one you are unlikely to stumble across unless you're a native Nutmegger and you happen to be around at Halloween time (and happen to also read this book!). ***Witch's Dungeon***

Classic Movie Museum (90 Battle St.; 860-583-8306; preservehollywood
.org) is now approaching its 50th season, and it all started with young Cortlandt Hull, who as an ill child spent time building model monster kits. As
he grew up, he became fascinated with the theatrical transformations from
human to monster. Soon Cortlandt grew bored with his models and hungered
for more. He was disappointed with visits to different wax museums that just
didn't do it for him, so he started creating his own full-size versions of his
favorite monsters, and they seemed to take on a life of their own. It was a
real family affair—Cortlandt's dad helped him with a building to house them
in and built the backgrounds, his mom re-created many of the famous costumes for his creatures, his uncle acted as engineer—and the rest is history.

By the '70s and '80s, Cortlandt's skills had improved, and his "little"
museum started to gain national attention from the likes of the *New York
Times, National Geographic,* and Ripley's Believe It or Not! Members of the
acting community took notice, too, and lent their support. Vincent Price,
John Agar, and Mark Hamill all did special recordings for the museum. People from all over the country have come to visit this Connecticut treasure.
Cortlandt's beloved creatures are now sought after and travel the country
to star in their own special displays. Cortlandt himself is well known as an
artist. Who knew all this would come from his interest in monster models?!

Open only during Oct, Sat and Sun from 7 to 10 p.m. Small admission
charge. Not wheelchair accessible at this time. The website warns you to
dress warmly and be prepared to wait in line for up to two hours. The tour
takes less than three minutes and only three or so people can go at one time.

Places to Stay in the Heartland

GLASTONBURY

Butternut Farm
1654 Main St.
(860) 633-7197
butternutfarmbandb.com
Moderate

So much more than just a
bed-and-breakfast, But-
ternut Farm is a labor of
love for innkeeper Don
Reid, who has owned
the property since 1959.
After spending years
renovating the home,
Reid opened it as a B&B
in 1977, and today the
inn offers 5 guest rooms,
each with private bath. A
full breakfast is served,
including fresh eggs from
the farm's chickens. All
the rooms are outfitted
with colonial furnishings,
so you may just feel as if
you've stepped back in
time. Enjoy!

Connecticut River Valley Inn

2195 Main St.
(860) 633-7374
connecticutrivervalleyinn
.com
Moderate to expensive
Beautiful at any time of
the year, the Connecticut
River Valley Inn offers 4
seasonally themed rooms.
A favorite for weddings
and other special occa-
sions, this inn is also
perfect for a romantic
getaway.

SIMSBURY

Simsbury 1820 House
731 Hopmeadow St.
(860) 658-7658
simsbury1820house.com
Moderate to expensive
This rambling, comfortable
house, built in 1820, was
the home of Gifford Pin-
chot, the man who raised
America's consciousness
about conservation. Today
the restored inn offers
32 guest rooms but still
looks much as it did in its
heyday, with shining oak
floors and glorious leaded
glass windows. All the
rooms are comfortably
furnished with antiques
and high-quality reproductions. Guests receive a
complimentary breakfast
in the beautiful dining
room from 7 to 10 a.m.

Linden House Bed and Breakfast

288/290 Hopmeadow St.
Weatogue
(860) 408-1321
lindenhousebb.com
Moderate
Located in the village of
Weatogue in Simsbury,
the Linden House B&B
offers 5 guest rooms in a
beautifully restored Victorian home. Near Talcott
Mountain State Park,
shopping, antiquing, and
historic sights, this B&B is
everything a New England
getaway should be.

Places to Eat in the Heartland

AVON

First & Last Tavern
26 W. Main St. (US 44)
(860) 676-2000
firstandlasttavern.com
Inexpensive to moderate
Comfortable pub-style
place offering casual Italian fare. The focaccia is
delicious.

CANTON

Bamboo Grill
50 Albany Turnpike
(860) 693-4144
bamboogrillcuisine.com
Inexpensive to moderate
A wonderful Vietnamese
restaurant with tasty, inexpensive, and healthy food.

COLLINSVILLE

Crown and Hammer Pub
3 Depot St.
(860) 693-9199
crownandhammer.com
Moderate to expensive
Great pub-style food, live
entertainment, and beautiful views of the Farming-
ton River and dam.

LaSalle Market & Deli
104 Main St.
(860) 693-8010
lasallemarket.com
Inexpensive
Great location with live
music, including open-mic
Friday starting at 6 p.m.,
rain or shine. The last
Saturday of each month
features "Band Jam Night"
starting at 7 p.m.

HARTFORD

Trumbull Kitchen
150 Trumbull St.
(860) 493-7412
maxrestaurantgroup.com
Moderate to expensive
One of the city's hippest,
coolest contemporary res-
taurants for fusion cuisine.
Reservations are a must.

PLAINVILLE

Cottage Restaurant and Cafe
427 Farmington Ave.
(860) 793-8888
cottagerestaurantandcafe
.com
Moderate to expensive
Family-owned and -oper-
ated restaurant serving
contemporary American
fare.

SIMSBURY

Brookside Bagels
563 Hopmeadow St.
(860) 651-1492
Inexpensive
Incredibly fresh bagels in
interesting flavors, awe-
some selection of cream
cheese and lox, creative
sandwich combinations,
fast and friendly service.
But be prepared—this
place can get busy during
rush hours and the line
can be long.

THE LITCHFIELD HILLS

West of Hartford is **Litchfield County,** an area largely synonymous with Connecticut's western uplands. Moving north and west through Litchfield, you get deeper into the **Litchfield Hills,** a forested spur of the Berkshires that typifies what comes to most people's minds when they think of New England.

Steepled white churches, romantic old inns, quaint antiques shops, and small establishments run by Yankee craftspeople still abound. In recent years, though, the Litchfield Hills have become home to many of the rich and famous: Dick Ebersol and Susan Saint James in Litchfield, Philip Roth and Dustin Hoffman in Roxbury, Henry Kissinger in Warren, Meryl Streep in Salisbury, Mia Farrow in Bridgewater, and Clinton Kelly in Kent, to name but a few. Their arrival has brought upscale shops and nouvelle restaurants that give the area a cosmopolitan flavor.

The southern portion of this hill mass merges into the region's "Alpine Lake" country, an area reminiscent of Switzerland, with cool forest-shrouded lakes and tranquil meadows. This region is home to some of the state's best inns. Cutting between the Litchfield Hills and New York's

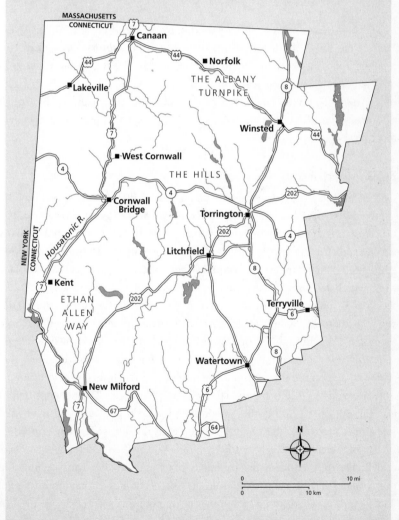

MASSACHUSETTS
CONNECTICUT

7

Canaan

44

44

Norfolk

THE ALBANY
TURNPIKE

8

Winsted

44

Lakeville

7

West Cornwall

THE HILLS

4

4

202

4

Cornwall
Bridge

Torrington

202

Housatonic R.

202

Litchfield

8

NEW YORK
CONNECTICUT

7

Kent

Terryville

6

ETHAN
ALLEN
WAY

202

Watertown

8

New Milford

7

67

6

64

N

0   10 mi

0   10 km

Taconic Mountains, from the extreme northwestern corner of Connecticut to Stratford on the coast, is the Housatonic River. In its northern reaches, the Housatonic is a wild freshet that is surely one of the prettiest rivers in New England. Litchfield County is bordered by Massachusetts on the north and New York on the west. To the south of the lake country are the populous counties of Fairfield and New Haven.

The Albany Turnpike

In the days before railroads and superhighways, Hartford and Albany, New York, were linked by a rutted roadway called the ***Albany Turnpike.*** This highway of sorts was the main route through the rugged northwestern uplands, and its location determined the patterns of settlement in this part of the state. Today the successor to the old turnpike is a gleaming asphalt ribbon dubbed Route 44, and any traveler through this part of Connecticut must pass over it.

New Hartford

One of the easternmost townships along the Litchfield portion of Route 44 is ***New Hartford,*** home to ***Satan's Kingdom State Recreation Area.*** The origin of this name has been the subject of debate for years, but it likely was named for the bandits who used to hide out in the rugged, wooded countryside that flanked the turnpike and offered a perfect hiding place from which to ambush and rob the Hartford–Albany stagecoaches. Today the area is best known for its whitewater tubing. ***Farmington River Tubing*** (92 Main St.; 860-693-6465; farmingtonrivertubing.com) operates from Memorial Day through Labor Day, offering a fun way to cool down. You start your adventure at their rental operation, where you receive a life jacket and a tube. You are then on your own until you reach the outtake point 2½ miles downriver. The company stresses "on your own": They do not help if you fall out of your tube, they recommend you do not leave the river until you finish the route, they highly suggest you do not try to stand up while in any of the three Class 1, 2, and 3 rapids you will encounter on your trip, and finally they explain that tubing is not for everyone. Did we mention that you're on your own? Minimum age suggestion is 10, minimum height and weight is 4 feet and 50 pounds, but the company leaves it up to your discretion. Operation is weather permitting, so it's always best to call ahead before making the trip. If tubing isn't for you, there are great hiking trails throughout the state park to explore.

Also located in New Hartford is the **Collinsville Antiques Co. of New Hartford** (283 Main St.; 860-379-2290; collinsvilleantiques.com). If you're wondering about the name (we were confused, too), it's because the company was formerly located in Collinsville, where it had operated since 1989. When new owners Doug and Cindy Szydlo purchased the business in 1995, they began to groom it and grow it into the wonder it is today. Often voted Best Antiques Shop by the *Hartford Advocate* and *Hartford Magazine,* the shop outgrew its space in the old Collins Company. The town didn't want to lose the business, and it caused quite a stir, but it was time. In 2005 the company had found its new home in New Hartford's Waring manufacturing building. The building received a huge overhaul and today includes a restaurant, the Cruisin Cafe, for breakfast and lunch, outdoor eating and lounging areas, and a simply huge assortment of antiques. Open daily 10 a.m. to 5 p.m.

Barkhamsted

North of New Hartford, Route 44 loops through **Barkhamsted.** If you're here during the cooler months, say, February or March, visit the **Kasulaitis Farm and Sugarhouse** (69 Goose Green Rd.; 860-379-8787) to watch the process and buy some tasty maple products. If you miss sugaring off, stop by anyway and watch the lambs frisk and frolic in the spring pasture. Such sights are good for the soul.

Something else that's good for the soul is watching New England's color change as she greets autumn in all her splendor. Barkhamsted's combination of sparse population, winding roads, heavy forest, and large lakes makes it one of the most dramatic parts of Connecticut for leaf peeping.

One of the best fall foliage jaunts through Barkhamsted starts north of the town at the junction of Routes 20 and 181 in Hartland. If you approach this intersection from the east on Route 20, you'll pass through West Hartland on the way. Don't let this confuse you; with typical Yankee contrariness, West Hartland is actually east of Hartland, so keep driving for another mile. At the intersection in Hartland, take Route 181 south. This road runs between the Barkhamsted Reservoir and the Farmington River, for much of the way under the limbs of the lovely People's State Forest. At the tip of the reservoir, Route 181 meets Route 318. Take 318 east to the **Saville Dam,** separating Barkhamsted and Compensating Reservoirs.

There's parking nearby and even on the dam itself; this is a great spot to stop for pictures or a picnic. From the dam, continue east to Route 219. From there you can drive south to pick up Route 44, return west for more leaf peeping, or loop up to Route 20 in Granby.

If you loop south, you'll pass the Compensating Reservoir on your right. Also known as **Lake McDonough** (860-379-3036 [in season] or 860-278-7850, ext. 3110; themdc.com/lake_mcDonough.shtml), this body of water is a state recreational area, with seasonal facilities for boating, swimming, picnicking, hiking, and fishing. Boating is allowed from mid-Apr through Sept; rowboats can be rented. Fishing is allowed mid-Apr through Labor Day. The beaches here are wheelchair accessible, as are most of the other facilities. There is also a fully accessible nature trail with Braille signs. Open weekdays, 10 a.m. to 8 p.m., weekends and holidays, 8 a.m. to 8 p.m. No admission; parking fee.

If after reaching Saville Dam you're still in the mood for more fall color, head back west on Route 318 for ½ mile beyond the intersection of Route 181. Turn right on E. River Road. This will take you directly through **People's State Forest** (860-379-2469) along the banks of the West Branch of the Farmington, where even on the hottest day the tall trees and pines keep the forest shady and glade cool. This forest has a whole bunch of trails to explore, including the yellow Jessie Gerard Trail, on which you will find the site of a village that existed more than 270 years ago. Established in 1740 by Mary Barber and her husband, James Chaugham, this village became a regular stop for stagecoaches traveling through the area. Barber and her husband decided to move to this area of wilderness to escape her father, who was not happy that she, a white woman, married Chaugham, a Narragansett Indian. They, their children, and their children's children lived quite happily there for the next 120 years. Now a State Archaeological Preserve known as the *Lighthouse Archaeological Site,* the former village is not much more than a few cellar holes, but it is a stop on the Connecticut Freedom Trail and a continuing reminder of the ongoing fight for freedom from oppression.

As you leave the forest on River Road, one of two roads that run along the riverbank, notice the other, W. River Road, which runs through the forest on the west bank, intersecting with Route 318 a few yards west of, and across the bridge from, E. River Road. The two roads don't quite intersect several miles north of the bridge in the village of Riverton, former home of the Hitchcock chair, first produced in 1825.

While other Connecticut entrepreneurs were experimenting with the use of interchangeable parts in the manufacture of rifles and clocks, Lambert Hitchcock set out in 1818 to mass-produce furniture in a little factory at the junction of the Farmington and Still Rivers. A decade later, Hitchcock was turning out 15,000 chairs each year, and his factory employed 100 people in the rapidly growing village of Hitchcocksville. The mass-produced Hitchcock chairs, selling for between 45 cents and $1.75, were an instant success. They were also extremely sturdy. Quality control consisted of dropping each assembled chair from a second-floor workshop into a waiting wagon; only those items that survived the drop unscathed were considered sufficiently sturdy to wear the Hitchcock label. Once the chairs were assembled, workers finished them by hand, often using multiple stencils that produced a colorful and distinctive look.

In the middle of the 19th century, Hitchcock's business foundered; in 1852 its owner died penniless. About the same time, the village that bore his name disappeared from the map. Tired of constantly being confused with nearby Hotchkissville, the residents of Hitchcocksville, in typically pragmatic Yankee fashion, changed the town's name to *Riverton.* Present-day Riverton (population a mere 300) is a sleepy, picturesque, quarter-mile-long village—little more than a quaint neighborhood tucked inside the larger town of Barkhamsted—where all three streets run alongside the Farmington River. Local stature and "image" were almost completely dependent on the venerable *Hitchcock Furniture Factory and Factory Store* (for bargain-priced chairs and other Riverton-made furnishings), both of which ceased operations in April 2006. But even without the Hitchcock-related attractions, the village is worth a leisurely visit.

Village attractions are easily reachable. It's only a 5-minute walk along Route 20 from the local Grange Hall on the banks of Sandy Brook at the west end of town to the bridge spanning the Farmington River at the east end. But that stretch of road abounds with enticing stores and snack shops. You might, for example, wrap up your visit with a bite at the ***Catnip Mouse Tea Room*** (Route 20; 860-379-3745; open Tues through Sat 11:30 a.m. to 2 p.m.) or grab a deli sandwich and Moxie at the ***Riverton General Store*** (2 Main St.; 860-379-0811; rivertongeneralstore.com; open daily 6 a.m. to 4 p.m.) and picnic along the river.

If you fish, mark your calendar for the first day of trout season (the third Sat in Apr). That's when Riverton holds its annual Fishing Derby on the Farmington River between Hogback Dam and Pipeline Pool. The Farmington is a National Wild and Scenic River, and probably offers the best fly fishing in Connecticut. Rainbow and brown trout don't exactly beg to be caught, but it's pretty easy to catch one. The contest runs from 6 to 10 a.m., rain, sun, or snow. There's no entry fee; all you need is a Connecticut fishing license. Prizes are awarded. Non-anglers are welcome to observe, and presumably applaud when a particularly promising catch is landed. Kids under 16 can fish in a specially stocked area. Breakfast is usually served at the Riverton volunteer fire department beginning at 4 a.m. for a small donation. For more information, call the Riverton General Store at (860) 379-0811 or visit rivertonct.com. Fishing licenses can be purchased at the store as well.

If you intend to overnight in this part of Connecticut, we recommend the ***Old Riverton Inn*** (436 E. River Rd.; 860-379-8678 or 800-EST-1796; rivertoninn.com). Established in 1796 (see what they did with their phone number there?), this inn originally opened as the Ives Tavern, a stagecoach stop on the old Boston-to-Albany Turnpike (US 44). Today the historic building retains its colonial charm.

The floor of the enclosed Grindstone Terrace is made of grindstones quarried in Nova Scotia, sent by sailing ship to Long Island Sound, then dispatched upriver to Hartford and hauled by oxcart from Hartford to Collinsville, where they were used to grind ax heads and machetes in the ***Collinsville Axe Factory*** (now an antiques store). The inn's dining room is decorated with Riverton's famous Hitchcock chairs. Located on the west bank of the Farmington River, the Old Riverton Inn is open year-round except the first three weeks in Jan. Each room has a private bath, and rates include a full breakfast on weekends, continental during the week. The restaurant serves dinner from 5 to 8:30 p.m. Fri and Sat, and noon to 3 p.m. Sun.

Norfolk

Located at the junction of Route 44 and Routes 272 and 182 and with **Campbell Falls** and **Haystack Mountain State Park** just north of the town center, **Norfolk** is a crossroads of tourism in northwest Connecticut. While outdoor recreation is popular, the activity for which the town is famous is the **Norfolk Chamber Music Festival** (20 Litchfield Rd.; 860-542-3000; music.yale.edu/Norfolk). Think of this annual summer event as a Tanglewood without the crowds. The Norfolk Chamber Music Festival and the **Yale Summer School of Music** perform summer concerts in the brown-shingled Music Shed on the grounds of the Stoeckel estate on Route 44, west of the Norfolk Green. The concert schedule varies from year to year, but the New York Woodwind Quintet, the New York Brass Quartet, and the Tokyo String Quartet have all appeared in the past. There are Fri and Sat evening performances throughout June, July, and Aug.

Norfolk has what many people consider the prettiest village green in the state. What better way to see the sights of charming and historic Norfolk than in a horse-drawn carriage? The **Horse and Carriage Livery Service** (Loon Meadow Drive, off Route 44; 860-542-6085; loonmeadowfarm.com) offers a horse-drawn tour of the town or a horse-drawn hayride with a bonfire afterward. In winter (snow permitting) you can arrange for a private

Three Civic-Spirited Families

The philanthropic, much-intermarried Eldridges, Battells, and Stoeckels have left their mark on Norfolk. Its shingle-sided, barrel-vaulted library (1889) was donated by Isabella Eldridge. High-society architect Stanford White designed that same year's village-green fountain, commissioned by Mary Eldridge and named in honor of her uncle, Joseph Battell. Mary Alice Bradford Eldridge paid for the 1892 town hall. The **Battell Memorial Chapel** (1928) features priceless Tiffany stained-glass windows depicting the four seasons, and Ellen Battell Stoeckel's estate now is home to Norfolk's summertime music festivals.

sleigh ride for two or for a larger sled that can handle groups on a romantic ride through snow-hushed woods. Warm up afterward with a cup of mulled cider in the woodstove-heated barn. Reservations are required and hours vary, so it's always best to call ahead.

James Mars was born into slavery in Canaan, Connecticut, in 1790. He and his family escaped and hid in Norfolk, Connecticut, for many months at the homes of abolitionists. At the age of 21 he gained his freedom thanks to new state laws. He became a deacon of Talcott Street Congregational Church in Hartford and worked for continuing civil liberties. A multimedia story of his life, *The Life of James Mars,* was produced by Puppetsweat Theater and has been shown throughout New England. Mars died in 1880 at the age of 90. He is buried in the **Center Cemetery** (15 Old Colony Rd.; 860-542-1775) in Norfolk alongside his father, Jupiter Mars, who served in the American Revolution. Their stones are located to the rear and left of the first entrance into the cemetery. To the right of this entrance, near the wall next to Old Colony Road, is the grave of Alanson Freeman, who served in the all-black Connecticut 29th Regiment of the Civil War.

Heading north on Route 272, you'll come to **Campbell Falls State Park** (Old Spaulding Road.; 860-482-1817), where you can see the Whiting River boil over rocks in a narrow gorge. You'll need to take a short hike to reach the falls; just follow the sounds of rushing water. The water drops in two levels, with a small pool in between and one at the bottom. The first level is a good place for a picnic among the weathered rocks. Campbell Falls is off Norfolk Road, just south of Southfield, Massachusetts, just before Spaulding Road. If you are traveling from the other direction, it's about 5 miles north of Haystack Mountain, on Route 272 in Norfolk.

northcanaan trivia

Milo Freeland is credited with being the first African American to volunteer for the Union army during the Civil War. Freeland died in 1883, while living in East Canaan. A stone was placed in the Hillside Cemetery on Route 44 in North Canaan in 1996 during a ceremony in his honor.

Canaan

Although the festival in nearby Norfolk tends to be better known, the tiny community of **Falls Village** in **Canaan** also boasts an excellent summer musical program. From mid-June to mid-September the town is home to the *Music Mountain Chamber Music Festival* (225 Music Mountain Rd.; 860-824-7126; musicmountain .org), the oldest continuous chamber music festival in the US. During the season a variety of string quartets play chamber music. Located off US 7. On Saturday evening there are folk, jazz, and baroque music performances.

Salisbury

Way up in the farthest northwest corner of Connecticut is the *Mount Riga area,* a system of peaks that marches north and west from Salisbury to the New York and Massachusetts borders. Mount Riga has a diverse and interesting history. For many years, its iron-rich depths were mined and supplied our nation with much-needed tools and weapons. People were needed to work these mines, and many came. A community emerged, and its people became known as the "Raggies," perhaps because they lived on Mount Riga. It is said that many of these people were immigrants, possibly from Latvia. They didn't know the culture, didn't speak the language, and kept mainly to themselves. And of course, we know how people generally feel about other people they don't understand. New England Yankees didn't go up and say, "Hey, tell me about your culture; I'd like to understand." Not feeling particularly welcome, the Raggies lived quietly on the mountain well into the 20th century and well after the iron forges cooled. Today there are myriad sources of information on this group of people, as descendants have begun to speak out and preserve their rich history and heritage.

salisburytrivia

The Appalachian Trail crosses the region, running over **Bear Mountain,** which at 2,316 feet is the highest peak in the state.

The highest point in the state is a shoulder of **Mount Frissel** that rises to 2,380 feet in the northwesternmost corner of Connecticut.

According to tourist brochures, you can stand on that mountain and (assuming that you are reasonably limber) place one foot in Connecticut and one foot in Massachusetts and bend over and put both hands in New York. If you succeed, please send us a picture!

There are many well-marked hiking trails on Mount Riga to choose from if you'd like to hike to the summit for the amazing views and one very curious sight (sound?). Near its summit is *Crying Child Rock,* which people say makes a soft crying sound just like an infant whenever the wind is right. Sit for a spell and listen.

Salisbury has always been a simple, pastoral village, with a small measure of sophistication and a lot of country charm. In recent years these qualities have made it a popular destination for weekending New Yorkers. The combination of a rustic setting and a sophisticated audience made this a perfect place for tea lover and importer Mary O'Brien to set up shop.

Chaiwalla (1 Main St.; 860-435-9758), whose name means "tea maker" in Hindi, serves light lunches and teas. The lunches are quite good, but high tea is what is done best. This is not your simple tea and a bun, but rather a bounty of scones and lemon curd and a selection of desserts. Fruit tarts glistening with fresh fruit on crisp, ultralight pastry are always a good choice, as are the butter cakes and a rich whiskey cake bursting with coconut and raisins. Chaiwalla serves 23 different teas, all of which are blended at the restaurant. The tea is proper tea, of course, not bag tea. Freshly brewed, it's available in half or full pots. In addition to conventional blends, tea enthusiasts can choose from such rare and exotic brews as banarshi, brewed with vanilla and cardamom, and Moroccan mint tea, made with—what else?— crushed mint leaves. Remember your cash, though; Chaiwalla does not accept plastic. Open 10 a.m. to 6 p.m. Wed through Sun.

Head south on Route 44 and CT 41 and eventually to Route 112, where you'll find **Lime Rock Park** (60 White Rd. [main entrance]; 860-435-5000; limerock.com) in the Lakeville section of Salisbury, probably Connecticut's most famous racetrack for NASCAR speedsters. From time to time, you can see celebrities behind the wheel. Tom Brokaw and Tom Cruise have made appearances. For us unfamous people, it's a fun place to spend the day. Home to the Grand-Am Championship Weekend and the traditional Memorial Day weekend season opener, Lime Rock goes out of its way to please the fans. Always wanted to drive a race car? Wannabe drivers can learn the ropes at Skip Barber Racing and Driving School.

Ethan Allen Way

Sharon

Audubon Sharon (325 Cornwall Bridge Rd.; 860-364-0520; sharon.audubon .org) in **Sharon** consists of almost 1,200 acres of woodlands, flower and herb gardens, and rural countryside, and includes the *Emily Winthrop Miles Wildlife Sanctuary.*

You'll also discover a pond, a swamp, and a marsh, and the entire area is crisscrossed by more than 11 miles of trails and nature walks. Both guided and self-guided nature walks are available. A large house on the property contains live-animal and other exhibits, a children's adventure center, a library, and a nature store. The center offers programs for both children and adults throughout the year.

The building is open 9 a.m. to 5 p.m. Tues through Sat and 1 to 5 p.m. Sun; closed Mon and major holidays. The Raptor Center and trails are open dawn to dusk. Admission for some parts of the center.

Cornwall

Up US 7 from Audubon Sharon, and only 1 mile south of the covered bridge at West Cornwall is another type of outdoor experience. *Clarke Outdoors* (163 US 7; 860-672-6365; clarkeoutdoors.com) is one of several outfitters along the Housatonic that offer kayaks, canoes, and rafts for those who want to try the river's whitewater. The staff here know what they are doing; a safety talk is given before each trip, and employees are happy to answer any questions you have. They offer guided tours on the Housatonic River, including a lovely trip under the covered bridge or a somewhat wilder whitewater rafting trip down Bull's Bridge Gorge. The Bull's Bridge trip is usually offered only in spring. Reservations for the guided rafting trips are a must. Tip: Prices are lower during the week. Shuttle service available. Be sure to check out the expressive anthropomorphic critters adorning Clarke's signs and vans. These are original Sandra Boynton paintings!

Clarke's is open Mar through Nov, 10 a.m. to 5 p.m. Mon through Fri, 9 a.m. to 6 p.m. Sat and Sun, closed Tues and Thurs.

On the west side of US 7, a couple hundred yards south of Cornwall Bridge, is something right out of an H. P. Lovecraft horror novel. There, jutting out from under a canopy of overhanging trees right along the side of the road is a big rock painted to resemble a most lifelike giant frog whose leering mouth seems to be reaching for the occupants of the passenger side of the car. But don't worry, the story behind the painting of this rock is not menacing. It all started more than 60 years ago when Margaret (Marge) Grusauski Wilson was on her way home from high school and noticed that a highway worker had painted two white eyes on the rock. The crew had recently painted the lines on Route 7, and the worker must have had a sense of humor. Marge went home and told her brother, John, about the rock, and the two of them decided to "do it up good." They went back later and added long rows of white teeth, ears, eyes, and a nose, adding black details. They chose a small black rock for the "monster's" hat. They were almost happy with their work, but something wasn't quite right. The next evening, Marge had a new partner in "crime" when she and her best friend, Marietta Baird, found a flat rock, painted it red, and gave the monster his tongue. *Monster*

OTHER ATTRACTIONS WORTH SEEING IN THE LITCHFIELD HILLS

Cricket Hill Garden
670 Walnut Hill Rd.
Thomaston
(860) 283-1042
treepeony.com

Elephant's Trunk Flea Market
490 Danbury Rd.
New Milford
(860) 355-1448
etflea.com
New England's largest outdoor flea market.

Golden Age of Trucking Museum
1101 Southford Rd.
Middlebury
(203) 577-2181
goldenagetruckmuseum.com

H.O.R.S.E. of Connecticut
43 Wilbur Rd.
Washington
(860) 868-1960
horseofct.org
Nonprofit rescue organization gives tours to view and feed horses.

Morris Historical Society Museum
Route 61
Morris
(860) 567-1776

Quassy Amusement Park
2132 Middlebury Rd.
Middlebury
(203) 758-2913
quassy.com

Silo/Hunt Hill Farm Trust
44 Upland Rd. (off Route 202)
New Milford
(860) 355-0300, (800) 353-SILO
hunthillfarmtrust.org
Everything you need for cooking, dining, or collecting.

Rock was complete. Throughout the next few years Marge and her merry band of helpers maintained the painted rock and here and there added a few new details. But no one ever talked about it. No one knew who the culprits were. Marge eventually moved to Florida, where she still resides today. She held her silence for a very long time, and a few other people took credit for painting the rock. Marge says she doesn't know who took over when she stopped, or how the rock came to be painted green, but she is tickled pink that something that started as a whim has continued for such a long time. She was amused to learn from friends who were on a leaf tour from New York City that the bus tour actually stopped at the rock. So, when you stop to take a picture, be sure to think well of Marge, her family, her friends, and her Monster Rock.

About 6 miles north on US 7 is the ***West Cornwall Covered Bridge,*** the largest and handsomest covered bridge in Connecticut, spanning the Housatonic at West Cornwall. Originally designed by Ithiel Town, the bridge has been in continuous service since 1864. Route 128 runs from US 7 across the one-lane bridge to become the main street of West Cornwall.

cornwalltrivia

In 1948 Mohawk Ski Area in Cornwall became the first ski resort in the country to make artificial snow. The first (unsuccessful) attempt involved trucking in 700 tons of ice from Torrington.

Be sure to hit the ***Cornwall Bridge Pottery Store*** (415 Sharon Goshen Turnpike; 860-672-6545; cbpots.com). Ever since Todd Piker started his pottery and store in 1972, this place has been selling world-class stoneware, much of it featuring a celadon glaze made from slag recovered from a local riverbed, where it was deposited by the ironworks that used to dominate the area's economy. None of the glazes, however, contain lead. Most items are decorated with simple blue or brown brushwork designs with an Asian flavor. The firing is done in a 35-foot wood-fired kiln at Piker's pottery in Cornwall Bridge, and the flames give the finished pieces distinctive two-tone markings. The workshop is open for visits, but it's always best to call ahead for the best hours. If you're lucky, you'll find some seconds available for sale here.

In addition to Piker's pottery, the two-floor, 5,000-square-foot Cornwall Bridge Pottery Store features an assortment of museum-quality crafts from other carefully chosen artists. The inventory changes often, so check in often. Open noon to 5 p.m. Fri and Mon; 10:30 a.m. to 5:30 p.m. weekends.

Housed in a rambling, high-ceilinged former Masonic hall at the top of the hill is *Barbara Farnsworth, Bookseller* (407 Rte. 128; 860-672-6571; farnsworthbooks.com). This establishment can be a near-religious experience for bibliophiles and collectors of old prints and maps. The bottom floor of the shop contains nonfiction, cookbooks, reference books, and a variety of antique prints and ephemera. The top floor contains the bulk of the store's 45,000 volumes, with the specialty being horticulture and landscape design. Open 9 a.m. to 5 p.m. Sat seasonally, and by chance or appointment. It's always best to call ahead and make sure someone is there, especially during inclement weather.

East of West Cornwall is *Mohawk Mountain State Park* (20 Mohawk Mountain Rd.; 860-491-3620). The big draw here is skiing, but if that's not your thing, avoid the crowds and take a scenic warm-weather 2½-mile stroll to the top of the 1,683-foot-high *Mohawk Mountain* instead. The view from the top is absolutely breathtaking. Why not pick up some sandwiches from Nodine's Smokehouse in Goshen (see p. 80) and enjoy them mountaintop?

Kent

Main Street (US 7) in the town of *Kent* is known as Ethan Allen Way, after the Connecticut hero who was born in the area. This street is lined for several blocks with restaurants, art galleries, antiques stores, craft shops, and the like. You'll also find interesting establishments on Maple and Railroad Streets. Businesses come and go fairly frequently, so if you want to know what's there currently, you'll just have to visit.

A mile and a half north of North Kent on US 7 is *Kent Falls State Park* (159 Macedonia Brook Rd.; 860-927-3238). The broad meadow and shaded picnic areas visible from the road are inviting enough, but you might be inclined to pass it by if you weren't specifically looking for a place to spread a picnic lunch. Don't. The best part of the park is a 250-foot waterfall that is easy to miss despite being one of the state's largest, especially when the foliage of high summer obscures it from view. If you like tramping through the woods, you can hike to the top of the falls, or if you prefer less demanding pleasures, you can simply sit out on the rocks in the middle of the falls and dangle your toes in the torrent. Even though the water may be a tad cool for toe-dangling come autumn, we highly recommend visiting the park after the leaves have turned and the summer crowds have thinned.

About a mile north of Kent, you'll find a big maroon L-shaped barn set back a short distance from the west side of US 7. The ground on which it sits used to be the Kent town dump, but all that changed back in the 1970s. At that time, New Britain's Stanley Tool Company was looking for a site for a museum to house a collection of American tools and implements collected by noted artist and author Eric Sloane. Stanley wanted the state of Connecticut to run the place, but the state would accept ownership only if the museum's site was somehow historically significant. As it turned out, down at the foot of the hill behind the town dump in Kent were the ruins of an old blast furnace that produced pig iron during most of the 19th century. The presence of this jumble of stone made the dump suitably historical,

Tall Tales of Ethan Allen

Ethan Allen is a favorite Connecticut hero, hence many stories have been passed down about the man. Here are a few of our favorites:

Ethan Allen was a big guy (6 feet 6 inches) with a big thirst. According to one "tall" tale, on a hot August afternoon, Allen and his cousin Remember Baker, having overindulged, repaired to nearby shady woods to sleep it off. A besotted Baker was awakened by a strange noise, and he watched in horror as a rattlesnake bit his drink-befuddled cousin over and over. Before Baker could find a weapon to subdue the serpent, it moved away from Allen, gazed at Baker with a certain drunken stare, then wobbled its way into the bushes, where it collapsed in a stupor. Allen awoke refreshed from his nap, except for complaints about "these eternal, damnable, bloodsucking mosquitoes," which had disturbed his rest.

It stands to reason that Ethan Allen would marry a woman as formidable as himself. His wife, Fanny, was, by all accounts, his equal in temper and independence. The story is told that Allen's friends became concerned about his drinking and decided to frighten him into leading a more temperate life. They wrapped themselves in sheets and hid beneath the bridge that Allen passed on his way home from his favorite tavern. Making the requisite booing, moaning, and keening sounds, they jumped out at their friend, only to scare his horse into rearing. Despite his snozzled state, Allen managed to control his mount and greeted the "apparitions" by proclaiming, "If you are angels of light, I'm glad to meet you. And if you are devils, then come along home with me. I married your sister."

so Stanley acquired the property and had Sloane design a building for his collection. Thus was born the Sloane-Stanley Museum, now known as the *Eric Sloane Museum & Kent Iron Furnace* (31 Kent-Cornwall Rd. [US 7]; 860-927-3849).

kenttrivia

Macedonia Brook State Park in Kent is the largest state park in Connecticut.

The one thing to understand about this place is that it is not so much a museum of artifacts as a gallery of art objects. The tools collected here, some of which date from the 17th century, probably do have some historical interest as a link with everyday life in America's past, but Sloane vehemently rejected the image of himself as what he called "a nurturer of nostalgia." The contents of this museum are oddly beautiful. Sloane personally arranged and lighted the displays, and the resulting jumble of wooden bowls and woven baskets, yokes and mallets and pitchforks, axes and scythes, and weathered sawhorses has an internal order that is both pleasing and restful. It's as if each arrangement were a small work of art in itself.

ethanallentrivia

Litchfield-born Ethan Allen is one of the most colorful personalities in American history. The guy was a crusty old coot. You probably learned in fifth-grade history that Allen ordered the British commander of Fort Ticonderoga to surrender by declaiming, "Surrender in the name of the great God Jehovah and the Continental Congress." What he really said was something like: "Come out of there, you goddamn old billy goat." Spin doctors, even then.

In addition to the fine tool collection, the museum also contains a re-creation of Sloane's studio with some of his works on display. And don't forget that historic blast furnace; it's the tumbled pile of rocks surrounded by the split-rail fence at the bottom of the hill behind the barn. Open May to June, Fri through Sun 10 a.m. to 4 p.m.; June through Oct, Thurs through Sun 10 a.m. to 4 p.m. Admission.

Located just off US 7 about 4 miles south of Kent, *Bull's Bridge* is one of only a few remaining covered bridges in Connecticut and one of two that are still open to traffic (the other is in West Cornwall, also off US 7 a few miles north).

Bull's Bridge was built in 1842 and spans the Housatonic River between New York state and Connecticut on the river's eastern bank. George Washington didn't sleep here, but he did pass over the bridge, and he (or a member of his party) did manage to lose a horse in the Housatonic while so doing. If looking at the bridge gives you a sense of déjà vu, it's because it's probably been the source of more quaint New England covered-bridge photographs on postcards and calendar covers than any other bridge in this part of the world.

After you cross the bridge, about 3 miles up the road on the **Schaghticoke Indian Reservation,** you'll find an old cemetery with many timeworn headstones, including one commemorating the last resting place of a "Christian Indian Princess." This tombstone belongs to Eunice Mauwee, born in 1756, the granddaughter of Chief Gideon Mauwee, a man generally considered to be the founder of the present-day Schaghticokes. She died in 1860 at the age of 104. Amazing. As you explore other tombstones here, remember to show proper respect and not take rubbings without permission.

The Hills

Goshen

They say that at one time, travelers passing through the Bridgeport area during the spring were shocked to see elephants plowing nearby fields; they were rented to local farmers by circus impresario P. T. Barnum. These days if you see an elephant strolling through a field along Route 4 in **Goshen,** it won't be plowing it—the various circus animals on the property belong to **Commerford Zoo** (48 Torrington Rd.; 860-491-3421; commerfordzoo.com), which operates kids' fun fairs and petting zoos throughout New England. Commerford's animals have also been known to make an appearance at birthday parties and weddings, and have even been in a movie or commercial or two. You can't tour Commerford's, but at any given time, a fair number of the residents will be exercising and thus visible from the road.

Just before you get to the rotary in Goshen, you'll see several large, intriguing stone cairns, surrounded by stout stone fences. You've reached the home of the 116-acre **Action Wildlife Foundation** (337 Torrington Rd., Route 4 West; 860-482-4465; actionwildlife.org). This former dairy farm–turned–game park is home to many exotic creatures, including zebras, yaks, miniature donkeys, and American bush llamas. The aoudad (wild sheep) live in one of the cairns called Aoudad Mountain and share quarters with fainting goats. Yep, when under stress, the goats go stiff and fall over in a faint just like a proper Victorian maiden. Visitors can tour the various animal areas on foot via walking paths throughout the acres of the park that are open to the public or on tractor-drawn wagons. If you are visiting with very small children, take the wagon tour, as the paths can get a little steep and the footing difficult. Action Wildlife has also recently added a drive-through safari. In addition to the exotic animals, the foundation has a picnic area and a petting zoo in the farm's former dairy. Admission. Open weekends only Nov and mid-Apr through late June, 10:30 a.m. to 5 p.m.; late June through Aug, Tues through Fri 10:30 a.m. to 4:30 p.m., Sat and Sun 10 a.m. to 5 p.m.; Sept and Oct, open Thurs and Fri 11 a.m. to 3 p.m., Sat and Sun 10:30 a.m. to 4:30 p.m.

Nodine's Smokehouse (39 North St.; 860-491-4009; nodinesmoke house.com) is one of the best smokehouses in New England. It's also something of a Connecticut institution. Nodine's (it's pronounced no-DINES) carries more than 80 specialty items, ranging from smoked hams, turkeys, and chickens to the more exotic smoked pheasants, shrimp, and venison sausage. Nodine's more common meats can be had in made-to-order sandwiches. Open 9 a.m. to 5 p.m. Mon through Sat and 10 a.m. to 4 p.m. Sun. If you see something you like but don't want to drag it along for the rest of your trip, never fear; they have a mail-order operation.

Torrington

No one driving past 192 Main St. in *Torrington* can possibly ignore the awe-inspiring symphony in Roman brick and rosy-red slate that occupies the property. At first, all you see is the big, round, three-story corner tower. Then the eye begins to jump from dormer to porch to porte cochere, taking in the Victorian carvings, the intricate sashes, the many small details that speak of another age, when decoration for its own sake was a common element of American home-building.

The magnificent, 16-room *Hotchkiss-Fyler House* is now the headquarters of the *Torrington Historical Society* (860-482-8260; torrington historicalsociety.org). It still displays the original mahogany paneling, hand stenciling, and parquet floors that made it such an opulent example of

Victorian excess when it was built by Orsamus Roman Fyler back in 1900. The original furnishings, on display here, are almost as extravagant as the house itself. Several of the rooms feature wonderful little collections of art objects, including gold Fabergé spoons, Sèvres porcelain, Victorian art glass, and Meissen porcelain figurines.

The Hotchkiss-Fyler House and an adjacent museum devoted to local history are open mid-Apr through the end of Oct, Tues through Sat from noon to 4 p.m. Admission for anyone older than 12.

One of the nicest places to take a leisurely fall hike is located in **Burr Pond State Park** (384 Burr Mountain Rd.; 860-482-1817). The circuit around the 88-acre pond in the park is a pleasant walk. There's history in the park, too; it was the site of Gail Borden's first American condensed-milk factory. In 1856 Borden, who was from Torrington, created a way to preserve milk by condensing it; his creation was called the "milk that won the Civil War." A bronze tablet marks the place where the factory once stood before being destroyed by fire. Some of the trails are perfect for little ones or those not up to a strenuous hike. The 436-acre park also offers swimming, fishing, swimming, boating, and picnicking. Admission.

torringtontrivia

Torrington was once known by the rather odd moniker of "Mast Swamp."

Connecticut Freedom Trail

Not far from Burr Pond are two turn-of-the-19th-century houses that quite possibly played a very important historical role. Both are reputed to have been stops on the Underground Railroad, and both were in the Tuttle family. The first one, at 4040 Torringford St., was built by Major Isaiah Tuttle in 1803 and was operated as an inn for many years. Built one year earlier, the second house was owned by Isaiah's eldest son, Uriel, and is located down the road at 3925 Torringford St. Uriel was very active in the abolitionist movement as the president of the Litchfield County Anti-Slavery Society as well as a member of the Connecticut Anti-Slavery Society. Records of his activities lend credence to the probability that his house was an Underground Railroad stop, and it follows that his father's would be as well. Both houses are currently in private ownership and are not open to the public.

Torrington is also the birthplace of notorious abolitionist John Brown. While he wasn't successful in his attempt to free the slaves at Harpers Ferry, and paid for his efforts with his life, Brown certainly left his mark on our state's and nation's history. The house where he was born on May 9, 1800, was destroyed by fire in 1918, but the site is marked with a stone wall and a small memorial. To find it, follow Route 4 west from Torrington center toward Goshen. Take a right onto University Drive. Follow for about 1 mile before turning left onto John Brown Road. The site is about ½ mile down the road on the right.

Harwinton

What was formerly known as the Farmington Antiques & Design Weekend has now become *Harwinton Antiques & Design Weekend* (80 Locust Rd.; 317-598-0012 [Jenkens Management]; farmingtonantiquesweekend.com), but it is still one of the most prestigious (and colossal) antiques shows in the country. Ralph Lauren, Steven Spielberg, and Barbra Streisand are style-setters who have been spotted here. Held the second full weekend in June and over Labor Day weekend, this show features dealers from all over the area and from as far away as Florida.

No matter whether you attend in the spring or fall, the Harwinton Antiques Weekend is one mammoth show. It's more likely the spring show will be washed out, but Labor Day is smack-dab in the middle of hurricane season, so be prepared. Umbrellas are okay, but a rain hat and poncho or foldable raincoat is better. Forget charge cards and even checks. You'll get the best deal if you pay in cash. Many dealers and the food vendors can't break large bills (and many are suspicious of counterfeit $50s and $100s), so bring along small bills. Various service clubs sell beverages and food at the show, but we usually tote along some extra water and save our money for the merchandise. Use your program to mark dealers and to take notes. Trust us, by the end of the show, you'll never remember where you saw the perfect Roseville vase at 10 a.m. If you snooze, you lose. When you find the absolutely perfect whatever, snag it.

Prices can be relatively high at this show, but if you ask, most dealers will do a little better on the price. Nonetheless, the discounts might not be as generous as you're accustomed to. The closer you get to the end of the show, the easier it is to dicker.

Litchfield

The *Litchfield Green,* which was laid out in the 1770s, is probably the best-known location in this part of Connecticut. The stark white Congregational church with the towering spire on the green's north side is almost certainly the most photographed church in New England.

For moderately fancy fare, *Litchfield*'s chic *West Street Grill* (43 West St.; 860-567-3885; weststreetgrill.com) on the green is the place. West Street Grill has become such a part of the Litchfield landscape that its changes in management and chefs make front-page news in the local newspaper. The frequent upheavals in the kitchen haven't hurt the food, which seems to get better with each passing chef. The cuisine is New American, meaning lots of fish and steak, with slight Asian and Irish influences. Reservations are a must for dinner, and you may need to call far in advance to get a table on a peak fall weekend. West Street Grill serves lunch and dinner daily, brunch on Sun, and bistro fare Thurs and Sun evening.

The heart of historic Litchfield consists of a block or two of North Street and the few blocks of South Street (Route 63) immediately off the green. There you'll find the 1760 home of *Benjamin Tallmadge,* once an aide to George Washington, and the house where Harriet Beecher Stowe was born. There's also the 1760 Sheldon Tavern, where George Washington really did sleep (he visited town five times), and the 1792 *Pierce Academy,* the first academy for girls in America. These buildings are all privately owned and only some are occasionally open to the public.

Much of Litchfield's historic heritage is summarized in an exhibit in the *Litchfield History Museum* (7 South St.; 860-567-4501; litchfieldhistorical society.org). Here you can trace the history of Litchfield from the first contact between Europeans and Indians back in the 17th century to the end of the town's "golden age" in the middle of the 19th century. The museum also features a display of antique furniture and a gallery of 18th-century portraits, plus several galleries of changing exhibits. There's also a research library and gift shop. The museum is open between mid-Apr and the end of Nov, 11 a.m. to 5 p.m. Tues through Sat and 1 to 5 p.m. Sun. The museum shop is open year-round, Tues through Sat from 11 a.m. to 5 p.m., Sun 1 to 5 p.m. Admission.

Admission to the historical society also includes admission to the *Tapping Reeve House & Law School,* located a block south of the museum at

82 South St. Founded in 1773, this was America's first law school. Here's a chance to tour the school that trained political conspirator and former vice president Aaron Burr. Of course, it also schooled the likes of John C. Calhoun and some 130 other congressmen and senators, not to mention three Supreme Court justices, six cabinet members, and a dozen governors. Today the Reeve House exhibits tell the story of students who attended the school.

Farther out Route 202 is the *White Memorial Foundation and Conservation Center* (80 Whitehall Rd.; 860-567-0857; whitememorialcc.org), whose 4,000 acres constitute Connecticut's largest nature center and wildlife sanctuary. This privately owned facility is administered by a nonprofit corporation, the White Memorial Foundation. It contains numerous picnic areas, 9 camps, 2 family campgrounds, a number of bird-watching platforms, 35 miles of riding and hiking trails (including a hiking trail for the blind with Braille signs), more than 70 acres of open water, and more than half of the Bantam Lake shoreline. The property is open year-round for fishing, canoeing, cross-country skiing, and similar activities.

The Conservation Center building is the focus for the White Memorial Foundation's work. The first floor features fluorescent rocks, a working beehive, and a variety of exhibits, including some stunning nature dioramas and a collection of more than 3,000 species of butterflies. The center is open 9 a.m. to 5 p.m. Mon through Sat, and noon to 5 p.m. Sun year-round. Admission.

A little more than 3 miles south of Litchfield center on Route 63 is *White Flower Farm* (800-420-2852; whiteflowerfarm.com), an establishment comprising more than 10 acres of cultivated plants and 30 acres of wildflowers, plus assorted greenhouses. Flowers bloom here all summer: From mid-May to mid-June, the Exbury azaleas and tree peonies are in flower; throughout June, you can see tall bearded iris and herbaceous peonies; and around the middle of the month, the Japanese iris take over—they last until the middle of July. The stars of the farm, though, are the tuberous begonias that bloom throughout July and August. These have to be seen to be believed; the pictures in the farm's catalog (written under the pen name of "Amos Pettingill") just don't do them justice. White Flower Farm also has a great gardening store. Open daily 9 a.m. to 5 p.m.

As you travel east from Litchfield on Route 118, just past the East Cemetery is the *Lourdes in Litchfield Shrine* (83 Montfort Rd.; 860-567-1041; shrinect.org/Lourdes_in_Litchfield/Welcome.html). For 32 years, Montfort

Missionaries have operated this 35-acre shrine, which features a replica of the famous grotto at Lourdes, France. An outdoor Stations of the Cross path winds its way to a spectacular crucifixion scene at the top of the hill. The grounds are open year-round sunrise to sunset daily, and include a picnic area and gift shop. In addition, outdoor services are conducted throughout the pilgrimage season (May 1 to mid-Oct), and the **Blessing of the Motorcycles** occurs the third Sunday in May. At the blessing, each person, biker or not, and his or her vehicle is blessed. In recent years, more than 500 bikers from as far as Maine and New York have attended the celebrations. Even if you aren't a biker, it's worth a visit to see some really fine bikes.

Haight-Brown Vineyard (28 Chestnut Hill Rd.; 860-567-4045; haight vineyards.com) may not be quite Haut-Médoc, but it is really quite a nice place for a Saturday afternoon vineyard walk, winery tour, and wine tasting. With vines that were first planted in 1975, this is Connecticut's oldest continuously operating winery and the first in the state to make sparkling wine using the French *méthode champagne.*

You can view the winemaking operation and vineyards from an outdoor balcony and picnic on the grounds. There's also a gift shop. The staff is friendly, knowledgeable, and eager to answer questions. Open Mon through Thurs 11 a.m. to 5 p.m., Fri 11 a.m. to 6 p.m., Sat 10:30 a.m. to 6 p.m., and Sun noon to 6 p.m.

Wisdom House Retreat Center (229 E. Litchfield Rd.; 860-567-3163; wisdomhouse.org), formerly a convent for the Sisters of Wisdom, is now the site of Connecticut's only outdoor labyrinth. Don't arrive thinking you'll find a high, boxwood maze like those in England or in Colonial Williamsburg. The low circular path is a symbol older than time and one that transcends religions. Walking the spiral path helps you meditate and heighten your awareness. You'll find a helpful pamphlet at Wisdom House suggesting different meditative approaches to walking the labyrinth. Whichever approach you take, it's a peaceful way to get in touch with your inner self, to find some peace in the silence, and to shed the cares of 21st-century life. Many visitors use the labyrinth for silent meditation, so it probably isn't a place to visit if you are accompanied by rowdy children. The center offers all sorts of services on the 70-acre site, including an outdoor swimming pool, overnight accommodations for 140, conferences, and more. Visit their website for the most up-to-date information.

South of Wisdom House Retreat Center is ***Topsmead State Forest*** (Buell Road; 860-567-5694), an estate-turned-park that looks as if it belongs in the British midlands. When Waterbury heiress Edith Morton Chase came home from a European tour enchanted with English manor houses, she was determined to build herself an authentic Cotswold cottage, complete with leaded-glass casement windows, hand-hewn beams, and buttery stucco exteriors. She found the right location in Litchfield. The Cotswold cottage of her dreams was designed by architect Richard Dana, who shared Miss Edith's love for English cottage architecture.

Topsmead, however, was more than a building. It was also a vast garden and a working farm. Miss Edith was as fond of English country gardens as of English architecture, and she surrounded her home with formal manicured gardens and cutting gardens full of the flowers most beloved by English gardeners: roses, sweet William, and phlox. Even in her late 70s, she reputedly walked a daily mile around these gardens, inspecting, issuing orders, and sipping from an ever-present glass of skim milk.

When Miss Edith died in 1972, she left her 511-acre estate to the State of Connecticut so that everyone could enjoy a touch of England in Litchfield. Topsmead State Forest is open all year for picnicking, sledding, cross-country skiing, and hiking; there's even a letterbox or two. You can tour the house on the second and fourth weekends of each month from June to Oct, noon to 5 p.m. (the last weekend of Oct, it closes at 4 p.m.).

John Morosani was only 2 years old when his father sold off the last cow from their dairy operation, but something must have clicked, because about 50 years later, he has reinstated cattle on his family's property and grown the farm, with the help of business partner Jim Abbott, into a thriving business. By starting off slow with 7 calves in the spring of 2003, and applying for various government grants to help with the fencing, Morosani and Abbott have built ***Laurel Ridge Grass Fed Beef*** (66 Wigwam Rd.; 860-567-8122; lrgfb.com) one step at a time. Today they manage 80 head on over 200 acres. The cattle are entirely grass fed, with a little kelp thrown in to give them the right minerals. The farm also offers pastured poultry and pork. Laurel Ridge meat is in such demand now that Morosani and Abbott have a hard time keeping up. They do sell at various farm stands, including their own housed in a windmill on their farm, and stores throughout the area; check their website for details.

Now, you might think that Laurel Ridge would be most famous for its beef, but it's not. It's really the flowers. Yep, that's right. Daffodils, in fact—thousands of them. It all started with Mr. and Mrs. Morosani way back in 1941 when they first moved to Litchfield and purchased the land that is now Laurel Ridge Grass Fed Beef. The Morosanis were purveying their property and decided that one pasture was just too rocky to be of much use as a crop field. So they planted 10,000 daffodil bulbs. Do you know what daffodil bulbs do every year? They multiply. Like rabbits. The Morosanis were diligent in digging up their multiplied flower bulbs and replanting them every fall for more than 20 years. By then, the daffodils had become something of a local legend and people came from miles away to see their beauty. The Morosanis started the Laurel Ridge Foundation to be managed and supported by their descendants to ensure the daffodils would be cared for. Lucky for John, the major work for the daffodils coincides nicely with hay season for his cows. To find the farm, take Route 118 east from Litchfield and then Route 254 south. The farm is near the village of Northfield. Just look for a patch of spring; you can't miss it.

On Route 209, in southwest Litchfield, you'll find the ***Bantam Cinema*** (115 Bantam Lake Rd.; 860-567-0006; bantamcinema.com), just south of Route 202. The Bantam Cinema is an old-fashioned movie theater that screens those offbeat, independent, or imported films that never seem to get much play at suburban theaters. Even though the screening rooms and sound systems are modern, it's a wonderfully intimate and kind of old-fashioned way to see a film.

From time to time, the cinema holds special programs with celebrities, such as Bridgewater's Mia Farrow, talking about their work and films. Be sure to check their website for dates and times.

It would be a mistake to bypass the ***Bantam Bread Company*** (853 Bantam Rd.; 860-567-2737; bantambread.com). This is the type of hearth-baked bread that people line up for in New York and Los Angeles. Pick the Holiday Fruit Bread, a whole-wheat sourdough loaf packed with toasted walnuts, plump and tender golden raisins, and tart dried cherries. The shop also turns out a variety of other breads—sourdough, semolina, rosemary-scented kalamata olive, sunflower and flaxseed, caramel swirl—plus biscotti, cookies, and memorable tarts, including a lemon-berry custard number that is to die for. Open 8:30 a.m. to 5:30 p.m. Wed through Sat and 8:30 a.m. to 4 p.m. Sun; closed Mon and Tues.

ANNUAL EVENTS IN THE LITCHFIELD HILLS

JANUARY

Winter Carnival
Woodbury
(203) 263-2203
woodburyskiarea.com
Almost anything you'd want to do on the snow—snowboarding, tubing, skiing. Good events for kids.

MAY

Annual Sports Car Championships & Royals Car Show
Lime Rock Park
467 Lime Rock Rd., Route 112, Lakeville
(800) 435-5000
limerock.com
Spend Memorial Day weekend at the largest race in North America. The racing world is well represented with some of the best drivers from the International Motorsports Association (IMSA) and the Sports Car Club of America (SCCA). Auto-racing-related booths, souvenirs, and food. For the best view, forsake the stands and sit on the slopes overlooking the track.

JULY

Annual Open House Day Tour of Litchfield
Litchfield Town Green
(860) 567-9423
ctjuniorrepublic.org/events_open.htm
Includes 5 beautiful properties of historic and architectural interest and other points of interest.

AUGUST

Goshen Fair
Goshen Agricultural Society Fairgrounds
Route 63, just south of Goshen Center
(860) 485-8586
goshenstampede.com
There are lots of old-fashioned touches, such as blue ribbons for the best corn relish, homemade quilts, and young 4-H kids exhibiting their sheep, cows, and pigs. Lots of midway action to occupy the kids and enough junk food to keep everyone happy.

If you're looking for something sweeter, don't pass *Love Heart's Bakery* (583B Bantam Rd.; 860-361-6526; loveheartsbakery.homestead .com), where you'll find a cozy little place that shares space with ChowderHeads. Named after owner Allison Barker-Croce's daughter, this bakery offers a wonderful assortment of cookies, brownies, baklava, cakes (chocolate, fruit, carrot, cheese), pies, and tarts (ummm, can we say chocolate macadamia nut?). You never know what is going to be on tap, so you have to be sure to stop in often.

Litchfield Jazz Festival
Goshen Fairgrounds, Goshen
(860) 361-6285
litchfieldjazz.com
Spend some of Connecticut's hottest summer nights enjoying one of the coolest jazz scenes around. This festival is a real showcase for up-and-coming jazz talent. Music, art, and photography shows, and lots of yummy food (or bring your own picnic).

A Taste of The Litchfield Hills
Harwinton Fairgrounds
litchfieldfestivals.com
The Taste of The Litchfield Hills is the oldest wine and food festival in New England. Since 1985, this annual event has attracted thousands of people who come to sample some of the best the region has to offer. Usually the last weekend in August, this festival takes place on the Harwinton Fairgrounds.

SEPTEMBER

Bethlehem Fair
384 Main St. North (Route 61)
(203) 266-5350
bethlehemfair.com
Old-fashioned country fair.

DECEMBER

Christmas in Riverton
rivertonct.com
Includes a local theater production of *A Christmas Carol,* a Champagne Tour (adults only), photos with Father Christmas, horse-drawn wagon rides, and more.

Bethlehem

For most of the year, ***Bethlehem*** (on Route 61 north of Woodbury) is just another quiet, pretty New England country town. During the Christmas holiday season, however, all that changes, and for a few brief weeks, Bethlehem bustles with activity.

The reason, of course, is the name. The local post office doubles its staff each December to accommodate the thousands of folks who want a Bethlehem postmark on their Christmas cards. If you're going to be passing through during early December, bring yours along and they'll be glad to add them to the bin. The **Bethlehem Christmas Town Festival** in mid-December also draws a lot of people to listen to the music, ride hay wagons, and look at holiday arts and crafts and a small festival of lights—a far cry, you will agree, from the days when the Puritans who wrote the colony's stringent blue laws prescribed a 5-shilling fine for "Christmas Keeping." For details call the town clerk's office during the morning at (203) 266-5557.

South of Bethlehem, about 1½ miles down Flanders Road (off Route 61), is the **Abbey of Regina Laudis** (273 Flanders Rd.; 203-266-7727; abbeyofreginalaudis.org), which operates the Monastic Art Shop, offering items handcrafted on the premises by Benedictine nuns. Among crafts represented are printing, potting, and blacksmithing. You can also buy beauty products, honey, herbs, and postcards showing the abbey grounds. The Sisters of the Abbey also produce *Women in Chant* CDs, which are available at the gift store. The abbey's holiday decorations include a nativity scene composed of 18th-century Neapolitan figures. Open by appointment. Call ahead or visit their website for hours and information on special events.

Woodbury

Situated in the south-central part of Litchfield County on US 6, **Woodbury** was one of the first towns established in inland Connecticut. During the early 18th century, it was home to **Moll Cramer,** the best known of Connecticut's witches. Known as the "Witch of Woodbury," Cramer resided in a hut she built on **Good Hill** and supported herself by begging. Good Hill got its name from the fact that while Moll lived there, storms and high winds never seemed to cross Woodbury.

After Cramer disappeared from Good Hill without a trace, Woodbury was hit by a series of destructive storms. Even today, old-timers speak of needing a "Moll Cramer storm" after a summer dry spell. If you enter Woodbury from Roxbury on Route 317 (Good Hill Road), you'll pass over the crest of the hill near the township line.

Today US 6 runs through the center of Woodbury past rows of 18th- and 19th-century houses, many of which have been converted into antiques and gift shops. In fact, in this neck of the woods, Woodbury's Main Street is nicknamed "Antique Avenue." Some travel guides create the impression that unless you roll up in a chauffeured Rolls, you won't get very good treatment at many of the antiques shops in Woodbury. Not so! Even if you show up in faded jeans and scuffed-up sneakers, you can look forward to being treated with great kindness and helpfulness.

It's a pleasure just to walk through **Mill House Antiques** (1068 Main St. North [US 6]; 203-263-3446), a restored mill house with imaginative displays of top-quality English and French furniture. Mill House also offers extraordinary gardens full of antique urns and statues. They promise you'll really feel as if you're strolling through Europe. Open daily 10 a.m. to 5 p.m. For a complete directory of Woodbury antiques dealers, visit litchfieldcty.com.

For a taste of the Woodbury that antiquers rarely see, visit the **Canfield Corner Pharmacy** (2 N. Main St.; 203-263-2595). It has an old-fashioned soda fountain and is crammed from floor to rafters with every nostrum and homemaker's convenience on the market. Open Mon through Fri 9 a.m. to 6 p.m., Sat 9 a.m. to 3 p.m. Also on Main Street is **Dottie's Diner @ Phillips** (740 Main St. South; 203-263-2545). The "@ Phillips" is a nod to former owners the Phillips family, who ran a diner here for years. Now Dottie Sperry offers the best of the old and so much more of the new, including to-die-for doughnuts, including the chocolate-frosted cinnamon ones, incredible chili that will warm you to your toes, and much, much more. Visit Dottie's Mon 6 a.m. to 3 p.m., Tues and Wed 6 a.m. to 8 p.m., Thurs and Fri 6 a.m. to 9 p.m., Sat 6 a.m. to 3 p.m., and Sun 7 a.m. to 1 p.m.

Good News in Woodbury

Road-foodistas Jane and Michael Stern adore Woodbury's **Carole Peck's Good News Cafe** (694 Main St. South; 203-266-4663; good-news-cafe.com), as do other restaurant critics and celebrity diners-out.

This gem of an eatery has been compared to Berkeley's Chez Panisse. For many epicures, it's like going home, except the food is better and you don't have to clean your plate to get dessert. Carole Peck buys most of her produce and other foods from local suppliers, so everything you get is fresh and high-quality, and the food is healthful without being grim or preachy. The desserts are as splendid as the entrees, so many from which to choose. The truth is, no matter what you order, the food is great, and the service remarkable, the art wonderfully watchable, and the atmosphere comfortable. Open Mon and Wed through Sat 11:30 a.m. to 10 p.m., Sun noon to 10 p.m.; closed Tues.

Although they are not antiques, the pewter plates, mugs, lamps, and other accessories at the **Woodbury Pewter Factory Outlet Store** (860 Main St. South; 800-648-2014; woodburypewter.com) look as authentic as any antique you would buy in Woodbury. Featured in *Victoria* magazine, Woodbury Pewter has been around since 1952, when it was a tiny shop tucked into a blacksmith's shop. Today it's a modern retail operation that features not only its own products but also the pewter work and jewelry of pewterers from across America. Open Mon through Sat 9 a.m. to 5 p.m., Sun 11 a.m. to 5 p.m. Woodbury Pewter also holds several very good sales throughout the year.

A glebe is the parcel of land granted to a clergyman during his tenure of office. The gambrel-roofed **1740 Glebe House** (49 Hollow Rd.; 203-263-2855; theglebehouse.org), off US 6 in the center of town, has always had ecclesiastical connections. Mere weeks after the start of the American Revolution, a group of clergy secretly assembled in the house to elect the first American bishop of the Episcopal Church, the Reverend Dr. Samuel Seabury. His election broke the American connection with the Church of England and laid the foundation for the separation of church and state in America. Today the old farmhouse is used as a museum and kept much as it was. The original paneling remains, and the rooms are stuffed with period furnishings collected locally. Open 1 to 4 p.m. Wed through Sun, May through Oct, and weekends only in Nov (other times by appointment). Admission.

Bridgewater

You'll want to visit **Olson's Bridgewater Corners Country Store** (5680 Rte. 4; 860-672-6241; bridgewatercornerstore.com) as much for the history as the inventory. This building has been serving travelers since 1890, sometimes as a store, for a long time as the town's first post office, but mostly as a gathering place. Today's owners, the Olsons, carry on the tradition, and they've kept the original post office window. You can come here for a quick sandwich, but you'll also find locally brewed beer, coffee, and wine; baked goods, specialty cheeses, cold cuts, and other groceries; books, magazines, and postcards; hunting, camping, and fishing supplies; motor oil and washer fluid; children's toys; and greeting cards. Did we forget anything? Probably, but you'll find it all at this great little piece of history. Where else can you pick up a sandwich and a snow shovel? Open 6:30 a.m. to 8:30 p.m. Mon through Thurs, 6:30 a.m. to 9 p.m. Fri, and 9 a.m. to 8:30 p.m. Sat and Sun.

Washington

Lake Waramaug State Park (30 Lake Waramaug Rd.; 860-868-2592) offers seasonal camping, fishing, swimming, car-top boating, and picnicking. With its surrounding forests and hills, the lake is often likened to Switzerland's Lake Lucerne, and the inns that ring its waters reflect the same alpine charm. The lake is named for Chief Waramaug, whose Wyantenock tribe hunted and wintered in the area. One of the best ways to see the area, especially during leaf-peeping season, is to take the 0.9-mile drive around the lake. The burning autumn colors of the surrounding hardwoods, reflected by the cool, crystal-clear lake, make this a picture-postcard setting.

The Legend of Chief Waramaug and His Great Lodge

About the time settlers first arrived in northwestern Connecticut, the Native Americans who lived along the banks of the Housatonic River were led by a great leader, **Chief Waramaug.** Waramaug lived in a lodge high above the west bank of the Housatonic, not far from the beautiful alpine lake that bears his name. The lodge was so majestic that it was called Waramaug's Palace and, in its time, was without a doubt the most elegant dwelling in Connecticut. According to legend, Waramaug's longhouse was 20 feet wide by 100 feet long. Native American artists from all over New England worked ceaselessly for months to create Waramaug's Palace. Using bark gathered from all over New England, they intricately painted the bark with sumptuous colors distilled from herbs and flowers. Although much of the decoration came from Waramaug's own people and from the Iroquois from nearby New York, the Hurons, the Delaware, and even the fearsome Mohawks all sent their greatest artisans to decorate Waramaug's great lodge.

The interior was as magnificent as the outside. Waramaug's council chamber was decorated with portraits of the great chief, his family, and the elders and wise men of the tribe. Other rooms were alive with pictures of the animals who shared the forests with Waramaug and his people. According to legend, Chief Waramaug died peacefully in his great lodge and was buried nearby. For years after his death, passing warriors would add a stone to his gravesite as a gesture of respect for the great leader.

The crossroads village of **New Preston** at the southeast tip of Lake Waramaug contains several delightful little shops that are well worth a short stop, especially if you like antiques. **Dawn Hill Antiques** (11 Main St.; 860-868-0066; dawnhillantiques.com) specializes in 18th- and 19th-century Swedish furnishings. Open 11 a.m. to 5 p.m. Thurs through Mon. Closed Tues and Wed. Right next to Dawn Hill Antiques you'll find **Upstairs Antiques** (11 Main St., 2nd Floor; 860-459-7924) and an amazing group of designers, artists, and antique connoisseurs who offer an equally amazing array of products from all over the world, including some at incredibly affordable prices. Open Thurs through Mon 11 a.m. to 5 p.m. **J. Seitz & Co.** (9 E. Shore Rd.; 860-868-0119; jseitz.com) handles both Southwestern antiques and reproductions, as well as other home furnishings and decor, apparel and accessories for both men and women, jewelry, and gifts. If you're lucky, you'll find yourself in town during the semiannual tent sale. Open Mon through Sat 9:30 a.m. to 5:30 p.m., Sun 11 a.m. to 5 p.m. You can't leave the area without visiting **Dynamite Angel** (13 E. Shore Rd.; 860-898-0347). Owned by none other than Carolyn Wallace (yes, that Carolyn Wallace), Dynamite Angel offers women's clothing and accessories including the likes of Fendi, Prada, Betsey Johnson, 7 for All Mankind, and Dolce & Gabbana. Inventory turns over quickly, though, so you never know what you're going to find. If you see something you like, grab it; don't wait. The shop is as funky as the rocker. Open Fri through Mon 11 a.m. to 5 p.m.

Southeast of New Preston off Route 199 is the **Institute for American Indian Studies** (38 Curtis Rd.; 860-868-0518; iaismuseum.org). Splendid Indian craft exhibits and authentic re-creations of Indian dwellings are among the features of this museum. The institute attempts, fairly successfully, to cover 10,000 years of Native American life; displays include a 17th-century Algonquian village and garden, a furnished longhouse, a simulated archaeological site, a prehistoric rock shelter, and a variety of nature trails. There's also a museum shop. The institute holds several special events throughout the year.

The museum is open 10 a.m. to 5 p.m. Mon through Sat and noon to 5 p.m. Sun. Be sure to keep a sharp eye out for signs directing you to the museum, because they are easy to miss.

Warren

The Hopkins Inn (22 Hopkins Rd.; 860-868-7295; thehopkinsinn.com) in ***Warren,*** overlooking the northern shore of Lake Waramaug, has welcomed travelers since 1847, and they are good at what they do. The food here is so stellar that people tend to recommend the inn solely for its cuisine and forget that it is a warm and comfortable hostelry in its own right, with 11 guest rooms and 2 private apartments at reasonable rates. The outdoor patio, open for dining spring through fall, provides a spectacular view of the lake. The cuisine is contemporary Austrian, complete with rich desserts. The inn is open year-round; the restaurant is open from late Mar through Jan 1. When the restaurant is closed, the inn operates as a bed-and-breakfast.

Except for the name, there's no connection between the inn and the ***Hopkins Vineyard*** (25 Hopkins Rd.; 860-868-1768; hopkinsvineyard.com). But the dairy farm–turned–winery and the inn do share spectacular views of Lake Waramaug and the surrounding countryside. The Hopkins family has farmed the land around the lake since the late 1700s but didn't plant its first grapevine until 1979. The vineyard produces a variety of wines, including a pretty good sparkling wine made in the traditional Champagne method. Try their off-dry cider as an ingredient for autumn recipes or as a celebratory drink before Thanksgiving. You'll find tastings, sales, and a gift shop in the winery's bright red barn. The winery also hosts special events throughout the year. Hours can vary, so it's best to check the website or call before planning your trip.

Places to Stay in the Litchfield Hills

KENT

Starbuck Inn B&B
88 N. Main St.
(860) 927-1788
starbuckinn.com
Expensive
Situated on 2 acres in gorgeous Kent, only steps away from many attractions. Six guest rooms, each with private bath, and 1 with its own entrance. Full breakfast is included from 8 to 9:30 a.m. daily, and homemade sandwiches, breads, and desserts are offered every evening starting at 4 p.m. in the living room. Numerous special packages are offered throughout the year. This is a nonsmoking inn, and pets cannot be accommodated.

NORFOLK

Manor House
69 Maple Ave.
(860) 542-5690
manorhouse-norfolk.com
Expensive
This beautiful Victorian B&B in the heart of Norfolk boasts spacious grounds, excellent breakfast, and gorgeous rooms. Within walking distance of concert venue Infinity Hall, great antiquing, museums, and outdoor activities, the area offers plenty to do. Of course, maybe you just want to sit in front of the fireplace and do nothing; that's okay, too!

WASHINGTON

Mayflower Inn & Spa
118 Woodbury Rd.
(Route 47)
(860) 868-9466
mayflowerinn.com
Expensive
Located less than 2 hours from New York in the middle of beautiful Washington, the Mayflower offers 5-star accommodations in your choice of 30 different rooms. This place is truly breathtaking in any season. Take the time to peruse their website to tailor your getaway to your desires.

WOODBURY

Curtis House
506 Main St.
(203) 263-2101
curtishouseinn.com
Inexpensive to moderate
Connecticut's oldest inn, in operation since 1754 in one way or another, offers 14 guest rooms, 8 with private baths. There are 2 large dining rooms and the rustic City Hall Pub, where lunch and dinner are served. This inn is only a 10-minute walk from the Glebe House Museum. Be sure to ask the owners about the secret entrance, rumored to have been used by the Freemasons once upon a time.

Places to Eat in the Litchfield Hills

BARKHAMSTEAD

Log House Restaurant
110 New Hartford Rd.
(Route 44)
(860) 379-8937
theloghouserestaurant.com
Moderate
Family-owned and -operated for almost 40 years, the Log House offers great entrees and a large variety of subs and sandwiches.

LITCHFIELD

@ the Corner
3 West St.
(860) 567-8882
atthecorner.com
Moderate to expensive
This gem of a place offers all the usual steak, seafood, poultry, and pasta dishes, and a variety of bakery items from their pastry shop.

NEW PRESTON

Nine Main Cafe
9 Main St.
(860) 868-1879
Moderate
Offers daily breakfast and lunch specials in a 19th-century building featuring a '50s theme.

NORFOLK

The Pub
14 Greenwoods Rd. West
(860) 542-5716
Moderate
Located in a castle-like brownstone adorned with stained-glass windows

and turrets with a menu beyond pub grub, such as veggie burgers (little patties of shredded veggies with a dipping sauce and a dollop of onion marmalade); good, filling soups, such as the baked potato soup; very good burgers; and salads, such as chicken, apple, and walnuts over baby greens.

RIVERTON

Sweet Pea's
6 Riverton Rd. (Route 20)
(860) 379-7020
sweetpearestaurant.com
Moderate to expensive
Located in an antiques-filled, yellow Victorian house, this restaurant offers New American cuisine featuring many fish dishes and fresh, in-season ingredients. There is also a children's menu, complimentary wine tasting, and outdoor dining. Open 11:30 a.m. to 2:30 p.m. and 5 to 9 p.m. Tues through Sat and 11:30 a.m. to 8 p.m. Sun.

WOODBURY

Curtis House
506 Main St.
(203) 263-2101
curtishouseinn.com
Moderate to expensive
This beautiful country inn serves typical Yankee fare, including chowders, potpies, steak, seafood, and wonderful desserts. Traditional pub fare is also served.

GATEWAY TO NEW ENGLAND →

For most of America, Connecticut's southwestern shore is truly the Gateway to New England, the place where mid-Atlantic names, customs, and speech patterns begin to drop away and we Yankees start to quietly assert our personality. Most visitors to New England form their first impressions of our region from what they see in the busy towns and cities of Fairfield and New Haven Counties.

Geographically, the Gateway country is really just one long, lightly wooded coastal plain, with elevations ranging from sea level along the shore to 800 feet inland. The coastline of this low-lying plain is broken by many small bays and inlets and by the mouths of five rivers: the Mianus, Saugatuck, Mill, Housatonic, and Quinnipiac. A few miles inland, numerous lakes and ponds dot the countryside. The neighboring Long Island Sound helps temper the climate, making for pleasant summers and relatively mild winters, with plenty of rain and moderate snowfall.

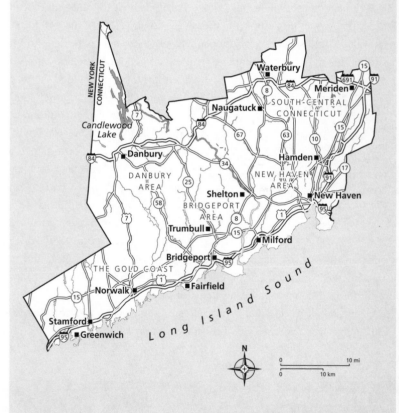

The Gold Coast

Greenwich

The southernmost of Fairfield County's towns, *Greenwich* is only 28 miles from Times Square, and many of its residents commute daily to jobs in the banks, brokerage houses, and corporate headquarters of Manhattan. So do thousands of others in the southwestern towns. The wealth they bring back to the state combined with that generated by the dozens of corporations that have headquarters here has helped earn this area the nickname of the Gold Coast. As you move north and east, the tony quality of the Gold Coast gives way to the working-class atmosphere of cities such as Bridgeport and Norwalk. This transition is complete by the time you cross the line into New Haven County, the bridge between the commuter towns of the southwest and the outlying communities of metro Hartford. New Haven is a mixture of town and gown, famed as the site of Yale University, but also revered by the cognoscenti as the home of Louis' Lunch, birthplace of the American hamburger. Across the Quinnipiac River from New Haven, population density begins to fall away quickly as one moves east, and the eastern townships of New Haven County are really more typical of the shore than of the populous southwestern part of the state.

greenwichtrivia

In 1640 European settlers gave Native Americans 25 coats in exchange for the land now occupied by the prosperous town of Greenwich.

As its mission statement proclaims, Greenwich's *Bruce Museum* (1 Museum Dr.; 203-869-0376; brucemuseum.org) "bridges the arts and

AUTHOR'S FAVORITES

Bruce Museum

Center Church on the Green

Discovery Museum and Planetarium

Military Museum of Southern New England

United House Wrecking Inc.

sciences for people of all ages and cultures to foster learning and to preserve the past for the future."

Sounds uplifting, to be sure. Fortunately, it's also fun. For big people, the collection includes works by some of Connecticut's famed impressionists, including Childe Hassam, plus a wealth of art honoring diverse cultures. For the youngsters, there are scads of well-thought-out interactive exhibits. There are also temporary exhibits throughout the year. Open 10 a.m. to 5 p.m. Tues through Sat; 1 to 5 p.m. Sun. Admission; free on Tues.

Little Bethel A.M.E. Church (44 Lake Ave.; 203-661-3099) and **First Baptist Church** (10 Northfield St.; 203-869-7988; firstbaptistchurch greenwich.org) are the first and second African-American churches, respectively, to be established in Greenwich. Before the 19th century, the African-American community really had no defined nucleus; they were not allowed such freedom. But as former slaves began to gain their freedom, this started to change. Neighborhoods began to appear, and many turned to religion for comfort and community. Little Bethel A.M.E. Church was established in 1883, while First Baptist came along in 1909, although the first official prayer meeting of the congregation occurred in 1897. Both churches are now listed on both the Connecticut Freedom Trail and the National Register of Historic Places.

When the **Merritt Parkway** was opened in 1938, it was praised for its beauty and efficiency. Today it is acclaimed as a scenic alternative to the newer, grittier, and truck-laden I-95. The Merritt, which is on the National Register of Historic Places, runs 37 miles, from Greenwich on the state line to Milford's border at the Housatonic River. At that point it becomes the Wilbur Cross Parkway, and the scenery and architecture become less distinguished.

Credit for the Merritt's unique charms goes especially to its landscape architect, Weld Thayer Chase, and to George Dunkelberger, designer of the 68 distinctive bridges. Watch closely and you will see the Connecticut state seal, an owl, a blue-and-white Yale textbook, and a pair of Nike's wings on the many Art Deco spans that cross the parkway. (If you're driving with restless children, point out the bridge ornamentation, urging them to see what will come next and choosing their favorites.) The grassy median that separates the Merritt's north- and southbound lanes is also a delight, with its varied landscape of trees and shrubs. Two bonuses: The Merritt is toll-free, and trucks are not allowed. One drawback: The Merritt is a two-lane highway, so if there are traffic issues, there's not a lot of room to maneuver; be prepared to wait.

Stamford

As you leave Greenwich and enter *Stamford,* watch for the *Stamford Cone* on the corner of N. State Street and Washington Boulevard. Stop for a visit and you'll feel like you're standing inside a giant kaleidoscope. This 45-foot-tall structure is made up of 204 panels of glorious stained glass. There's something magical about standing inside and watching the play of light and color. The cone is open to the public from 9 a.m. to 4 p.m. After dark, the cone is lit inside until dawn.

Be sure to stop in at *United House Wrecking Inc.* (535 Hope St.; 203-348-5371; unitedhousewrecking.com). Just look for a rambling collection of buildings surrounded by a chain-link fence and guarded by a bunch of stone yard animals and lots of other junk . . . er, treasures.

Inside are more than 2½ acres of every type of antique something or other you can (or can't) imagine. The main display area contains antique furniture, some salvaged from Gold Coast mansions, some from manor houses in England and France; others are quality reproductions. While they are no longer in the demolition business, the owners travel the world to bring back a wide variety of unusual architectural items. There's so much that they organize it in sections: tables here, cabinets there, chairs over yonder; there are doors, fireplace mantels, patio furniture, weathervanes, fountains, gates. If you need it, you're likely to find it throughout their 43,000 square feet of retail space. The establishment's discovery by both Oprah Winfrey and Martha Stewart has caused the size of weekend crowds to balloon. If you really want to browse, go during off-peak hours. Open 9:30 a.m. to 5:30 p.m. Mon through Sat; noon to 5 p.m. Sun.

Jackie Robinson Park (Richmond Hill Avenue and W. Main Street), on the city's west side, is dedicated to the baseball hall of famer who broke the color barrier on April 15, 1947, when he became the first African American to play major league baseball. Within the park is a bronze statue of the man who called Stamford his home for nearly 20 years. The statue declares COURAGE, CONFIDENCE, AND PERSEVERANCE—words to live by.

The *Stamford Museum and Nature Center* (39 Scofieldtown Rd.; 203-322-1646; stamfordmuseum.org) is something of a hybrid, with plenty to appeal to a variety of tastes. For many visitors, the animals on the small working farm are the main attraction. Wheelchair-accessible paths wind gently around pastures and barns with cows, oxen, sheep, goats, pigs, llamas, alpacas, horses, donkeys, and barnyard fowl. One of the neatest exhibits includes a microscope/television system for viewing the mysteries of pond life. The nature center's 118-acre woodland site also includes galleries for interactive exhibits, a planetarium, picnic tables on a meadow overlooking the pond, a state-of-the-art observatory with research telescope, 2 stores, and a vast hardwood forest with miles of hiking trails.

Norwalk

During the 1930s, unemployed artists were commissioned under the Works Progress Administration (WPA) to paint murals, many portraying the art of everyday life in America, in public buildings. Most of the structures that once housed these underappreciated masterpieces have fallen victim to the wrecking ball, but some of Connecticut's Depression-era buildings, especially post offices, still display these modern wonders. *Norwalk,* however, has retained and restored one of the largest collections of Depression-era murals in the US. Maintained by the *Norwalk Transit District* (275 Wilson Ave.; 203-852-0000; norwalktransit.com), these murals were originally painted on the walls of the old high school. When that building was torn down, the art was carefully preserved, restored, and rehung in municipal buildings throughout the city. You'll find them at the city hall, community college, Maritime Aquarium at Norwalk, the public library, and of course, the transit district.

If you're looking for some on-the-water time, the *Small Boat Shop* (144 Water St.; 203-854-5223; thesmallboatshop.com) offers guided tours of the beautiful and privately owned Norwalk Islands. You must make reservations in advance; the tours carry a fairly hefty per-person price tag.

SoNo, shorthand for South Norwalk, was once an all-too-common decaying inner-city neighborhood, but that all started to change in 1949 when a man named Roger Wilcox and his family built a community. This community, they decreed, would be "a different type of community with a completely democratic character, [with] no discrimination because of race, color, creed or politics." This was a new idea in 1949; it pleased some folks and greatly displeased others. But the community has survived and is officially on the National Register of Historic Places, as well as gaining a mention on the Connecticut Freedom Trail. The community known as Village Creek Historic District includes Dock Road, Outer Road, and Split Rock Road. Today the area around Washington and S. Main Streets has pulled itself up by the bootstraps to become a home to artists and artisans, much like Manhattan's trendy SoHo. This restored waterfront is now home to dozens of galleries, specialty shops, and restaurants.

The centerpiece of the SoNo revival is the **Maritime Aquarium at Norwalk** (10 N. Water St.; 203-852-0700; maritimeaquarium.org). At the center, part museum, part aquarium, and part theater, what ties it together is life on (and by) the sea. The building also contains restaurants and a nice gift shop. Open daily 10 a.m. to 5 p.m. (until 6 during July and Aug). Closed Thanksgiving and Christmas. Admission.

The **SoNo Switch Tower Museum** (77 Washington St.; 203-246-6958; westctnrhs.org) is an interesting part of the district's thriving cultural scene. Run by the Western Connecticut chapter of the National Railroad Historical Society, the museum was originally the switch tower in the timing building. Now it is a participatory museum. Some memorabilia is on display, but the main attraction is standing above the tracks and watching the trains roar by beneath you. Visitors can also pull the levers that move the switches and signals on the main line. The museum is open May through Oct, noon to 5 p.m. Sat and Sun. Admission is free, but donations are appreciated.

norwalktrivia

At one time Norwalk was the oyster capital of Connecticut. Severe pollution changed all that for a while. Today, thanks to tough environmental legislation that is cleaning up Long Island Sound, Connecticut is once again one of the country's top oyster producers. And the new home base for Connecticut's oystering industry is, once again, Norwalk.

At **Calf Pasture Park** on Calf Pasture Road, families loll on the beach, picnic, or wander the shore looking for seashells. Open daily from 7 a.m. to 10:30 p.m. with a lifeguard on duty from 10 a.m. to 6 p.m. A food concession, restrooms, changing areas, and eating areas are available. If you're an out-of-towner, there's a fairly stiff parking fee. Pets are not allowed.

Just a short ferry ride off Norwalk, the historic **Sheffield Island Lighthouse** (203-838-9444;

lighthouse.cc/sheffield) is a pretty cool place to spend a hot summer day. Sheffield is the outermost of Norwalk's 13 islands and offers scenic views of both Long Island Sound and the Norwalk River. The *G. W. Tyler,* a 49-passenger ferry, leaves for the island from Seaport Dock (corner of N. Water and Washington Streets in South Norwalk) twice a day on weekdays and three times on weekends. Weekend and holiday service starts Memorial Day weekend; daily service runs from late June through Labor Day. Dates and times are posted on the website. On the round-trip cruise, the ferry's crew offers lively commentary on Norwalk's oystering past and the island's sometimes racy history and folklore. Island clambakes are held Thurs evening throughout the summer. There are also Haunted Lighthouse and Christmas in July weekends. Whenever they choose to go, visitors can tour the lighthouse, picnic, or walk to the trail of the McKinney Wildlife Refuge. Fee for ferry ride and clambake. The light, which is now on the National Register of Historic Places, was constructed in 1868 and was an active working light until 1902.

Westport

Downtown **Westport,** with its collection of boutique shops, has its own charm, although the streets and stores can get crowded on peak shopping days. The shops come and go, so just park and go where your fancy takes you.

One of the best reasons for visiting Westport even on the busiest days is a place called **Coffee An'** (343 Main St.; 203-227-3808), a world-class doughnut shop. The doughnuts are made from scratch, and they keep coming fresh out of the oven all day. They also serve breakfast, salads, and sandwiches. Open Mon through Fri 7 a.m. to 3:30 p.m., Sat 7 a.m. to 3 p.m., and Sun 8 a.m. to 1 p.m.

One of the oldest nature centers in Connecticut is a good place to walk off doughnuts from Coffee An'. **Earthplace, the Nature Discovery Center** (10 Woodside Ln.; 203-227-7253; earthplace.org) offers more than 2 miles of trails (open dawn to dusk) and an excellent display of native plants on this 62-acre sanctuary. On weekends the hands-on aquarium exposes kids to marine life, and the Discovery Room has many hands-on natural-history activities, puzzles, artifacts, and scientific equipment to use. Since 2005 the exhibit hall has featured activities for kids. There is also an animal rehabilitation center where injured and abandoned animals are cared for. The center also has a wheelchair-accessible trail. The center is open 9 a.m. to 5 p.m. Mon through Sat and 1 to 4 p.m. Sun. Admission.

In 1802 Henry Munroe purchased 8 acres of land in Westport. Four years later, he and his wife, Lyzette, moved from Fairfield into their new house in Westport. While this is a significant accomplishment for the times, it is even more significant considering the Munroes were African American. Theirs is one of the few houses in the area known to be built by a free black man in the 19th century. The house and barn still stand today and are a stop on Connecticut's Freedom Trail, but are privately owned and not open to the public. While you cannot visit their home, you can visit their final resting place in **Green Farms Burying Ground** (Sherwood Island Connector and Green Farms Road) in Westport. This cemetery holds some beautiful headstones that are a window into the past. You'll find the Munroes in the far southwest corner.

Fairfield

The **Connecticut Audubon Birdcraft Museum** (314 Unquowa Rd.; 203-259-0416; ctaudubon.org/birdcraft-museum) is housed in the first privately owned songbird sanctuary in America. It was established in 1914 by Mable Osgood Wright, a pioneer in the American conservation movement and founder of the Connecticut Audubon Society. Recognized as a National Historic Landmark in 1993, the Birdcraft Museum is undergoing a major interior renovation, which will include new interactive exhibits, refurbished dioramas, and other exciting changes that will bring the museum to life even more. While the museum will be closed during renovations, the nature store and visitor center will remain open Tues through Fri 9 a.m. to 1 p.m. The sanctuary will also be open daily, year-round, dawn to dusk.

fairfieldtrivia

Wiffle ball was invented by David N. Mullaney of Fairfield in 1954. By the way, "wiffle" comes from the sandlot baseball term "whiff" (strike), which is what you usually do when you try to hit that crazy plastic ball with all those holes.

Bridgeport Area

Bridgeport

Phineas Taylor (P. T.) Barnum is quite possibly the country's most famous entertainment entrepreneur. Born in 1810, in an era when entertainment was pretty much divided along class lines between the cultural and the popular, Barnum revolutionized showbiz by presenting entertainments designed to appeal to people of all classes. Over time his name came to be linked with three things: showmanship, the circus, and a legendary quote that he never said, "There's a sucker born every minute."

Barnum also served as the mayor of *Bridgeport* in 1875, and today that city is repaying him by working hard to rebuild the museum that honors his work and memory. The *Barnum Museum* (820 Main St.; 203-331-1104; barnum-museum.org) was heavily damaged when an F1 tornado blew through the city on June 24, 2010. The path of the tornado was only about 300 feet for less than ²⁄₁₀ of a mile, but damage was extensive. Thousands of artifacts and exhibits had to be carefully sorted through and moved to safer storage before architects and engineers could even begin to evaluate the damage to the museum's building, which is a jewel on its own.

bridgeporttrivia

Famous last words: On his deathbed, P. T. Barnum is reported to have said, "How were the receipts today at Madison Square Garden?"

Recovery efforts are ongoing, and in an attempt to keep visitors abreast of how the process is going, the folks at the museum have created an exhibit called Recovery in Action! Located in the museum's massive storage area, the exhibit is presented Thurs and Fri from 11 a.m. to 3 p.m. Visitors will be able to view some of the unique artifacts as they are carefully cleaned and restored. Tours of the storm-damaged building are not possible, but you might have the opportunity to watch a conservator work on some of the exhibits. There is suggested donation for entry to the exhibit.

Bridgeport has another museum that is definitely worth a visit. Someone once described the *Discovery Museum and Planetarium* (4450 Park Ave.; 203-372-3521; discoverymuseum.org) as "more fun than a basket of puppies." It is indeed a splendid place for kids of all ages.

This 20,000-square-foot museum offers permanent and changing exhibits throughout the year. While some museums are "don't touch" places, the Discovery is a "please touch" place. You can make a variety of delightful things happen by simply pulling a lever, turning a crank, or pushing a button. When your hands have had enough pulling, turning, and pushing, you can enter an anechoic chamber and hear what things sound like without an echo or play the drums remotely using optical sensors or interact with the museum in what seems like a zillion and one other ways. As part of a special program, school groups can even suit up and go to Mars as crew members aboard a spaceship. For a small additional charge, kids age 10 and up can participate in one of the Challenger mini-missions that are held most weekends.

The Henry B. duPont III Planetarium offers shows starting at 1 p.m. for children 7 and under, 3 p.m. for 8 and older. There are more shows on the weekend, so check the website or call for details. Planetarium admission is included in the general admission.

Be sure to check out the gift shop; it's thoughtfully stocked with lots of low-priced goodies. The museum is open 10 a.m. to 5 p.m. Wed through Sun. They are open Mon, too, in July and Aug. Admission.

bridgeporttrivia

A fun-loving bunch of students, who have remained nameless, are sometimes credited for inventing the game of Frisbee by tossing back and forth empty pie tins from Mrs. Frisbie's Bridgeport bakery.

Bridgeport's **Beardsley Zoo** (1875 Noble Ave.; 203-394-6565) is Connecticut's largest zoo, featuring large North American mammals in addition to various exotics. There is also a children's zoo set up like a New England farm within the main zoo, a 36-acre rain forest, and an indoor carousel museum. The facility includes a picnic area, snack bar, and gift shop. It is open daily from 9 a.m. to 4 p.m. Admission.

When sisters Mary and Eliza Freeman purchased neighboring lots in Bridgeport and eventually each built a home, they did not intend for those houses to serve as a symbol of American freedom more than 150 years later. They could not have known that the community would come together to save their homes with the wish to create an important cultural exhibit that will teach future generations the history of African Americans in our state, help revitalize the surrounding community, and serve as a role model to other communities. I'm sure they had no idea, but that is exactly what happened. The **Mary & Eliza Freeman Center for History and Community** (freemancenterbpt.com) is still in the planning stages, but it is well on its way. The Main Street houses that belonged to Mary and Eliza had slipped into such a state of disrepair that they were in danger of being demolished. But once again Yankee ingenuity kicked in, grants were secured, people pitched in, and the houses were saved. The houses, along with the **Walters Memorial A.M.E. Zion Church** (12 Gregory St.), are all that remain of a free black community referred to as Little Liberia that thrived in the 19th century. The women's history is as amazing as the homes they built. Neither sister ever married, and they were successful at a time when being a woman and being black were not in their favor. For a bit, they both lived in New York City and amassed huge real estate portfolios. At the time of her death in 1862 at the age of 57, Eliza had $3,000 in real estate. Mary subsequently grew that investment to more than $30,000, possibly up to $50,000, an amount second only to P. T. Barnum. At the time of this writing, the homes were buttoned up for the winter and awaiting work to resume in spring 2013. We can't wait to see how things come along.

Trumbull

Trumbull resident Nero Hawley's life is chronicled in the book *From Valley Forge to Freedom: A Story of a Black Patriot,* published in 1975. He was one of the many slaves who fought in the Revolutionary War for freedoms they could only imagine they would eventually enjoy. Hawley did gain his freedom at the end of the war and lived to be 75 years old. He is buried in Riverside Cemetery, a short walk from Daniel's Farm Road near Route 127 in Trumbull. You'll find his final resting place in the center of the far end of the small graveyard.

Shelton

The Jones family believes if you are good to the land, the land will be good to you. In fact, those words have been passed down for generations by Phillip James Jones, founder of **Jones Family Farms** (606 Walnut Tree Hill Rd.; 203-929-8425; jonesfamilyfarms.com) in **Shelton.** And that was 150 years ago, so they must be doing something right. The family currently farms 400 acres and offers pick-your-own opportunities throughout the year—pumpkins in the fall, strawberries and blueberries in the summer, Christmas trees in the winter. The family also owns and operates Jones Winery, and its wine was voted Best Connecticut Wine by *Connecticut Magazine* in 2010 and 2011. Special events are offered throughout the year, including hayrides, Halloween parties to benefit UNICEF, and wine tastings. The farm is generally open Mon through Sat 9 a.m. to 5 p.m., and 8 a.m. to noon on Sun, with longer or shorter hours depending on the season. Everything is weather-dependent, so be sure to call or check their website before traveling.

Stratford

Do you have a future pilot in the family? Then the ***National Helicopter Museum*** (2480 Main St.; 203-375-8857; nationalhelicoptermuseum .org), located in Stratford Eastbound Railroad Station, should be on your itinerary. Here your budding aviator can learn all about how these whirlybirds were developed. There are pieces designed by Stratford's own Dr. Anselm Franz, inventor of the gas turbine engine in the 1950s. Igor Sikorsky's career is chronicled and a model of his first craft is on display. From the dragonfly and hummingbird to today's incredible flying machines, it's all here. Open Memorial Day through mid-Oct, Wed through Sun 1 to 4 p.m. or by appointment.

connecticut freedomtrailtrivia

Stratford resident Asa Seymour Curtis was a farmer with a huge heart. His home at 2016 Elm St. was a known stop on the Underground Railroad. When he died in 1895 at the age of 82, he was remembered for his efforts, with an obituary reading " . . . a number of runaway slaves it is said found a safe refuge with him and were passed on their way to Canada." Visit ctfreedomtrail.org for more information.

Milford

Milford bills itself as the "little city with a big heart." With a population of more than 52,000, Milford has a rich and varied history along with a vibrant beach community. Originally purchased from Paugusset Chief Ansantawae, Milford became home to settlers beginning in 1639. Pirates are said to have

Connecticut Freedom Trail

There are two stops on the Freedom Trail in Milford. One is the **Soldiers Monument** in Milford Cemetery (Prospect Street), which honors 46 soldiers who contracted smallpox and were abandoned by a British ship on a Milford beach. One of the doctors who volunteered to try to help the men contracted the disease himself and is buried with them in the common grave. The other stop is **First Baptist Church** (28 North St.; 203-878-1178), which contains a memorial marker honoring six African Americans who fought in the American Revolution.

roamed the area's waters and rumor is that buried treasure is hidden on a small island off the shores of Silver Sands Beach. In Revolutionary times, the city hosted George Washington as he made his way across the area. The city saw the ravages of the Civil War and helped slaves to freedom on their way through the Underground Railroad.

Oysters have been an important industry to this city, and every year they are celebrated at the **Milford Oyster Festival** (milfordoysterfestival .org), which has been a tradition since 1975. On the third Saturday in August, this event, the largest one-day festival in the state, attracts more than 50,000 people to downtown Milford. There are arts and crafts, boat races, a car show, entertainment from all over (local and nationally known), and tons and tons of food. It is an opportunity for many of the local nonprofit organizations to raise money for their causes, which means lots of good stuff for visitors.

Milford also has beautiful beaches. **Silver Sands State Park** (203-735-4311) is located off Route 1 and offers free parking (hard to find in this area!). There is a long wooden boardwalk to be enjoyed, and at low tide you can sometimes walk all the way out to Charles Island (remember, hidden treasure?).

New Haven Area

Orange

If you like to hunt for bargains, the **L.L. Bean Outlet** (560 Boston Post Rd.; 203-795-3500; llbean.com) store in **Orange** is the place for you. You never know what you will find here. From a canoe filled with mis-monogrammed backpacks, Bean bags, and lunch boxes, to returned catalog purchases, to off-season sale items, there's usually something you need. They offer great sales, too, on the discounted items. And if you know L.L. Bean, then you know their products are high-quality. Open Mon through Sat 9 a.m. to 9 p.m., Sun 11 a.m. to 6 p.m. There is also a Trader Joe's in the same plaza.

New Haven

New Haven's Yale University is one of those American treasures that can be measured only in terms of firsts, bests, and similar benchmarks. In 1861 it granted the first doctor of philosophy degree in the US.

In 1869 its School of Fine Arts, the first in the country, opened its doors. Yale numbers among its graduates men of the caliber of Eli Whitney and Noah Webster, and since 1789 almost 10 percent of major US diplomatic appointees have been Yale grads.

Yale boasts some of the must interesting architecture in the country. Start at *Phelps Gate* on College Street. Beyond the gate is the *Old Campus,* ringed with gothic buildings. *Dwight Hall* introduced Yale to this type of architecture in 1842. Built as the college library for the then mind-boggling sum of $33,253, it was a strange marriage of spare New England Puritanism with opulent overindulgence. It boasts 32 carved heads of man and beast mounted on turrets on its 90-foot tower. Over the next 70 years, other architects designed additional gothic buildings for the Old Campus. Bingham and Vanderbilt Halls on Chapel Street and the bridge over High Street all have their own menagerie of mythological beasties.

Yale graduate James Gamble Rogers's 221-foot 1921 *Harkness Tower* on High Street honors people and events associated with Yale history, including university founder Eli Yale and graduates Samuel F. B. Morse, Eli Whitney, John C. Calhoun, Noah Webster, Nathan Hale, and 18th-century fire-and-brimstone preacher Jonathan Edwards. James Fenimore Cooper also attended, but was asked to leave after two years.

Higher on the tower are figures from ancient history, such as Phidias, Homer, Aristotle, and Euclid. Rogers also designed the *Sterling Memorial Library,* the Sterling Law complex, and the Hall of Graduate Studies. The library's decorative sculpture has a surprisingly whimsical theme, with its bookworm perched above the Wall Street entrance. The *Sterling Law*

School complex is a veritable jungle of legal symbols, including Minerva and her owl. A feisty bulldog serves as the school mascot. Free student-guided tours of Yale are available through the **Yale Visitor Information Office** (149 Elm St.; 203-432-2302; yale.edu/visitor/tours.html). Tours run Mon through Fri at 10:30 a.m. and 2 p.m. and on weekends at 1:30 p.m.

Yale University's **Beinecke Rare Book and Manuscript Library** (121 Wall St.; 203-432-2977) is like no other building you've ever seen. To protect the fragile documents inside from sun damage, it was built without windows. Instead, the exterior walls are made of wafer-thin marble slabs. When the sun shines, the building's interior has a cloudy amber glow. The library, which is open to the public, has 5 major collections. The permanent exhibit on the mezzanine features the Gutenberg Bible. Printed in about 1455 in

The Boulevard for Bargains

You'll sometimes hear Nutmeggers whisper, "Oh, I got it at the Boulevard." There will usually be some winking and smiling going on during said conversation. That's because the **Boulevard** (500 Ella T. Grasso Blvd.; 203-772-1447; fleact.com) is a year-round flea market where bargains abound. We caution you, however, to go with your eyes open. While you will find great deals, you will find cheap knockoffs. Most of the time people are good with that as long as the knockoff is good, but you need to know what you are looking for so you don't get bamboozled. Do your research. The vendors here are hard-core. They don't bargain much, but we, of course, encourage you to try—you never know. Bring cash; that's all they deal with. If you don't see it, ask. You may or may not get an honest answer. We suspect the Boulevard has been raided a time or two, so any truly name-brand merchandise is often sold quickly and quietly. For a while North Face jackets and UGG boots were hot items, but you'll also find MAC makeup, "Tiffany" jewelry, "Pandora"-like beads galore, furniture, toys, blankets and other bedding, dollar items, jeans, shoes, phone cases, and oh so much more. In season you'll often find fresh vegetables. You just never know. There are a few food vendors, too. Bathrooms are sketchy. The flea market is held on an open field, and there is limited paved parking; the rest is on bumpy ground. They open at 7 a.m., but if you get there too early, they'll still be setting up. It gets busy fast, too. If you see something you like, we recommend you don't wait. If you do, it may be gone when you go back. There are, however, several vendors who sell the same or similar items, so be sure to look around, too. Open year-round, Sat and Sun 7 a.m. to 4 p.m.

Mainz, Germany, it is regarded as the first book printed from movable type in the Western world. *Audubon's Birds of America* is also on display. This is a great place to visit, but maybe not one for toddlers or younger children. While it's okay to walk through with them, it's a very quiet place with many glass cases—just a word of warning. Open 9 a.m. to 7 p.m. Mon through Thurs, to 5 p.m. Fri, and noon to 5 p.m. Sat.

They call it **The Tomb** (64 High St.), and the name fits. If you walk down High Street between Chapel and Elm Streets in downtown New Haven, you will come across a spooky stone edifice with no windows. This is the headquarters of Skull and Bones, the infamous secret society at Yale University. Its alumni include George H. W. Bush and his son George W., plus a host of CIA agents and big-shot dignitaries. Skull and Bones had an unwanted national spotlight shined upon its Greco-Egyptian facade during the 2004 presidential campaign, which featured the eerie coincidence of two "Bonesmen" (Bush the younger and US senator John Kerry) running against each other. Neither of them would discuss his membership in this elite group that supposedly practices secret rituals involving coffins. According to folklore, Geronimo's skull is inside the building. If you're contemplating trying to get inside, forget about it. Just walk on and wonder.

Yale is also home to several of America's finest museums. A showcase for British art and life, the **Yale Center for British Art** (1080 Chapel St.; 203-432-2800; yale.edu/ycba) was built around the extensive collection of Paul Mellon, a 1929 Yale graduate who spent 40 years amassing works by a host of British artists. Mellon's holdings have been expanded since the center opened in 1977, and the building now houses the largest collection of British art outside of Great Britain. It also houses a 13,000-volume research library. Open 10 a.m. to 5 p.m. Tues through Sat and noon to 5 p.m. Sun.

yaletrivia

The **Yale Bowl,** completed in 1914, was the first enclosed football stadium in the US, and while it wasn't quite the Final Four, the first intercollegiate basketball game was played in New Haven in 1896.

On the opposite corner of Chapel and York Streets is the **Yale University Art Gallery** (1111 Chapel St.; 203-432-0600; artgallery.yale.edu). Founded in 1832, this is the oldest university art museum in the US, and its collection spans various eras, cultures, and art styles. The museum has gone through many changes and expansions over its long history. The museum's most recent expansion promises to enhance visitors' experience and learning, With more than 200,000 objects on display, how can a visit not be enlightening? There's also a sculpture garden, with works by Moore, Nevelson, and others, that makes an awfully nice setting in which to dream away a spring afternoon. Open 10 a.m. to 5 p.m. Tues and Wed (until 8 p.m. on Thurs), 10 a.m. to 5 p.m. Fri and Sat, and 1 to 6 p.m. Sun.

The *Yale Peabody Museum of Natural History* (170 Whitney Ave.; 203-432-5050; peabody.yale.edu), at the intersection of Whitney Avenue and Sachem Street, is the largest natural history museum in New England. Big deal, you say. Ah, but all children and those adults who are truly tuned in to "kid kool" know that "natural history" is just an adult euphemism for what it's really all about: dinosaurs. The big guys. The all-time king bad boys of the natural kingdom. T-Rex, Raptor Red, and their buddies.

The Peabody has the largest collection of mounted dinosaurs in the world, including a 67-foot apatosaurus. It also boasts the original *Age of Reptiles* mural by Pulitzer Prize winner Rudolph Zallinger. Sure, it has been reproduced countless times in books from coast to coast, but it's the biggest mural of its kind in the world, and nothing beats the overwhelming experience of standing in front of the real thing.

The Yale Peabody is open 10 a.m. to 5 p.m. Mon through Sat and noon to 5 p.m. Sun. Admission. There's loads of great info about visiting the museum on their website, including information on how to get in free, so be sure to check it out.

But there's much more to New Haven than Yale University. For starters, there's the crypt under *Center Church on the Green* (250 Temple St.; 203-787-0121; newhavencenterchurch.org). For tourists who are truly committed to getting off the beaten path, this attraction is hard to beat. It's not so much creepy as it is historic.

These graves are believed to be unique to America. Nowhere else, historians say, was a church built over a colonial graveyard, a decision that helped protect the graves from the elements. The original graveyard dates to the 1600s. Here lie the remains of up to 1,700 early New Havenites, including Benedict Arnold's first wife and the family of President Rutherford B. Hayes, and Yale's founder, Rev. James Pierpont, among others. Headstones and tomb "tables" abound in the cold, subterranean expanse. The crypt's visiting hours are Apr through Oct, Thurs and Sat 11 a.m. to 1 p.m. The tours are free, but donations are accepted to help preserve the crypt and its remarkable contents. The church is also on the Connecticut Freedom Trail for its role in supporting the Mende African *Amistad* captives.

newhaventrivia

You probably know that Connecticut inventors produced the submarine and anesthesia, but did you know that the Nutmeg State was also quite possibly the birthplace of the lollipop? Some sources credit New Haven resident George Smith with the creation in 1908. The name (maybe) is a nod to the famous racehorse of the time, Lolly Pop. Who knew?

The remaining area of the graveyard became the New Haven Green. Instead of moving all the bodies, it is said, residents simply built up the ground over them and moved the headstones to an existing cemetery. The bodies were left in peace until 2012, when Hurricane Sandy visited Connecticut. The winds took down a tree that had been planted hundreds of years ago on the green. When it toppled, its roots pulled out of the ground, bringing with it a human skeleton. The skeleton is believed to belong to one of the original residents of the graveyard.

Connecticut pizza lovers claim that **Frank Pepe Pizzeria Napoletana** (157 Wooster St.; 203-865-5762; pepespizzeria.com) in New Haven makes the best clam pizza in the Western world. There is some reason to accept that claim. Pepe's special white clam pizza, prepared by hand on the premises, like everything else here, is topped with fresh littlenecks, olive oil, garlic, oregano, and Romano cheese. For other types of pies, if you want cheese, you have to ask for it; otherwise, you get a marvelous pie crust topped with tomato sauce. The splendiferous pies are baked in a coal-fired oven to emerge as flat, crisp circles of dough with a firm, chewy crust.

Pepe's in New Haven is open 11:30 a.m. to 10 p.m. Sun through Thurs, 11:30 a.m. to 11 p.m. Fri and Sat. (Pepe's also has other locations in Connecticut and one in New York; check the website for details.) If you can't handle the line at Pepe's (and there will be one), you can always try **Sally's** (237 Wooster St.; 203-624-5271), but chances are there might be one there, too. You can't go wrong at either place; Sally's rivals Pepe's in the quality of pizza it serves.

The ***Five-Mile Point Light*** (1 Lighthouse Rd.; 203-946-8005), located at the eastern point of New Haven Harbor, was built in 1847. The 65-foot-high stone lighthouse was functional until it was taken out of service in 1877. Now it dominates ***Lighthouse Point Park*** (2 Lighthouse Rd.; 203-946-8019; cityofnewhaven.com/parks/parksin-formation/lighthousepoint.asp#info). The park includes lots of nature trails, a bird sanctuary, and a 1916 carousel that is one of the largest in America (52 feet in diameter) and holds 72 figures: 69 horses, 1 camel, and 2 dragons. The park is free; there's a small admission for the carousel. Carousel rides are available noon to 4 p.m. weekends and holidays from Memorial Day through Labor Day.

New Haven is justifiably proud of its role in liberating the captives aboard the ship ***Amistad.*** In 1839 a group of Africans who had been kidnapped from their homes in Sierra Leone by slave traders mutinied and took over the ship. But they were seized by naval authorities and taken to New Haven for trial.

newhaventrivia

New Haven is affectionately called the "Elm City" because of the stately elm trees that dotted the New Haven Green and Yale University in the late 18th century, creating a leafy canopy over the downtown area. Gradually these majestic trees succumbed to Dutch elm disease, but in recent years many have been replaced with a hardier species of elm.

After being imprisoned in a jail on the New Haven Green, where abolitionists took up their cause, the prisoners were acquitted, first in Connecticut courts and then by the US Supreme Court. This amazing and courageous saga received wide attention when Steven Spielberg's movie *Amistad* was released in 1997. Three years later a reproduction of the *Amistad* was completed in Mystic and arrived at its home port of New Haven in July 2000. The storied ship is available for tours when it is docked at Long Wharf, alongside ***New Haven Harbor*** (389 Long Wharf Dr.). But during many times of the year, it's on tour at other ports or in winter storage. Call Amistad America at (203) 495-1839 to find out if the *Amistad* is in port.

You can also visit the ***Amistad Memorial*** (165 Church St.) and read about Joseph Cinque (also known as Sengbe Pieh), one of the passengers on the ship. The 11-foot bronze statue was created by Ed Hamilton and was dedicated in 1992. It stands in the location of the New Haven jail at the time of the trials.

The museum grounds are open 10 a.m. to 5 p.m.; the museum is open daily except for May, Sept, and Oct, when it is open weekends only. Be sure to check their website for ways to save on tickets.

newhaventrivia

Famous New Haven inventions include the meat grinder, the corkscrew, and Isaac Strouse's misogynistic little torture device: the corset.

Fairhaven Furniture (72 Blatchley Ave.; 800-404-4754; fairhaven-furniture.com) was voted one of the *Hartford Advocate's* Best of New Haven in 2012. We know why. Husband-and-wife owners Kerry Triffin and Elizabeth Orsini

Arts in New Haven

New Haven likes to call itself the cultural capital of Connecticut, and it's a sobriquet that is well deserved. Besides the well-known museums mentioned elsewhere, the Elm City has nearly a dozen smaller museums and galleries, many nestled off the beaten path in residential neighborhoods and old factories. Below is a partial list. We recommend you check their websites for a sense of the kind of work each exhibits. Also, call ahead for hours of operation.

All Gallery
319 Peck St.
(203) 671-5175
allgallery.org

ArtSpace
50 Orange St.
(203) 772-2709
artspacenh.org

City Gallery
994 State St.
(203) 782-2489
city-gallery.org

Creative Arts Workshop
80 Audubon St.
(203) 562-4927
creativeartsworkshop.org

Gallery 81
81 Chestnut St.
(203) 785-9130
gallery81.com

John Slade Ely House
51 Trumbull St.
(203) 624-8055
elyhouse.org

Sumner McKnight Crosby Jr. Gallery
Arts Council of Greater New Haven
70 Audubon St., 2nd Floor
(203) 772-2788
newhavenarts.org

White Space Gallery
1020 Chapel St.
(203) 495-1200
whitespacegallery.com

work together to create an amazing furniture store that is so much more. Kerry is the furniture designer of the team and says there is "pretty much nothing we can't make for you in wood." That's a tall order! Elizabeth handles the gift and accessory side of the store, and is always on the hunt for new and interesting merchandise. Stop in and check out what they've come up with. The store is open Mon, Thurs, and Fri 9 a.m. to 6 p.m., Sat 10 a.m. to 6 p.m., and Sun noon to 4 p.m.

connecticut freedomtrailtrivia

There are so many stops in New Haven for the Connecticut Freedom Trail that if we listed them all, we'd have to add another chapter. New Haven is rich in its history and we hope you will visit the trail's website (ctfreedomtrail.org) for a listing and explanation of all the stops here.

East Haven

The **Shore Line Trolley Museum** (17 River St.; 203-467-6927; shoreline trolley.com) in **East Haven** maintains nearly 100 vintage trolleys and other vehicles. For detailed descriptions of which ones are on display, visit their website; it's a wealth of information. There are also some interpretive displays, including hands-on exhibits and audio-video displays at the museum. We suspect, though, that most people will be drawn by the trolley rides. The museum offers 3-mile round-trip rides in vintage trolley cars on the Branford Electric Railway, the nation's oldest operating suburban transportation line. Hard-core trolley freaks are also welcome to hang around the car barn watching the restoration process. You can picnic on the grounds, and there's also a gift shop. Your ticket entitles you to ride all day on all trolley cars, which depart from the station building every hour on the half hour beginning at 10:30 a.m. with the last departure at 4:30 p.m.

Hamden

Traveling north from New Haven, you'll come to suburban **Hamden.** The town's **Eli Whitney Museum** (915 Whitney Ave.; 203-777-1833; eliwhitney .org) includes displays tracing two centuries of industrial growth on the site plus various technology-oriented interactive hands-on exhibits. The museum is mainly devoted, however, to the achievements of Eli Whitney, one of the towering figures of the Industrial Revolution. Whitney was a local firearms manufacturer who pioneered the use of interchangeable parts. He also changed the course of American history by inventing the cotton gin, a device that became the foundation of the Southern plantation economy, spurred the spread of slavery, and contributed mightily to the political crisis that ended in America's Civil War. You'll find a waterfall, a covered bridge, and walking trails behind the museum. Open noon to 5 p.m. Wed through Fri and Sun, and 10 a.m. to 3 p.m. Sat, with shortened hours during the winter. Be sure to check the website or call before planning a visit.

Hamden also contains some great picnic spots, most of them located within the confines of *Sleeping Giant State Park* (200 Mt. Carmel Ave., Route 10; 203-287-5658). According to legend, the basalt mountain where the park is sited is actually an evil giant by the name of Hobbomock, who was put to sleep to prevent him from doing harm to local residents. When you approach it from the north, the chain of high, wooded hills that make up the park really does resemble a sleeping giant. Today, people climb all over the giant. Many of Sleeping Giant's 11 color-coded trails lead to gentle or moderate hikes, so even if you're out of shape you can still get in a good walk. All told, the park's 13,000-plus acres include more than 28 miles of trails, some with spectacular views. There are parking fees for weekends and holidays Memorial Day through the end of Oct. The park is open 8 a.m. to sunset.

After your hike, visit *Wentworth Homemade Ice Cream Company* (3697 Whitney Ave., Route 10; 203-281-7429), located just down the road. Wentworth's occupies a yellow-sided house on your right as you're leaving Hamden. Wentworth's makes all of its own ice cream on-site. Incredibly dense and not too sweet, Wentworth's products seem to capture the essence of each of the dozens of flavors in the ever-changing repertoire. Almond amaretto (one of many "adult" flavors that use real liquor) will win you over even if you don't care for sweet liqueurs.

The best flavor of all, though, is the peach, a gift of ambrosia lovingly crafted from fresh, tree-ripened fruit. For kids, there are silly flavors such as Cookie Monster, neon-blue vanilla with cookie bits. There's even Canine Crunch for your fur-children.

Wentworth's is open Mon through Thurs noon to 9 p.m., Fri and Sat noon to 9:30 p.m.

South-Central Connecticut

Cheshire

The **Farmington Canal Greenway** is a Connecticut attraction that is quite literally off the beaten path. It's also a marvelous example of recycling on a grand scale. In the early 1800s New Haven was a thriving port city, but there was a problem: The goods that arrived by boat couldn't be transported easily to the north. So in 1828 a canal, engineered by Eli Whitney and others, was built. It ran a total of 83 miles, from the harbor through Hamden, **Cheshire,** Plainville, and Farmington and up to Northampton, Massachusetts. The Farmington Canal became the economic lifeline of central Connecticut. But just 20 years later it was replaced by a railroad that ran adjacent to the canal.

The railroad operated until 1982, when floods washed out a portion of the line. For years the railroad beds lay abandoned and neglected. At best, they became overgrown with grass and weeds. At worst, sections became eyesores, piling up with fast-food packaging, soda cans, old tires, and discarded shopping carts. But as the national rails-to-trails movement gained momentum, a grassroots effort emerged in southern Connecticut to restore this historic rail-canal corridor for recreational use. The result is a linear park for walkers, joggers, cyclists, and cross-country skiers that starts in southern Hamden and runs into Cheshire with entrances in Hamden at **Brooksvale Recreation Park** (Brooksvale Avenue) and on Todd Street (350 feet west of the intersection with Route 10) and in Cheshire at Cornwall Avenue (0.6 mile west of the Cornwall Street and Route 10 intersection) and N. Brooksvale Road (1 mile west of the intersection with Route 10). Parking is available at each trail entry point. The trail is also wheelchair accessible and has benches every so often for resting. One more thing, if you're walking or have younger children, be aware of the sometimes numerous bicyclists and Rollerbladers on the trail. Most will shout an "On your left" or "On your right" before they come up behind you, so don't be alarmed, but be aware. The trail is open year-round dawn to dusk.

On Route 42, you'll find a restored section of the canal at **Lock 12 Historical Park** (487 N. Brooksvale Rd.; 203-272-2743). In addition to the canal, the grounds contain a museum, a lockkeeper's house, a helicoidal bridge, and a picnic area. The park is open year-round, dawn to dusk. The museum is open the first Sun of each month.

At *Roaring Brook Falls* (203-272-2689; cheshirelandtrust.org), just off Roaring Brook Road (west of the junction of Route 70 and I-84), you'll find a wonderful hiking trail and overlook—the perfect place for a spring or fall picnic—and the foundation of an old mill to explore. But the draw here is Connecticut's highest single-drop waterfall. The Cheshire Land Trust's website makes the distinction between Roaring Brook Falls's single 80-foot drop and Kent Falls's 250-foot drop of multiple cascades.

Your kids might think that animation starts with the Simpsons and ends with SpongeBob, but a visit to the *Barker Character, Comic, and Cartoon Museum* (1188 Highland Ave., Route 10; 203-699-3822; barker museum.com) will widen their (and your) horizons. Herb and Gloria Barker, the museum's guiding lights, are longtime collectors of 'toon memorabilia, and they've packed a lot of history into this jewel-box museum. You'll find, among other things, many cartoon cells on view, a collection of lunch boxes and pull toys featuring cartoon characters from days gone by, and McDonald's Happy Meal toys, once giveaways, now pricey collectibles. Animators and illustrators such as George Wildman of Popeye fame often visit the museum for talks and special events. The museum is open noon to 4 p.m. Wed through Sat. Admission.

Waterbury

Ten miles or so northwest of Cheshire is the city of *Waterbury.* The brass industry moved into the city in the mid-1800s, and the Brass Capital of the World, as it was then known, was built largely on wealth derived from brass manufacturing. In the years since, the industry has moved elsewhere, but its architectural legacy remains. During the heyday of brass, Waterbury residents erected hundreds of rambling Victorian mansions and imposing public buildings. Entire neighborhoods of these buildings are preserved almost intact, and as part of an ongoing renaissance program, other neighborhoods have been restored to their former glory. As a result, much of modern-day Waterbury is a living museum of 19th- and early 20th-century architecture.

waterbury**trivia**

In 1790 the Grilley brothers of Waterbury made Connecticut's first buttons.

Timekeeping also helped to put the Waterbury area on the map. In the 1850s Waterbury Clock and Waterbury Watch made clocks and watches inexpensively, which made giving the gift of a timepiece (once prized and expensive) possible for everyone. Around 1900 watchmaker Robert Ingersoll partnered with Waterbury Watch to make the popular $1 "Yankee" watch. In just two short decades, almost 40 million Yankees were sold.

You can see the history of timekeeping and watch the industrial progress of this part of the Nutmeg State at the *Timexpo Museum* (175 Union St.; 203-755-8463; timexpo.com) in Brass Mill Commons (exit 22 off I-84). The museum traces the history of timekeeping with an emphasis on the Waterbury-based Timex Corporation. You'll see about 150 years' worth of clocks and watches, as well as those famous John Cameron Swayze commercials of our youth ("Takes a licking and keeps on ticking"). Interactive displays and games keep kids interested and occupied. There's also an exhibit of watches created by students in a competition to see who could create the best watch for the year 2154. Cool.

Perhaps the strangest part of the museum is a 40-foot replica of an Easter Island Moai statue and an interactive display that challenges visitors to guess the origin of the Easter Island inhabitants. We're sure you're going to ask (everyone does) what this has to do with watchmaking. Well, as it turns out, legendary explorer Thor Heyerdahl was friends with the owners of Timex, and they funded part of his overseas expeditions. His discoveries are explored in the museum's "Gallery of Exploration." The museum is open Tues through Sat 10 a.m. to 5 p.m. Admission.

If you're interested in architecture, you'll want to visit the *Hillside Historic District,* once home to Waterbury's captains of industry. Now listed on the National Register of Historic Places, the district includes 310 structures dating from the 19th

waterburytrivia

Preserving food in tin cans was a great idea, but getting the food out of those tins needed another. So when in 1858 Ezra J. Warner of Waterbury found a way to quickly open tins, tummies all across America thanked him. Unfortunately, his invention looked more like something from a slasher movie than the latest housewife's helper. You stuck a rather intimidatingly big, curved blade into the tin and rammed it around. Since the opener tended to open the user as well as the tin, about 10 years later, someone else invented the less dangerous cutting-wheel can opener.

and early 20th centuries. The center of Waterbury's restoration program, however, is the tree-lined city green, one of the most beautiful greens in any northeastern city. Within a few blocks of the green, you'll find scores of lovingly restored structures. Among the more interesting are a marvelously misplaced railroad station modeled on the Palazzo Pubblico in Siena, Italy. There are also 5 municipal buildings designed by prominent American architect Cass Gilbert.

The modernized and expanded *Masonic Hall* on the northwest corner of Waterbury's green houses the *Mattatuck Museum* (144 W. Main St.; 203-753-0381; mattatuckmuseum.org). This establishment is an oddly satisfying combination of industrial museum and art gallery. The gallery portion includes items spanning three centuries and is devoted to the works of American masters who have an association with Connecticut. The museum portion contains displays of household items and furnishings dating from 1713 to 1940 as well as exhibits dealing with local history, especially the history of the region's industrial development. Its holdings include collections of 19th-century furniture, novelty clocks and watches, early cameras, and Art Deco tableware. The most curious item is Charles Goodyear's rubber desk. The museum is open 10 a.m. to 5 p.m. Tues through Sat. Except during July and Aug, it is also open noon to 5 p.m. Sun. There is a gift shop and cafe on-site.

Souvenir hunters should check out what used to be the *Howland-Hughes Department Store,* a downtown stalwart built in 1890 and renowned throughout the state as the oldest freestanding department store in Connecticut. Today it operates as *The Connecticut Store* (140 Bank St.; 203-753-4121; shop.ctstore.com), well named because the management focuses on inventory that consists exclusively of made-in-Connecticut merchandise.

It's your chance to browse for Woodbury pewter, wristwatches and buttons produced right here in Waterbury, Bovano enamelware from Cheshire, Liberty candles from Bolton, Allyn neckwear from Stamford, and Lego building blocks from Enfield—plus made-in-Shelton Wiffle balls, made-in-Orange Pez candy dispensers, and made-in-Norwich Thermos bottles. Also in stock are clothing, housewares, games, puzzles, and wood carvings. This one-of-a-kind place has weathervanes, too, custom-crafted in Meriden. The store is open 10 a.m. to 3 p.m. Tues through Sat.

Meriden

Way before there were golden arches on every street corner, the central Connecticut towns of **Meriden** and Middletown had developed a local specialty called the "steamed cheeseburger." Steaming the burgers makes them incredibly juicy and reduces the sharp Wisconsin cheddar to just the right degree of molten wonderfulness. Locals know to order theirs in the form of a "trilby" (a regional term for anything served up with mustard and onions). Your best bet is undoubtedly **Ted's Restaurant** (1046 Broad St.; 203-237-6660; tedsrestaurant.com), where they've been serving, and we kid you not, world-famous steamed cheeseburgers since 1959. And it's been run by the family since Ted opened it. His son, Paul, took over when his dad passed away, and now Paul's nephew Bill Foreman operates the restaurant. Bill knows his stuff and has been able to open additional locations in Cromwell (43 Berlin Rd.; 860-635-8337) and New Haven (344 Washington Ave.; 203-234-8337). Stop by any of them for this Connecticut must. Open Sun through Wed 11 a.m. to 9 p.m., Thurs through Sat 11 a.m. to 10 p.m.

Wallingford

If you're in Wallingford—no, if you're anywhere in the state on a weekend in October and you like to be scared—set your sights for **Wallingford**'s **Trail of Terror** (60 N. Plains Hwy.; trailofterror.com). While our wonderful New England town is predestined to be filled with spooky extravaganzas at this time of the year, this Trail of Terror is like no other we've been to. It's scary. Really scary. (This is *not* a children's activity.) You travel outdoors through more than 30 "very interactive" fright scenes. Some you'll recognize and love. Some not so much. *But* it's all for a good cause! Yep, this is a totally volunteer-run operation and they donate all the proceeds to charity. Over the years, the trail has donated $500,000 to the local Red Cross chapter. They also support the Community Revitalization Efforts of Wallingford and other local charities (a complete list is on their website). Their donations for 2012 exceeded $850,000. Way to go!

The trail is not easy to get into. It's very popular and hence very busy. They sell out just about every night they are open. There are two ways you can go about gaining entrance. If you're feeling lucky, you can just head on over and wait in line. If you make it before they sell out, you can buy a $10 general admission ticket and have at it. If you're not feeling so lucky, you can go to their website and purchase a $20 speed pass. This works much like the Disney speed pass. You will be given a time and date at which you are to arrive at the trail for your turn. Not much waiting. The trail is weather dependent and will close for heavy rain and/or wind. They keep

OTHER ATTRACTIONS WORTH SEEING IN GATEWAY TO NEW ENGLAND

Bishop Farms
500 S. Meriden Rd.
Cheshire
(203) 272-8243
bishopfarmscheshirect.com

Bovano
830 S. Main St.
Cheshire
(203) 272-3200
bovano.com
Gift shop includes Bovano enamelware.

Knights of Columbus Museum
1 State St.
New Haven
(203) 865-0400
kofcmuseum.org
Art, artifacts, and archival material relating to the history, formation, and activities of the Knights of Columbus.

Lockwood-Mathews Mansion Museum
295 West Ave., Mathews Park
Norwalk
(203) 838-9799
lockwoodmathewsmansion.com

Meeker's Hardware
86–90 White St.
Danbury
(203) 748-8017

Railroad Museum of New England
176 Chase River Rd.
Waterbury
(860) 283-7245
rmne.org

St. James Church
25 West St.
Danbury

St. Peter Church
Main and Center Streets
Danbury

Stepping Stones Museum for Children
303 West Ave., Mathews Park
Norwalk
(203) 899-0606
steppingstonesmuseum.org
Focusing on the arts, science and technology, and culture and heritage. Rain forest exhibit.

Tarrywile Mansion and Park
70 Southern Blvd.
Danbury
(203) 744-3130
tarrywile.com

their Facebook page and Twitter up to date, so it's best to watch there if you're thinking of heading out. The trail opens at 7 p.m. Fri, Sat, and Sun. Last entry is 11 p.m. Fri and Sat and 10 p.m. Sun. Parking can be a little difficult. You can pay $5 to park in the Polish National Alliance parking lot, but everything else is at your own risk. Happy scaring!

Tucked away on the back industrial roads of Wallingford is a very cool little consignment shop. ***Twice as Nice Consignments*** (169 N. Plains Hwy.; 203-626-0423) offers everything from Vera Bradley bags and Department 56 to furniture and children's toys. The inventory changes constantly, so you never know what you might find. We've seen handmade quilts, antique lamps and cookbooks, many name-brand items at rock bottom prices, Boyd's Bears, American Girl items, and more. Prices are reasonable, and many items are marked down the longer they are there. There's so much to look at in this compact space that it's not hard to spend an hour or two just browsing. Open Mon through Wed, Fri, and Sat 10 a.m. to 5 p.m., Thurs 10 a.m. to 6 p.m. Closed Sun.

Danbury Area

Weston

Weston is an especially pretty town smack-dab in the middle of Fairfield County, thanks to tough zoning regulations and restrictions on development. According to folklore, old Mr. Scratch himself left some hoofprints on the rocks thereabouts. Lucifer's purported stomping grounds are now the site of the ***Lucius Pond Ordway/Devil's Den Preserve*** (203-226-4991) on Pent Road (take Godfrey Road, which is off either Route 53 or 57, to Pent Road). Owned by the Nature Conservancy, Devil's Den consists of more than 1,756 acres with 20 miles of hiking trails. This is a great place to scout out examples of rare or unusual plant species, including hog peanut and Indian cucumber root. Or you can just have a pleasant hike. If you plan to do so, be sure for your own safety that you pick up a map at the Pent Road entrance and sign in. Special programs and guided walks are held on some weekends, with attendance by reservation only. The park is open from dawn to dusk daily. There are no restrooms, and dogs and bicycles are not allowed.

Wilton

When J. Alden Weir saw his first impressionist painting in a Paris gallery, it gave him a headache, but by 1881 the American artist was honing his own distinctively impressionistic style. Today his **Wilton** home, **Weir Farm** (735 Nod Hill Rd.; 203-834-1896), is a National Historic Site. Weir designed his farm as he would a painting, mixing and matching visual elements until everything was perfect.

The farm, which he called "the Land of Nod," provided inspiration for his own paintings of late 19th-century family life and for the works of fellow artists Childe Hassam, John Twachtman, and John Singer Sargent. The self-guided Painting Sites Trail is a living landscape. It's well marked to highlight a series of views from Weir's paintings, including Weir Pond, which he built with the prize money from his 1895 painting *The Truants*. Admission is free, as are ranger-led tours. The grounds are open year-round dawn to dusk; the visitor center is open 10 a.m. to 4 p.m. Thurs through Sat, Apr through Nov; 10 a.m. to 4 p.m. Sat and Sun, Dec through Mar.

connecticut freedomtrailtrivia

Abolitionist William Wakeman owned a home in Wilton before the Civil War. Old newspapers give accounts of Wakeman's late-night journeys spiriting fugitive slaves to freedom. It is said that a trapdoor leading to a tunnel once existed inside his house, which is now privately owned and not open to the public.

Ridgefield

Nearby **Ridgefield** was the site of a minor 1777 skirmish known as (what else?) the **Battle of Ridgefield**, in which Benedict Arnold led the colonists against General William Tryon's British. The historic 1733 Keeler Tavern still carries a legacy of the battle in the form of a British cannonball embedded in the wall. Now the **Keeler Tavern Museum** (132 Main St.; 203-438-5485; keelertavernmuseum.org), the inn has been restored and furnished with authentic 18th-century furniture, appointments, and artifacts. Guides in colonial dress conduct 45-minute tours Feb through Dec. Open 1 to 4 p.m. Wed, Sat, and Sun (last tour is at 3:20 p.m.). Gift shop. Admission.

A short distance down Main Street is the **Aldrich Contemporary Art Museum** (258 Main St.; 203-438-4519; aldrichart.org), the only museum in our state that is dedicated to contemporary art. Before its 2004 reopening, the museum underwent a huge renovation. Formerly housed in a historic building known as "Old Hundred" (due to its 100-year history in the town), the museum received a facelift that charged architect Mark Hay with "the challenge of expanding a contemporary art museum located in a historic district with colonial roots." He did a fine job. This private facility is definitely contemporary and includes a screening room, performance area, education center, project space with 22-foot-high ceilings, and more. This close to New York, it tends to get works from the best of America's young artists. Often the artists represented are relative unknowns whose first important exposure comes at the Aldrich.

Behind the museum is the most exciting part of the Aldrich. Sloping away from the building is a broad green lawn dotted with several dozen pieces of modern sculpture. Most are massive, towering over the strollers in their midst. All are imbued with a special strangeness that comes partly from their staid colonial surroundings. Scattered about this sculpture garden are wrought-iron tables and chairs where visitors can sit and relax.

The Aldrich is open noon to 5 p.m. Tues through Sun. The garden is always open, even when the museum is closed. Admission. The museum offers great special deals, including free admission on Tues, which are listed on their website. Be sure to check it out.

If inns were film stars, Ridgefield's **Stonehenge Inn & Restaurant** (35 Stonehenge Rd.; 203-438-6511) would be Cary Grant: nothing ostentatious, just impeccable, gracious, and charming, with a tiny touch of reserve—the perfect mix for an extended stay or an exquisite dinner. Located on US 7 in Ridgefield, only an hour north of Manhattan, the inn features 16 rooms of understated opulence designed for grace and comfort. The 10 acres of landscaped grounds, including a duck pond and gardens, are almost as inviting as the elegant interior.

The food follows the same path. Fresh and well prepared, the tastefully presented cuisine is matched by professional service. Prices are in the high range. Dinner reservations are a must. Open for dinner 6 to 9 p.m. Tues through Sat.

Redding

When Washington's Northern Army went into winter quarters at the end of November 1778, it was dispersed in an arc from New Jersey to Connecticut

ANNUAL EVENTS IN GATEWAY TO NEW ENGLAND

MAY

Dogwood Festival
Greenfield Hill Congregational Church
1045 Old Academy Rd.
Fairfield
(203) 259-5596
greenfieldhillchurch.com
Stroll amid drifts of dogwood and welcome spring. Lots of good stuff to see and do, including garden tours, arts and crafts, a plant and garden sale (very good prices), historic walks, tag and rummage sales, picnic lunches, and an indoor luncheon (reservations required).

JUNE

International Festival of Arts and Ideas
New Haven
(888) ARTIDEA (278-4332)
artidea.org
Two weeks of free and ticketed events throughout the city, featuring some of the finest entertainers and most provocative thinkers from around the world, plus lots of kids' events.

JULY

Annual Craft Expo
New Haven
(203) 453-5947
guilfordartcenter.org/expo.html
Connecticut's oldest outdoor juried art show.

Great Connecticut Traditional Jazz Fest
Meriden
(800) 468-3836
greatctjazz.org
The largest festival in the Northeast showcases New Orleans–style Dixieland jazz, big-band sounds, and swing and jug-band music being played simultaneously in 4 venues throughout the weekend.

to ring the British garrison in New York. Three of the army's brigades had their winter encampment at **Redding**, where they were strategically positioned to defend the region from British raiders. Their commander was Major General Israel ("Old Put") Putnam, a larger-than-life hero, who is often called Connecticut's Paul Bunyan.

That winter was relatively mild, but the harvest had been poor, and supplies were scarce. The men, many of whom had been through the hell

AUGUST

New Haven Open at Yale

Connecticut Tennis Center at Yale
New Haven
(203) 776-7331
newhavenopen.com
Professional women-only tennis
tournament played on outdoor hard
courts, featuring top tennis players.

SoNo Arts Celebration

Washington and S. Main Streets
Norwalk
(203) 866-7916
For 3 days the heart of SoNo (South
Norwalk)—site of innumerable
boutique shops, galleries, and neat
restaurants—turns into one huge
block party alive with outdoor arts,
entertainment, and food.

SEPTEMBER

Norwalk Oyster Festival

Veterans Memorial Park
Norwalk
(203) 838-9444 or (888) 701-7785
seaport.org
Honoring Norwalk's seafaring past and
present, this event features oyster-
shucking and slurping contests, tall
ships, adult and kid entertainment, and
a nice fireworks display. If you prefer to
savor bivalves under less competitive
conditions, you'll find plenty of oysters
at the food court.

NOVEMBER–DECEMBER

Brookfield Craft Center Holiday Exhibition and Sale

Route 25
Brookfield
(203) 775-4526
An exhibition of quality American
crafts, gifts, and holiday decorations
displayed throughout 3 floors of a
restored gristmill.

of Valley Forge the previous year, began to mutter about a similar privation
winter in Connecticut. Then in December the state experienced one of the
worst winter storms in New England history. Two days after it ended, the men
of one brigade mutinied and prepared to march on the colonial assembly in
Hartford to demand overdue supplies and wages. Putnam was able to break
up the protest only with the greatest of difficulty. Thus began the winter
encampment at Redding that came to be known as Connecticut's Valley Forge.

The original encampment is now the site of ***Putnam Memorial State Park*** (203-938-2285; putnampark.org), Connecticut's oldest state park, at the junction of Routes 58 and 107 in West Redding. These days the 12-man huts are just piles of stone where their chimneys stood, and the old magazine is only a stone-lined pit. The officers' barracks have been rebuilt, though, and there is a museum containing exhibits dealing with the Redding encampment. There's also a great statue by the front gate showing Old Put riding his horse down a flight of stairs to escape capture during a British raid in February 1779. Open daily, 8 a.m. to sunset.

Bethel

The ***Bethel Cinema*** (269 Greenwood Ave.; 203-778-2100; bethelcinema .com) screens art and independent films, attracting a large audience wanting more than the latest blockbuster sequel. The 2-screen theater is known for showing films long before the rest of the world hops on the bandwagon. Generally 2 films are shown during a run, and mainstream movies are shown as well. The matinees are kind to tight budgets, and local restaurants offer discount deals. The theater publishes a newsletter with information about upcoming features and film-related lectures.

Readers of a certain age might have spent their teen years hanging out at drive-in restaurants where the uniformed carhops roller-skated out to your car and delivered the food on steel trays that clipped to the window. At the ***Sycamore*** (282 Greenwood Ave.; 203-748-2716; sycamoredrivein.com) those readers can relive those memories, or introduce them to younger generations. In continuous operation since 1948, the Sycamore is an old-fashioned drive-in restaurant that has been become a ***Bethel*** landmark. Carhop service is available spring, summer, and fall. Just pull in and flash your lights. It's not all atmosphere, either. The burgers are juicy and tasty. The brewed-there root beer (the recipe for which is a deep, dark secret) can taste sweet and full or sparkly and dry, depending on its age. The malts are made with real malt powder. The Sycamore sponsors Cruise Nights through-out the summer, but you might see a vintage car pull in at any time (with Sunday often having a regular traffic in these vehicles). Open 6:30 a.m. to 8:30 p.m. Mon through Thurs and to 9 p.m. Fri, 7 a.m. to 9 p.m. Sat, and 7 a.m. to 7 p.m. Sun.

Danbury

There was a time when a good hat was an essential wardrobe item, and you weren't really dressed without a good topper. In those days, Connecticut was hatmaker to America, and **Danbury** was the center of the hatmaking business. Today the glory days of hatmaking are remembered along with other Danbury history in the **Danbury Museum and Historical Society** (43 Main St.; 203-743-5200; danburymuseum.org). There are actually several buildings at this address, and exhibits are scattered among them. The oldest building, the Rider House, was saved from demolition in 1941 thanks to the efforts of Danbury's citizens and is now part of the museum. Exhibits deal with early American life, the Revolutionary War, and the history of Danbury. Another highlight is the recording studio of opera singer Marian Anderson, who was a Danbury native and the first African American to perform at the Metropolitan Opera in New York. One year before she and her husband purchased this house in Danbury in 1940, Anderson performed her famous concert on the steps of the Lincoln Memorial after being denied permission to sing at Constitution Hall. An astounding 75,000 people watched. The studio is a stop on the Connecticut Freedom Trail and houses many artifacts from her career and life. Museum hours are Tues through Fri 8 a.m. to 3 p.m., Sat 10 a.m. to 4 p.m. summer and spring, Fri and Sat 10 a.m. to 4 p.m. fall and winter.

Star Power in Connecticut

Because it offers suburban living in close proximity to New York, a host of celebs from the world of entertainment have made their homes in Connecticut. Connecticut is also the birthplace of many well-known actors. Maybe it's something in the water.

Bridgeport: Robert Mitchum, Peter Falk, Brian Dennehy, and John Ratzenberger

Darien: Chloë Sevigny

Fairfield: Meg Ryan

Greenwich: Glenn Close

Hamden: Ernest Borgnine

Hartford: Sophie Tucker, Linda Evans, Katharine Hepburn, and Louis Nye

Redding Ridge: Hope Lange

Stamford: Christopher Lloyd

Waterbury: Rosalind Russell

The *Military Museum of Southern New England* (125 Park Ave., just off I-84, exit 3; 203-790-9277; usmilitarymuseum.org) is the result of a volunteer army of helpers who don't want the sacrifices of those who served in World War II forgotten.

Inside the museum you'll find enough dioramas, maps, models, pictures, and paraphernalia of war to occupy your attention for several hours. The most impressive items are fully restored weapons and vehicles exhibited against realistic backgrounds, complete with mannequins dressed in authentic period uniforms. The experience is enhanced by World War II–era background music. The museum also holds monthly open-turret days when visitors can enter the tanks. There's also a gift shop. Open 10 a.m. to 5 p.m. Tues through Sat and noon to 5 p.m. Sun, Apr through Nov; 10 a.m. to 5 p.m. Fri and Sat, 1 to 5 p.m. Sun, Dec through Mar. Closed Mon and holidays. Admission.

Adults commuting into Manhattan may think of trains as something to be endured, but some of us will always see trains as romantic and vaguely magical. At the *Danbury Railway Museum* (120 White St.; 203-778-8337; danbury.org/drm), housed in a restored 1903 train station and adjoining a 6-acre railyard at Danbury's Union Station, a group of dedicated volunteers is doing its bit to keep that magic alive. They've transformed the old station into a museum of train paraphernalia and restored trains. Call ahead and ask about special events.

The museum holds some neat events, such as shopping trips to Manhattan, Christmas and Halloween trips, and "rare mileage" trips (their term for trips along tracks not in regular use). Near the front of the museum is a small but interesting gift shop. If Union Station looks familiar, it should. Alfred Hitchcock used it in *Strangers on a Train* as the setting for his own cameo appearance. Open June through Aug, Mon through Sat 10 a.m. to 5 p.m., Sun noon to 5 p.m.; Sept through May, Wed through Sat 10 a.m. to 4 p.m., Sun noon to 4 p.m. Admission.

If you're hungry and like Hungarian, the spot to stop is *Goulash Place* (42 Highland Ave.; 203-744-1971). Roadfood.com editor Michael Stern calls Goulash Place "a treasure-trove of Eastern European gastronomy." Located in a mostly residential neighborhood, this restaurant surprises a lot of people, and the restaurant is not often filled. But this is not a sign of the quality of the food. Once people have visited here, they often come back again and again. But don't be in a hurry; when you're here, you're like family, and the staff will take their time making you feel welcome. On the menu, among many others, are Hungarian beef goulash with dumplings, chicken paprikash, Transylvanian goulash, and delicious soups. While the wine and beer selection isn't huge, prices are reasonable, and you won't leave hungry.

Brookfield

The **Brookfield Craft Center** (286 Whisconier Rd.; 203-775-4526; brookfieldcraft.org) north of Danbury on Route 25 houses a school of contemporary arts and crafts within 6 colonial buildings (including a 1780 gristmill) set on the banks of Still River. The associated arts-and-crafts gallery and retail shop is open 11 a.m. to 5 p.m. Mon through Sat and noon to 4 p.m. Sun; closed major holidays.

If your kids normally gag at being dragged off to a craft center, try bribing them with a visit to **Mother Earth Gallery & Mining Company** (806 Federal Rd.; 203-775-6272; motherearthcrystals.com). It's a great way to occupy kids during school vacations. You and the kids can suit up with natty lighted miners' helmets and buckets and go digging for amethyst, quartz, mica, pyrite, tourmaline, peridot, and galena. The best part: You get to keep whatever you find. The fluorescent mine, glowing with green, red, orange, and blue rocks, is spooky but neat. The complex includes a gift shop that is well stocked with products from conservation organizations. Mother Earth is one cool place for a kid's birthday party. Admission; open to kids 5 and older. Open 10 a.m. to 6 p.m. Mon and Wed through Sat, and noon to 5 p.m. Sun.

You don't have to travel to Napa for an authentic wine tour. **Brookfield's DiGrazia Vineyards & Winery** (131 Tower Rd.; 203-775-1616; digrazia.com) is one of New England's smaller wineries, but it's also one

danbury trivia

Zadoc Benedict founded the nation's first hat factory in Danbury in 1780. It produced a dizzying three hats a day! By the mid-1800s, the Hat City led the world in hat production, and by 1949 more than 66 percent of the nation's hats carried a "made in Connecticut" label. From 1949 to 1977, Connecticut honored the hat industry with Hat Day, and both houses of Connecticut's legislature would be filled with examples of the hatmaker's art, from tough-guy fedoras to Miss Porter's–perfect pillboxes.

of the most interesting. The grapes come from vineyards in New York as well as Sharon and Southbury, but it all comes together at the **Brookfield** site, which is a family-run boutique winery. While other area vintners make fruit wines or grow the French hybrids traditional to New England, Dr. Paul DiGrazia and family focus on specialties. You might find Beaujolais, port, mead (honey wine), or wines made from pears, sugar pumpkins, raspberries, or apples. If you're sensitive to sulfides, ask about the wines made with honey. This vineyard has been around since 1978, and the original line has expanded greatly. Tours and wine tastings are available, as well as a gift shop and picnic area. Open daily 11 a.m. to 5 p.m., May through Dec; weekends only Jan through Apr.

Newtown

East of Danbury is **Newtown,** where the **Second Company of the Governor's Horse Guards** (4 Wildlife Dr.; 203-426-9046; thehorseguard.org) practice, usually in full uniform. A horse guard practice is something no horse- or animal-loving kid can resist. Chartered in 1808, the Second Company of the Governor's Horse Guards was used mainly to escort the governor and distinguished visitors on ceremonial occasions. Today the troop is a cavalry militia designated by the governor to serve the people of southwestern Connecticut. The troop's horses, which are donated, are a variety of breeds.

The public is invited to watch the drills. Fall and winter drills begin at 10 a.m. Sun; spring and summer drills begin at 7 p.m. Thurs. Tours of the

Connecticut Haunts

Connecticut's most famous ghost, the **"White Lady,"** is said to haunt the **Stepney Cemetery** on Pepper Street in Monroe and the **Union Cemetery** down the road in nearby Easton. Visitors to the cemeteries report that the apparition wears a white nightgown with a bonnet. Others say they've seen not only the White Lady but also shadowy specters who try to grab her. The late Ed Warren of Monroe, a legendary ghostbuster who, incidentally, is also buried in Stepney Cemetery, believed her name was Mrs. Knot, and her husband was murdered near Easton in the 1940s. Mrs. Knot is said to have met the same fate as her husband shortly after his unfortunate demise. As with any cemetery, visit with respect and only during its operating hours.

barns are often available. The guard also participates in parades across the state and other special events, including visiting area hospitals, attending local fairs, and making a presence at official state ceremonies. Check the website for a complete list. (The First Company of the Governor's Horse Guards, headquartered in Avon, also holds public drills and special events. See "The Farmington Valley" in "The Heartland" chapter.)

Southbury

Not so long ago, your chances of seeing eagles hunting and soaring in the wild were somewhere between slim and none, and Slim was out to lunch. Today, thanks to the Endangered Species Act, the American eagle population is itself soaring. In winter Connecticut bald eagles find the **Southbury** area much to their taste. In fact it's such a popular place that their eagle buddies from as far away as Canada and Maine flock there, too. The **Shepaug Dam Bald Eagle Observation Area** (800-368-8954; shepaugeagles .info) is a wonderful place to watch for these majestic birds. Supported by First Light Power Resources, this observation area is staffed by knowledgeable guides to coach you in observing these beautiful birds— some of whom have a wingspan of 7 feet—while they fish, hunt, and soar. To use a worn-out phrase, they take your breath away. Eagle observations are held Tues through Fri 9 a.m. to 3 p.m., from early Dec through mid-Mar, although the season can vary; please check the website for current conditions. It also has a page with essential tips for planning your visit.

southbury trivia

Kettletown State Park in Southbury gets its name from the story that settlers paid the Native Americans who originally lived on the spot one brass kettle for the land.

By the way, bald eagles aren't really bald. In truth, they have a glorious head of white feathers. The bald part comes from the word *piebald,* which means "white."

When you have your fill of the eagles (is that even possible?), you'll want to bring your camera with you to **Southford Falls,** where you'll find the lovely cascade of Eight Mile Brook as it rushes to meet the Housatonic River. The park also includes the remains of the Diamond Match factory, which was destroyed by fire in 1923. The ruins include an old steam engine foundation, a grinding stone, and some of the sluice pipe. The little covered bridge, built by carpenter Ed Palmer with the help of author/artist Eric Sloane, is based on an 18th-century arch design. There are picnic tables by the bridge, just the place for a romantic spring picnic, or you can perch on a rock by the falls and spend some time just listening to the water or reading. The park also includes a lookout tower, great for viewing fall foliage. Southford Falls State Park is located just south of Southbury on Route 188, south of I-84.

Oxford

Rich Farm Ice Cream Shop (691 Oxford Rd.; 203-881-1040; richfarmice cream.com) on Route 67 has been serving up delicious, creamy concoctions made with milk from Dave and Dawn Rich's own herd of Holsteins since 1994, but the farm has been in Dave's family for five generations. In summer the place is packed, and you might wait in line a good 15 to 20 minutes. You won't be bored because this is a real farm with real farm looks and real farm smells. At haying time during the summer, just a whiff of the fresh-cut hay distills summer. As for the ice cream, you can choose from among 25 flavors with seasonal favorites, such as pumpkin, and kid flavors, such as Cookie Monster. Or keep things simple and stick with a good old-fashioned chocolate cone. The shop also makes ice cream cakes and seasonal treats, such as ice cream Yule logs. They also now serve lunch Mon through Fri. Bring cash; they don't accept plastic, and please leave Fido in the car so he doesn't scare the cows. Open daily Apr through Oct, 11:30 a.m. to 8 p.m.

Places to Stay in Gateway to New England

GREENWICH

Homestead Inn
420 Field Point Rd.
(203) 869-7500
homesteadinn.com
Very expensive
Four-star luxury hotel in ritzy Greenwich offering 18 rooms and suites with amazing furniture. The adjoining restaurant, and entire reason the Henkelmanns purchased the property, is the domain of German chef Thomas Henkelmann. Come for dinner, or stay the weekend; the choice is yours.

Places to Eat in Gateway to New England

MILFORD

Rainbow Gardens Restaurant and Bar
117 N. Broad St.
(203) 878-2500
rainbowgardens.org
Moderate to expensive
New American cuisine served in a lovingly restored Victorian on the Milford Green, emphasis on freshness and quality. Open 11 a.m. to 3 p.m. Mon, 11 a.m. to 9 p.m. Tues through Thurs, 11 a.m. to 10 p.m. Fri and Sat, and noon to 7 p.m. Sun. Truly a community place.

NEW HAVEN

Claire's Corner Copia
1000 Chapel St.
(203) 562-3888
clairescornercopia.com
Moderate
Vegetarian, organic, sustainable, and kosher with items, such as gazpacho, salads, soups, sandwiches, and sauces, all with their homegrown heirloom tomatoes. Outdoor seating available with views of the green. Several gluten-free options available. Open Mon through Thurs, 8 a.m. to 9 p.m., Fri 8 a.m. to 10 p.m., Sat 9 a.m. to 10 p.m., Sun 9 a.m. to 9 p.m. for breakfast, lunch, and dinner.

Marjolaine Pastry Shop
961 State St.
(203) 789-8589
marjolainepastry.com
Inexpensive
This bakery and coffeehouse is a great place to stop to satisfy your sweet tooth. Open 7 a.m. to 6 p.m. Tues through Fri, 8 a.m. to 5 p.m. Sat, and 8 a.m. to 1 p.m. Sun. Closed Mon.

NEWTOWN

King's Breakfast & Lunch

271 S. Main St. (Route 25)
(203) 426-6881
kingsofnewtown.com
Inexpensive
This is your quintessential food joint with lots of options and good food. Open daily 8 a.m. to 3 p.m.

NORWALK

La Taverna

130 New Canaan Ave.
(203) 849-8879
Moderate to expensive
Serves Italian food in a romantic Old World atmosphere; offers a sizable international wine list and easy-to-find central location. Lunch is served from noon to 3 p.m.; dinner, 5 to 9 p.m. (10 p.m. on weekends).

Pasta Nostra

116 Washington St.
(203) 854-9700
pastanostra.com
Moderate to expensive
SoNo is known for its fine restaurants, and this is one of them. The style and the prices are high, but the food is worth it. All pasta is made fresh on-site; there's also a take-out pasta store. The lunch and dinner menus, which change daily, feature high-quality dishes, such as a zesty linguine puttanesca. Open for dinner starting at 5:30 p.m. Thurs through Sat., at 6 p.m. Wed.

STAMFORD

Long Ridge Tavern

2635 Long Ridge Rd.
(203) 329-7818
longridgetavern.com
Moderate to expensive
New American cuisine served in a historic tavern. Open noon to 9 p.m. Mon through Fri, until 10 p.m. Sat, and for Sunday brunch 11 a.m. to 2:30 p.m. Check their website for coupons.

WATERBURY

Bacco's

1230 Thomaston Ave.
(203) 755-1173
baccosrestaurant.com
Moderate to expensive
The best Italian food has to offer at this family-run restaurant. Open Tues through Sun 11:30 a.m. to 10 p.m. Closed Mon.

COAST & COUNTRY

Connecticut has 253 miles of shoreline, all of it bordering the Long Island Sound. This coastline was settled shortly after the first towns were built in the Connecticut River Valley. Today the southwestern portion of the state's coastal plain has been largely urbanized, while much of the eastern portion has been given over to tourism. It is the less densely populated portion of this coastline (between New Haven and Rhode Island) that most people envision as the Connecticut shore. Home to clam shacks and posh inns, popular sandy beaches and lonely old lighthouses, modern submarines and ancient whalers, riverboats and coastal mail packets, the Connecticut shore reflects the romance of the sea like few other places on earth.

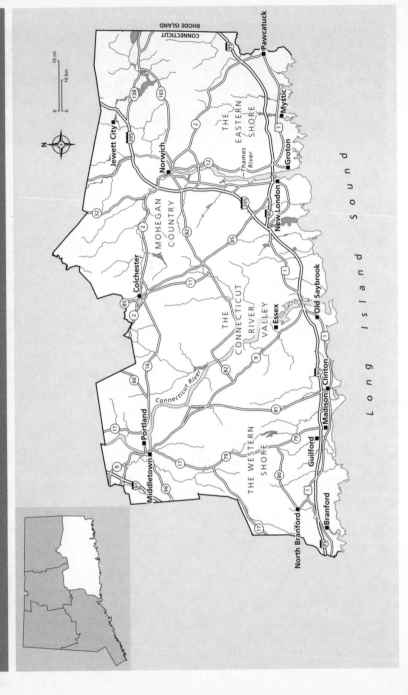

COAST & COUNTRY

AUTHOR'S FAVORITES

Gillette Castle

Goodspeed Opera House

Ledge Lighthouse

Mashantucket Pequot Museum and Research Center

Thimble Islands

Even if you're not a big fan of the sea, this part of Connecticut has much to offer. The inland portion of the coastal plain and the lower reaches of the Thames and Connecticut Rivers, in fact all of New London and Middlesex Counties and the easternmost part of New Haven County, are all part of what we call "the Shoreline." Here you'll find attractions as disparate as Stonington's Old Lighthouse Museum and a classic diner in Middletown, the glorious wedding-cake architecture of the Goodspeed Opera House and the gothic extravagance of Gillette Castle, or the famous hunt breakfasts at the Griswold Inn and the renowned chili dogs and shakes at Higgies in Higganum.

The Western Shore

Branford

According to legend, Captain William Kidd was a black-hearted pirate and bloody-handed murderer who savagely preyed upon America's eastern coast. Well, not exactly. As a matter of public record, the real Captain Kidd was a Scottish-born merchant transplanted to America who was commissioned in 1695 to hunt down the pirate Thomas Tew (of Newport) in the Indian Ocean. While pursuing Tew, Kidd stretched the limits of his commission, which embarrassed his prominent British backers (including the Crown). When he returned home, Kidd was seized and, after a rigged trial in which evidence of his innocence was suppressed, convicted of murder and piracy and hanged in 1701.

Whether your view of Captain Kidd leans toward the mythical or the historical, it's hard to resist the tantalizing legends of pirate gold and buried treasure. Many of these tales are linked to the state's ***Thimble Islands,*** just off the coast of ***Branford's*** Stony Creek, and local residents nurture the

Kidd mythology. The residents of High Island, for example, refer to their home as "Kidd's Island" and enhance its piratical flavor by flying the skull and crossbones. And on Money Island, where Kidd is widely supposed to have buried some of his treasure in a cave, shovels and spades get a good workout every summer as people try to locate the buried booty.

The Thimble Islands were discovered in 1614 by Adrien Block and have been used for everything from farming to quarrying granite. Today many of the islands play host to wealthy out-of-towners who have built opulent vacation homes on them. There are a variety of ways to see the islands. You can travel with Captain Bob Milne on his **Volsunga IV** (203-481-3345; thimbleislands.com), which leaves from Stony Creek Town Dock on Indian Point Road. There are various options, from a reasonable walk-on tour (you'll need cash or a check, though; no plastic is accepted) to the more pricey private charter. Either way, Captain Bob will supply a lively running commentary about the area, past and present.

thimbleislands trivia

Even though colonial maps labeled them the "Hundred Islands," there are actually 325 islands in the Thimble Islands. Their name comes not from their small size, but from a type of wild blackberry—thimbleberries—that once grew there.

Captains Mike Infantino Jr., his son Justin, and the crew of the **Sea Mist** (203-488-8905; thimbleisland cruise.com) also offer a variety of tours (they don't accept credit cards, either) and lively stories of the area in which they grew up. They also offer seal-watch tours in Mar and Apr. As many as 40 seals—harbor, harp, hooded, and gray seals—have been spotted on the popular 2-hour excursions.

One note: All the islands are privately held. Unless you're an invited guest, don't plan on getting off the boat to explore; uninvited guests are understandably not welcome.

If you're hungry for seafood after your cruise, try **Lenny's Indian Head Inn** (205 S. Montowese St.; 203-488-1500; lennysnow.com). Lenny's offers lobsters fresh off the boat and fish and seafood so fresh it practically swims into the kitchen. It's a comfortable place with wooden booths and customers from all walks of life, from Creekers to tourists, looking for a real New

England seafood place. Open daily at 11:30 a.m. year-round, they offer lots of specials, so be sure to check the website.

The **Stony Creek Market** (178 Thimble Islands Rd.; 203-488-0145) is another local hangout. It's good for lunch or for picking up sandwiches and salads for an impromptu picnic. Also serves super pizza! Open Mon through Fri 8 a.m. to 9 p.m., Sat 9 a.m. to 5 p.m., Sun 10 a.m. to 4 p.m.

You can tell a lot about a town by its library—one reason Branford is a special place. Not only is the *James Blackstone Memorial Library* (758 Main St.; 203-488-1441) in downtown Branford breathtaking in design and decor, it's been lovingly restored, reflecting the justifiable pride that town residents take in this unique building.

stonycreektrivia

People from Stony Creek like to call themselves "Creekers," probably to distinguish themselves from the "Yorkers" who swarm the place in summer. We also have it on good authority that Indian Neck residents are referred to as "Neckers." We're seeing a trend here.

The Blackstone Library was built in 1896 at a cost of $300,000. The centerpiece is the octagonal rotunda, paved with a marble and mosaic floor. The 50-foot dome is decorated with large murals that provide a pictorial history of bookmaking, from *Gathering the Papyrus* to *First Proof of the Gutenberg Bible*. The paintings are illuminated by an ornamental skylight that forms the eye of the dome. Medallion portraits of famous American authors, including Emerson, Hawthorne, Longfellow, Whittier, and Stowe, also adorn the room. The whole building is studded with elegant period detail, including wide marble staircases leading to the second floor and a large, inviting fireplace in the main reading room. Open year-round 9 a.m. to 8 p.m. Mon through Thurs, to 5 p.m. Fri and Sat, and Sun 1 to 4 p.m. Sept through mid-May.

branfordtrivia

Salt produced in Branford was used to preserve meat for the Revolutionary army.

The hospice movement in America began in Branford in 1974.

A tiny, unassuming pizza place tucked into a strip mall, *Born in America Restaurant and Pizza Kitchen* (4 Brushy Plain Rd.; 203-483-0211) is divided into two parts:

One half serves takeout, and the other half is a small sit-down restaurant. Chef Darrell Janis won the gold in the 1997 Pizza Olympics in Las Vegas. His creations range from the Full House pizza (white sauce, duck, portobello mushrooms, and spicy chorizo sausage topped with smoked Gouda, mozzarella, roasted garlic, tomatoes, and scallions) to a few veggies, sweet and flavorful red sauce, and just a tad of mozzarella on the chewy and tender crust. Born in America also offers appetizers, salads, grinders, and daily specials. Open Sun through Thurs 11 a.m. to 9 p.m., Fri and Sat 11 a.m. to 9:30 p.m.

Guilford

In *Guilford,* Fair Street, from the *Boston Post Road* (US 1, but called Route 1) to the green, offers a nice walk. It's less than a city block long, but in that short distance, you'll see a converted foundry, a former one-room schoolhouse, and homes representing a variety of architectural styles.

If sidewalks aren't your thing, Guilford has many scenic foot trails. The *Anne Conover Nature Education Trail* sits amid 235 acres of tidal wetlands that form the heart of the *Guilford Salt Meadows Sanctuary* (Meadow Lands Road; 203-869-5272; guilford.audubon.org). The 1-mile walking trail is a family-friendly outing and popular bird-watching location. Many educational displays are located along the trail, and guides are available at the trail kiosk. The *WestWoods Trail System* (Sam Hill Road; 203-457-9253; guilfordlandtrust.org/wordpress/properties/westwoods), maintained by the Guilford Land Conservation Trust, is the largest recreational area for hiking in Guilford. It contains 39 miles of trails featuring cave structures, waterfalls, salt marshes, and an inland tidal lake.

Guilford boasts that its green is the largest in New England. It's certainly big and beautiful, and there's a lot to explore. Visit guilfordgreenct.com for a list of what you'll find, or stop, park for free, and explore it all on foot.

North of the green is the *Guilford Art Center* (411 Church St.; 203-453-5947; guilfordartcenter.org), a small school of arts and crafts with a gallery that does about 10 shows per year, and a shop that is open year-round. Open 10 a.m. to 4 p.m. Mon through Sat, noon to 4 p.m. Sun. There are many special events here throughout the year.

On Whitfield Street, you'll find the *Henry Whitfield State Museum* (248 Old Whitfield St.; 203-453-2457). Built in 1639 as a combination minister's home, stronghold, and meeting hall, the Henry Whitfield House is

Something Cold in New Haven County

Whether you're coming from the beach, off a boat, home from the theater, or whatever fun you've found in New Haven County, consider stopping by one of **Ashley's Ice Cream**'s 5 locations for a delicious, all-natural treat. They've got all the flavors and toppings you've come to expect from a place that's raised ice cream production to an art form, plus a few surprises. You'll find no artificial colors or flavors at Ashley's, only freshly whipped cream, fresh-baked cones, and delectable chocolate. They are obviously doing something right: The *New Haven Advocate* has voted them Best Ice Cream for the past 27 years—that's right, we said 27. Ashley's is located in New Haven, Hamden, Branford, Madison, and Guilford; all locations are open Mon through Sat 11 a.m. to 11 p.m., Sun noon to 11 p.m. For more information, visit ashleysicecream.net.

reputedly the oldest stone house in New England. Today it's a showcase for 17th- and 18th-century antique furnishings. There's also a pretty fair herb garden on the grounds. Open 10 a.m. to 4 p.m. Wed through Sun, May through mid-Dec; other times by appointment. Admission.

If you like old houses or antique furnishings, there are two other houses worth looking at in Guilford, both on Boston Street. The 1690 ***Hyland House*** (84 Boston St.; 203-453-9477; hylandhouse.com) is a classic colonial saltbox noted for its unusual woodwork and for no less than 3 walk-in fireplaces. The house is maintained by the Dorothy Whitfield Historic Society and is open June through Sept, noon to 4:30 p.m. Tues through Fri, 11 a.m. to 4:30 p.m. Sat, and noon to 4:30 p.m. Sun. Admission is free, but donations are accepted.

The 1774 ***Thomas Griswold House*** (171 Boston St.; 203-453-3176) is another saltbox that has been turned into a museum of local history. In addition to the usual collection of furnishings, this house has some period costumes, a barn full of tools, an outhouse, and a restored blacksmith shop. It is maintained and operated by the Guilford Keeping Society and is open June through Sept, Tues through Sun 11 a.m. to 4 p.m. Open on weekends as well in Oct, 11 a.m. to 4 p.m.

For a beautiful water view, follow Whitfield Street south from the green to Guilford Harbor. You'll find some comfortable, thoughtfully placed benches, just right for sitting a spell. If you're of a mind to see some more beautiful scenery, follow Mulberry Point Road (off Route 146) to its end. You can't park at the point, but you can see the lighthouse on Faulkner's Island off in the distance.

Faulkner's Island Lighthouse was built in 1802. In 1976 the keeper's house was destroyed by fire. The Coast Guard replaced the valuable Fresnel lens in the tower with a modern plastic optic, and the lighthouse became automated. While that move toward modernity may have cost the lighthouse some of its romance, you can still see the old light faithfully announcing its presence from many parts of Guilford and adjoining towns, as well as on vessels navigating Long Island Sound.

And when you see this beacon of Faulkner's Island Lighthouse, be grateful. If it weren't for the determination of the ***Faulkner's Light Brigade*** (faulknerslight.org), you might not see anything but a slim strip of land. In the early 1990s, this historic lighthouse, located 3 miles off the Connecticut coast in Guilford, seemed doomed. A series of storms had worn away the island on which it stood. The structure was on the brink of toppling into the sea until a coalition of local volunteers lobbied their legislators. Eventually Congress allocated more than $4 million to stabilize the island and save the lighthouse.

The island is part of the Stewart McKinney National Wildlife Refuge and a sanctuary for the rare roseate and common terns that end their long flight from winter homes in South America and the Caribbean to nest and breed there. This means that Faulkner's is off-limits to the public, except for the annual open house in September coordinated by the brigade. Ferry service

Sam Who?

While looking for something lost, have you ever muttered, "Now where in the Sam Hill is it?" And did you ever wonder who Sam Hill was? Well, he was a real guy who lived in Guilford (1678–1752). Old Sam was the town clerk for 35 years, judge of the probate court for 12 years, and deputy to the general court for at least 22 sessions. He ran for so many offices that people used to say "running like Sam Hill" when they meant someone was persistent. Poor Sam's name—which had become known throughout the country and sounds so much like the common name for the nether regions—eventually lost that connotation and became a polite euphemism for "hell."

is offered to the island from the Guilford Town Marina, or visitors can use their own watercraft.

Cider fanciers, don't leave the Guilford area without stopping at ***Bishop's Orchards Farm Market & Winery*** (1355 Boston Post Rd., Route 1; 203-453-2338; bishopsorchards.com). Started in 1910 as a produce stand, Bishop's has grown to become a sizable cider mill and pick-your-own/cut-your-own farm with sidelines in Vermont cheeses, local honey and eggs, fresh herbs, and more recently, wine. The cider mill makes splendid apple cider, but try the pear cider, too. It's a little thicker than apple cider and maybe a little sweeter, but the fresh pear taste is quite unusual and invigorating. Their wines are inventive, smooth, and lively. Our favorite is the original Stone House White. The farm market is open 8 a.m. to 7 p.m. Mon through Sat and 9 a.m. to 6 p.m. Sun. The winery is open 10 a.m. to 7 p.m. Mon through Sat, 11 a.m. to 6 p.m. Sun.

Madison

The 1785 ***Allis-Bushnell House & Museum*** (853 Boston Post Rd.; 203-245-4567; madisoncthistorical.org) in ***Madison*** is noted for the unusual corner fireplaces and original paneling that grace its period rooms. The Madison Historical Society maintains the house and its collections of toys, dolls, costumes, kitchenware, and china. The museum is organized in such a way to allow visitors to travel through time from the colonial period, through the Revolution, into the Civil War, and then on to the colonial revival era. What a neat idea. The grounds to the museum, including the herb garden in the back, are open to the public year-round 8 a.m. to sundown at no cost. The house is open by appointment and for special events and open houses throughout the year. More information is contained on the website.

Another historic home in Madison comes complete with a family ghost. The 1685 ***Deacon John Grave House*** (581 Boston Post Rd.; 203-245-4798; deaconjohngrave.org), located at Tunxis Farm, was owned and occupied for 300 years by the descendants of Deacon John Grave. Throughout its history it has served as an inn, a tavern, a military hospital, and even a courthouse, but it is the military hospital where this house's ghost story originates. During that time, Anne Grave lived in the house and helped nurse wounded soldiers back to health. She fell in love with one of these soldiers, and when he was well and had to leave, he promised to return but never did. Every once in a while someone will report seeing the form of a woman walking through the house, items will not be where they were originally placed, a presence will be felt, noises heard. Some speculate that Anne still roams the house waiting for her love to return. Do you believe the ghostly tale? You'll have to visit and see for yourself. The house is open mid-June through Columbus Day, 1 to 4 p.m. Fri and Sat.

Madison is also home to the *Meigs Point Nature Center* (203-245-8743). Located in *Hammonasset Beach State Park,* the center gives visitors an introduction to the sea life found in Long Island Sound, including horseshoe crabs, lobsters, and a variety of fish. It also has some reptiles found in Connecticut, as well as some mounted animals, including a deer and a black bear. The staff is knowledgeable and dedicated; everyone in your party is sure to learn something. A calendar of family and children's activities is offered. Nature walks are held at 9:30 a.m. Tues through Sat. Open 10 a.m. to 5 p.m. Tues through Sat Apr through Oct, 10 a.m. to 4 p.m. Tues through Sun, Nov through Mar. Hammonasset can get busy during the summer season, so if you can visit in the off-season, we highly recommend it. Parking fees apply in season, too.

Clinton

Chamard Vineyards (115 Cow Hill Rd.; 860-664-0299; chamard.com) in *Clinton* is one of the shoreline's hidden jewels. Owned by famed geneticist Dr. Jonathan Rothberg, Chamard produces 6,000 cases of wine a year. The vineyard grounds are beautiful and the lodge rustic and charming. They also have a barn where they host live music and other events, and a bistro where they serve "simple, wholesome, classic food influenced by products readily available from the property and in the region." What a wonderful way to support local businesses. You can also, for a fee, create your own wine, from choosing the grapes to fermentation to corking—the process is up to you. We love this place! The vineyard and wine bar are open Tues through Thurs 11 a.m. to 5 p.m., Fri and Sat 11 a.m. to 9 p.m., and Sun 11 a.m. to 6 p.m.

Westbrook

Crowded and touristy, *Lenny and Joe's Fish Tale Restaurant* (86 Boston Post Rd.; 860-669-0767; ljfishtale.com) still has the best fried clams around, and the servings are huge. If you've never eaten whole-belly clams, this is a good place to start. But be forewarned: You'll never again be satisfied with those sad little strips with which the rest of America gets stuck. Lenny and Joe's also has good lobster rolls, fresh coleslaw, and grand onion rings and fried zucchini. In the spring you can get a Connecticut River shad dinner. Be prepared to wait, though. Most days, there's a line. Open daily 11 a.m. to 10 p.m. (until 11 p.m. Fri and Sat). Shorter hours in cooler weather. There's a second restaurant at 1301 Post Rd. in Madison (203-245-7289).

The Connecticut River Valley

Old Saybrook

If you're a hardy New Englander, then you know that the best time to visit the beach is in the winter—no crowds, no traffic, no fees. Unfortunately, most of the clam shacks and ice cream stands close in the off-season. That's why it's good to know that *Johnny Ad's* (910 Boston Post Rd.; 860-388-4032; johnnyads.com) is open year-round. Johnny Ad's is something of a shoreline landmark. In the summer it's a popular destination for tourists; in the winter the locals have it all to themselves.

Depending on the season, you can eat inside or take your food out-doors to the picnic tables and fight the seagulls for it. The lobster roll is the genuine, butter-drenched shore favorite, and the fried whole-belly clams are crunchy and briny. Open daily at 11 a.m.

Once you've had your fill at Johnny Ad's, head to Main Street in **Old Saybrook** and check out the *James Soda Fountain* (2 Pennywise Ln.; 860-395-1781; tissascountrymarket.com). Built in 1790, the James Pharmacy was originally a general store to the inn of the time, the Humphrey Pratt Tavern. In 1877 the building was moved to the corner of Pennywise Lane and became a pharmacy; the soda fountain was added in 1896 by Peter Lane. When Mr. Lane was called away to serve our country in WWI, his sister-in-law, Ada Louise James, took over the business and ran it until 1967. Wait, what? A woman in business in the early 20th century? Yep, but not just any woman—Miss James was Connecticut's first African-American female pharmacist. She lived in an apartment in the back of the store until her death in 1977. Also of note here is that James's niece Ann Lane Petry spent a lot of time at the pharmacy. Born in 1908, Petry was the first African-American

oldsaybrook trivia

female writer who sold more than a million copies of a novel. She was the author of six published works, including *The Drug Store Cat,* which is based on her time at the pharmacy.

Today, Tissa's Le Souk du Maroc operates the James Soda Fountain and offers exceptional Moroccan fare. Open for lunch and dinner, Tissa's offers such lunch menu items as Moroccan lemon chicken wraps and roast lamb sandwiches with balsamic onion marmalade, as well as a variety of vegetarian options. For dinner, choose from five-vegetable tagine, roast duck with apple and cranberry compote, or lamb shanks. For dessert, don't leave without choosing one of the 24 flavors of ice cream, including Moroccan Delight. Open Mon through Thurs 10 a.m. to 4 p.m., Fri and Sat 10 a.m. to 8 pm., and Sun 11 a.m. to 6 p.m.

If you or people you're traveling with love trains, don't miss **Pizzaworks** (455 Boston Post Rd.; 860-388-2218; pizzaworksct.com), located at the Old Saybrook Railroad Station. The restaurant is literally next to the train tracks, so if you time your visit right, you'll be sure to see a train pull into the station.

Pizzaworks capitalizes on its location with a railroad decor in the main dining room. The big attraction is two working model trains that weave their way through meticulously re-created miniature villages. The menu features red and white pizzas, pasta dishes, and salads. The pizza is good and goes well beyond plain and pepperoni. Some of the more exotic toppings include Hawaiian (pineapple and Canadian bacon), shrimp and sun-dried tomatoes, Thai chicken, Tex-Mex, pesto mushroom, and clams casino. Open 4 to 9 p.m. Mon and Tues, 11:30 a.m. to 9 p.m. Wed, Thurs, and Sun, and 11:30 a.m. to 10 p.m. Fri and Sat.

If you follow Main Street its southernmost distance, you'll come to **Saybrook Point,** where the Connecticut River flows into Long Island Sound. This is ecologically protected National Conservancy topography, and the perfect place for lodgings that rank among coastal New England's best—namely, **Saybrook Point Inn and Spa** (2 Bridge St.; 860-388-1111; saybrook

.com), in business since 1989. The layout includes a dock and marina (large enough for 125 moorings) as well as a spa for fitness workouts, massages, a whole slew of sophisticated beauty treatments, and indoor/outdoor swimming pool plunges. All 80 guest rooms are tastefully furnished (Chippendale and Queen Anne styles predominate), with sizable bathrooms, fluffy robes, and ample storage space. If you'd like romantic intimacy, choose one of the 2 suites nestled in the marina's mini-lighthouse. The inn also recently purchased a historic building that they are calling Three Stories, with plans to turn it into a 7-suite B&B. Renovations are under way, and updates are on the website. Fresh Salt is the on-site restaurant here, serving breakfast, lunch, and dinner with a beautiful waterfront view. Brunch, served 10 a.m. to 2:15 p.m. Sun, is very popular. They are also only 4 miles from the Florence Griswold Museum (see write-up later in this chapter).

Essex

With one of the best anchorages on the Connecticut River, *Essex* has always had intimate ties with the river. Essex's Main Street still looks very much like it did in the 18th century. Clapboard houses, fan-shaped windows, and fences abound, and in the shops that line the street, purveyors of antiques, clothing, and gifts ply their trade to tourists from around the world.

There used to be two shipyards in the town, and from 1754 there was a West Indies warehouse next to the town dock where goods from Africa and the Indies were unloaded for redistribution across the state. It was next to that warehouse at the Hayden Shipyards that America built its first warship, *Oliver Cromwell,* in 1776.

It is therefore fitting that the **Connecticut River Foundation's Connecticut River Museum** (67 Main St.; 860-767-8269; ctrivermuseum.org) is located at Steamboat Dock. The museum chronicles the history of Connecticut by tracing the evolution of the Connecticut River and of steam power. Among the exhibits is a full-scale working replica of David Bushnell's 1775 *American Turtle.* This is the first submarine ever constructed. The museum also contains nautical paintings, shipbuilding tools, and memorabilia. Special events are held here throughout the year, including an annual holiday model train show, and foliage and other sightseeing cruises. The museum itself is open year-round from 10 a.m. to 5 p.m. Tues through Sun. Gift shop. Admission. The research archive is open by appointment only.

Groundhog Day Parade & Winterfest

Can't make it to Punxsutawney, Pennsylvania, for Groundhog Day on February 2? Head on down to Essex for the *Groundhog Day parade,* which features Essex Ed, their homegrown version of Punxsutawney Phil. Usually held the Sunday preceding Groundhog Day, this parade is the kickoff for Essex's *Winterfest,* a 7-week celebration that includes eagle watches, train rides, and tons of family fun. At the parade, be sure to get a photo of the larger-than-life Essex Ed papier-mâché sculpture; he sports a different outfit every year, and it's always a deeply guarded secret what he plans to wear. Organized by the Essex Board of Trade, the parade is a sight to behold. For more information, visit essexct.com.

If you've never visited the 1776 *Griswold Inn* (36 Main St.; 860-767-1776; griswoldinn.com), don't leave Essex without doing so. People who know and love this place often call it the "Gris" (pronounced "grizz"). Located about 100 yards from the river, the inn offers 33 guest rooms, a full-service restaurant, and a taproom with menu and delicious brews.

The Gris is open daily for lunch and dinner, plus a Sunday brunch in the form of the justly famous Hunt Breakfast. This tradition goes back to the War of 1812, when officers of the British army, which was then occupying Essex, forcefully suggested that the establishment start serving a regular Sunday hunt breakfast. Today the Hunt Breakfast table groans with an array of food that includes fried chicken, lamb kidneys and mushrooms, and creamed ham and eggs over English muffins. It's almost, but not quite, enough to make you forgive the British for burning New London during the same war.

A number of the inn's downstairs rooms have been turned into dining rooms. You can, for example, eat in the book-lined library or in the Steamboat Room, with its lifelike mural of steamboating on the river. No matter where you land, you'll have an interesting experience. The owners even hold art tours and talks about the amazing collection of art that was always at the inn, but never received much attention. Visit the website for available dates; reservations are required. The Gris is open throughout the year except for Christmas Day.

Once you have had your fill at The Gris, be sure to walk it off as you browse the wonderful shop *A Pocketful of Posies* (12 N. Main St.;

860-767-1959; apocketfulofposies.com). The owners are so incredibly talented and this gift store so incredibly beautiful that you may never want to leave. But you can't stay here in this lovingly restored 19th-century home, so you'll just have to buy something to bring home with you. And then come back for more! Open Apr through Dec 11:30 a.m. to 4:30 p.m. Wed, Thurs, and Fri; Sat 11 a.m. to 5 p.m., and Sun noon to 4 p.m. Jan through Mar open weekends only (11 a.m. to 4 p.m. Sat and noon to 3 p.m. Sun).

If the river formed Essex's early history, the railroad had much to do with its later development. The ***Essex Steam Train and Riverboat*** (1 Railroad Ave.; 860-767-0103 or 800-277-3987; essexsteamtrain.com) off Route 154 was chartered in 1868. It still runs a steam train, with an optional riverboat ride, along the Connecticut River. Four or more trains per day make the 12-mile round trip from Essex to Deep River, and all but the last train connect with the riverboat. Boats make a round trip from Deep River to Gillette Castle and East Haddam. If you happen to see Captain Paul Costello, be sure to tell him hi for us. Before or after the excursion, guests can tour a variety of vintage train cars and visit the gift and snack shops (both in old railroad cars). The railroad runs a varying schedule from May through Oct and from Thanksgiving through Christmas. Tickets can be purchased at the station in Essex. The North Pole Express and Thomas the Tank Engine special events require reservations and can fill up fast. Also check out the Rack, Rail & Sail special event they offer in conjunction with the Gris.

Essex used to be famous for manufacturing piano keys, and nearby ***Ivoryton*** was the center of the ivory trade that supported that industry. In fact the town's name derives from the fact that it used to import "ivory by the ton."

Both the legal ivory trade of olden days and the local piano works have ceased to be. But a salute to music of a different sort can be found at the ***Museum of Fife & Drum*** (63 N. Main St.; 860-399-6519; companyoffifeanddrum.org), where the Company of Fifers and Drummers is headquartered. Exhibits trace the development of military parades in America from the Revolutionary War to the present day and include many uniforms and musical instruments, including drums dating from 1793. There's a special display of Civil War–era musical instruments. This museum is truly unique. Open weekends, 1 to 5 p.m., June 30 through Labor Day weekend or by appointment. The museum is closed the third weekend of July and fourth weekend of August. Admission.

The *Ivoryton Playhouse* (103 Main St.; 860-767-7318; ivorytonplay house.org) was the first self-supporting summer theater in the nation. Although cozy and unpretentious, the Ivoryton can boast some of the most famous names in American theater: Marlon Brando, Ginger Rogers, Carl Reiner, Groucho Marx, Helen Hayes, Jerry Orbach, Alan Alda, Mary Astor, and Gene Hackman all graced the playhouse's stage. Katharine Hepburn, who was born in Hartford and lived nearby in the Fenwick section of Old Saybrook, launched her career at the Ivoryton. Today the theater offers a full schedule of great plays—musicals, comedies, and dramas, as well as a wonderful children's summer program of theatrical entertainment.

essextrivia

David Bushnell, designer of the *American Turtle,* coined the word "submarine" to describe his invention.

Ivoryton is also home to one of the state's beautiful inns. Named for a spectacular 200-year-old tree that graces its front yard, the *Copper Beech Inn* (46 Main St.; 860-767-0330; copperbeechinn.com) offers two styles of accommodation. For the traditional-minded, the elegant, 1890-vintage main building boasts 4 guest rooms with antique and country furnishings. The carriage house in the rear has 9 rooms with a mix of more modern amenities and traditional furnishings; some have the original post-and-beam ceilings. On the newer side, there's the Comstock House, which offers another 9 rooms. A continental breakfast is included with the room rates, and the inn's award-winning country-French restaurant, Pip's at the Copper Beech Inn, opens to the public for dinner daily starting at 5:30 p.m.

Deep River

Settled in 1635 as part of Old Saybrook, the sleepy village of *Deep River* is known throughout the state as the site of the *Deep River Ancient Muster,* "the oldest and largest gathering of fife and drum participants and enthusiasts in the world," according to Deep River's website. Held annually the third Saturday of July, this is truly a family-friendly event. The muster is preceded by a parade that starts at 11 a.m. at the corner of Main and Kirtland Streets, proceeds down Main Street, and ends at Devitt's Field, where

Connecticut Freedom Trail

Daniel Fisher was a slave. William Winters was a free man. And somewhere in between the two was a trip from North Carolina to Philadelphia to New York to New Haven and eventually to Deep River. On this journey Daniel was helped by numerous people, including Deacon George Read of Deep River, along the Underground Railroad. During this journey, Daniel became William. He lived a good life with friends and family in Deep River along Winter Avenue, which was eventually named for him. William Winters died in 1900 at the age of 92. He is buried in Fountain Hill Cemetery on High Street.

the muster commences. Roads close at 10:30 a.m., and people arrive early to claim spots along the route. Visit deepriverct.com for more information.

Down the road from Fountain Hill Cemetery, you'll find the *1840 Stone House* (245 Main St.; 860-526-1449), where the local historical society maintains a small museum filled with such items as 19th-century furnishings, maritime memorabilia, locally made cut glass, and Indian artifacts. Hours can vary, so it's best to call ahead and make an appointment to visit. Donation requested.

Killingworth

Hugh Lofting, the man who gave the world the character *Dr. Dolittle,* rests in a little cemetery in rural *Killingworth,* unseen by virtually all who pass by. Lofting was a native of England but moved to tiny Killingworth in 1928 at the height of his popularity as the author of a series of books about a kindly, eccentric veterinarian who could talk to animals. According to a town historian, Lofting wrote some of his books while living here, in a house on River Road. Lofting died in 1947 and was buried in *Evergreen Cemetery,* across the street from his house, now privately owned by another family. The cemetery is on Green Hill Road, and Lofting's tombstone is in the back right-hand corner.

Haddam

The real name of the *Merchant House* (1583 Saybrook Rd.; 860-345-4195 or 800-613-0105) on Route 154 is Ye Olde Tyler Merchant House, but you're welcome to call it Arts and Crafts Heaven. In that rarified category of antique furniture, the Stickley reputation looms large. But pick any name from the Arts and Crafts and Mission movements, and you'll most likely find high-quality reproductions at the Merchant House. You might eye an oak Harvey Ellis writing desk or perhaps Prairie settles. There's too much on display to do justice to the overall selection, so just drop by to browse and drool.

Besides the glorious furniture, the Merchant House offers gift items such as potpourri and fragrant lotions, creams, and potions. The Christmas shop carries some of the most interesting and unusual ornaments and decorations around. Stuff from the Christmas shop starts flying off the shelves in early October, so visit early. Take a minute to peruse the watercolors of historic and well-known Connecticut attractions; they make wonderful souvenirs or presents to commemorate special occasions. You'll see drawings of lots of the places described in this book—why not start a collection? Open 10 a.m. to 7 p.m. Mon through Sat, 10 a.m. to 6 p.m. Sun. Don't forget to ask the owners about the cave of Connecticut's Leather Man that is located on the property.

haddamtrivia

Heading south from Middletown toward Haddam, taking Route 9 to Route 154, you'll come upon a large rock set well back from the road. This is **Bible Rock** and its cleft marks the line between Middletown and Haddam. Look carefully because the rock is well back from the road and easy to miss when leaves cover the trees.

Another local institution on Route 154 in **Haddam** is the **Pilot House** (1364 Saybrook Rd.; 860-345-2945), which has also been around since 1945. Its claim to fame is a secret relish served with sandwiches. This is one of those ramshackle drive-in restaurants to which families make annual pilgrimages. Open 11 a.m. to 8 p.m. Tues through Sun from May through late Oct, although the hours vary depending on the season, so you might want to call ahead.

Located about 0.3 mile from the junction of Routes 81 and 154 on Route 154 north of Higganum Center is a Connecticut institution known as **Higgies** (236 Saybrook Rd.; 860-345-7777). This restaurant has been around since 1945 and has a reputation for the "best dogs and shakes" in the area. The owners pride themselves on using only top-quality products. A shake flanked by a couple of chili dogs makes a perfect nostalgic lunch, but the steamed cheeseburgers and pulled pork sandwiches are also popular. The best way to enjoy a Higgies lunch is outside at a picnic table under the trees. Open daily 11 a.m. to 8 p.m. early Apr until late Oct.

On Route 154 you'll pass some beautiful Victorian, Beaux Arts, and gothic revival houses. About 2 miles out of Higganum Center, there's a former Catholic church, now a private residence, overlooking the Connecticut River, the perfect brooding realization of gothic architecture.

Sundial Gardens (59 Hidden Lake Rd.; 860-345-4290; sundialgardens .com) on Brault Hill Road in the Higganum section of Haddam is actually a collection of formal gardens, including a 17th-century knot garden, an 18th-century-style garden, and a topiary garden with a fountain. There's also a tea and gift shop and tearoom on-site, and on Sunday the owners offer "tea talks" that include a tour of the gardens followed by tea and dessert. The tea shop is open Jan though mid-Oct, 10 a.m. to 5 p.m. Sat., noon to 5 p.m. Sun. It re-opens after Thanksgiving for the holidays through Christmas Eve, Thurs through Sat 10 a.m. to 5 p.m., and noon to 5 p.m. Sun. The gardens are open for browsing from mid-May through mid-Oct, 10 a.m. to 5 p.m. Fri and Sat. Admission.

Durham

Durham is one of those New England treasures tucked almost exactly halfway between New Haven and Hartford, with its main street being Route 17, which then splits into Routes 79 and 77 and points to the shore (Madison and Guilford, respectively). It's a small town with a little more than 6,500 residents, but it's home to Connecticut's largest agricultural fair. The **Durham Fair** (24 Town House Rd.; 860-349-9495; durhamfair.com) is held annually the last full weekend in September. It's been a Durham tradition since 1916, when the first fair was held on the town green. It's grown steadily since then and now attracts thousands of people every year. But the truly remarkable thing about this fair is that it's run entirely by volunteers, and has been since the beginning. The Durham Fair Association is able to award hundreds of dollars every year in scholarship money thanks to the efforts of these volunteers, and myriad civic groups from the surrounding towns count on the fair as their only fund-raiser. This is true community spirit.

A Main Street landmark for almost 40 years, **Carolyn Adams Country Barn** (352 Main St.; 860-349-1737) sells a variety of home furnishings, cool

Morse & Otte

People in town still call the **Durham Market** (238 Main St.; 860-349-1785) Morse and Otte. That was its name when it was opened by John C. Otte and Perley S. Morse in the early 1930s. The store was then passed down from generation to generation, and it was a fixture in town. When the letter S fell off the sign some-time in the 1980s, it was never replaced, and the store came to be known as the "elf-service market." The building hasn't changed all that much in the ensuing years (although it has received a new sign). In fact, when the current owner, Bob Mounts, was recently doing some renovations to the building, he discovered old handwritten receipts from the original owners, dated between 1936 and 1939. The market is still a fixture in town, and we think Morse and Otte would approve. Open Mon through Fri 7 a.m. to 7 p.m., Sat and Sun 7 a.m. to 6 p.m.

primitive knickknacks, and other high-quality novelties. You'll find brands such as Country Expressions, Clayton Marcus, Southern Craftsman, Lt. Moses Willard Lighting, and more. The business is still family-owned and -operated, and you'll often find Mrs. Adams herself behind the counter. With 2 floors and multiple rooms, it's easy to lose yourself here. Be sure to check out daughter Alana's full-service showroom, Alana Adams' Window Treatments & Area Rugs, in the same building. Alana has been following the family tradition since 1989. Open Tues through Fri 10 a.m. to 5 p.m., Sat 9:30 a.m. to 5 p.m., Sun noon to 4 p.m.

If you stop at Carolyn Adams, be sure to pay a visit to **Wild Wisteria** (354 Main St.; 860-349-1550) in the same plaza. This is an adorable little gift shop with a bent toward the seasonal. You never know what you'll find here. Open Wed through Fri 11 a.m. to 5:30 p.m., Sat 10 a.m. to 5 p.m., Sun noon to 4 p.m. Closed Mon and Tues.

If you're hungry, visit **Perk on Main** (6 Main St.; 860-349-5335; perkonmain.com) for delicious coffee, crepes, and so much more. Run by the brother-and-sister team of Mark and Katie Hughes, Perk on Main has been steadily growing since it opened almost 10 years ago. Their crepes are light and fluffy and include such fillings as spinach, eggs, tomato, onions, garlic, and feta or egg, smoked salmon, red onion, cream cheese, and tomato. They have egg sandwiches and omelets for those looking in that direction. Lunch brings quesadillas, soups, heartier crepes, sandwiches, wraps, and creative, fresh salads. Dinner is available as a set take-out menu depending on the day (vegetable lasagna on Tues, roasted turkey on Thurs, etc.). If you'd rather eat in, it's BYOB. There is also live entertainment on some nights. Be sure to check their website.

And while they serve delicious food in a cafe-type setting, that's not what is so cool about the place. What you might not know is that the Hugheses run their restaurant as green as possible. They compost and recycle all they can, thereby generating the same amount of garbage as an average single-family home. Now that's good business. A second location, **Perk on Church** (20 Church St.; 860-689-5060), is in Guilford. Both restaurants are open 6:30 a.m. to 4 p.m. Sat through Mon and 6:30 a.m. to 8 p.m. Tues through Fri.

If you're looking for a cake for a special occasion or just something to satisfy your sweet tooth, or maybe a gift, be sure to stop by **Kim's Cottage Confections** (16 Main St.; 860-349-2256; kimscottageconfections.com). With more than 20 years of experience in the confection industry, owner Kim

durhamtrivia

When the New York Giants squared off with the New England Patriots in 2012 for Super Bowl XLVI, Durham found itself in the middle. Exactly the middle. The small central Connecticut town is equidistant from the Giants' MetLife Stadium in East Rutherford, New Jersey, and the Patriots' Gillette Stadium in Foxborough, Massachusetts. Sports channels, newscasters, and sports fans descended on the small town in the wee hours of the morning to celebrate the rivalry.

A Sweet Treat on the Way to the Beach

So many travelers use Route 17 to Route 79 to get from points inland to Hammonasset Beach State Park. It's become a tradition to stop on the way back for an ice cream at **Durham Dari Serve** (13 Main St.; 860-349-3367). In business for more than five decades, Dari Serve still packs them in. It can get very busy on a summer night, so be prepared to wait a little bit. It's worth every minute, though. Bring cash; they don't accept credit cards. There's also no indoor seating; it's walk-up window only. Open daily noon to 9:30 p.m. from about mid-May to about mid-Oct, when the GONE FISHIN' sign goes in the window.

Terrill is up to just about any challenge you can throw at her. We've seen some pretty amazing cakes come out of her kitchen, and her other confections, well, they're just so good. As she says on her website, she does it all—from cookies to tea parties and everything in between. And it's all made right there on the premises. Open Tues through Fri 10 a.m. to 5 p.m., Sat 10 a.m. to 3 pm., Sun 9 a.m. to noon, and by appointment.

If you're looking for a sub, the place to go is *Lino's Market* (472 Main St.; 860-349-1717; linosmarket.com), an Italian specialty market tucked away at the end of Durham's Main Street. The parking is tough here, especially around noon and 5 p.m., so be aware. You'll find all sorts of fresh bread, Italian pastry, and other authentic Italian dishes prepared by Lino's mom and dad. Open Mon through Fri 7 a.m. to 7 p.m. and Sat 7 a.m. to 6 p.m.

Middlefield

Middlefield is home to *Lyman Orchards* (32 Reeds Gap Rd.; 860-349-1793; lymanorchards.com), which all started way back in 1741 when John and Hope Lyman purchased 36 acres of farmland here. Now, eight generations later, that acreage has grown into a huge enterprise comprising 1,100 acres that include the Apple Barrel store, 2 golf courses and a teaching facility, and farm and orchard land. Lyman's offers many special events throughout the year, including the Peach Festival in August, a corn maze in the fall, a winter festival in February, and so much more. They have pick-your-own fruits with the season as well. Open daily 9 a.m. to 6 p.m. Nov through Aug; 9 a.m. to 7 p.m. Sept and Oct.

While in Middlefield, be sure to check out *New Guida's Restaurant* (484 Meriden Rd., 860-349-9039; newguidasrestaurant.com), home of the famous 10-inch pedigreed hot dog. Guida's has been serving up these delicious dogs since 1946. You can order them plain (but why would you?) or with "everything" (mustard, relish, and onions). Or if you are a true diner aficionado, you can order a chili and cheese dog. They also have all the diner staples—wonderful breakfasts that are popular with the locals, ice cream, fried clams, and more. Open Mon through Sat 7 a.m. to 8 p.m., Sun 8 a.m. to 8 p.m. This place can get wicked busy on summer days during lunch, so please plan accordingly.

Down the road from Guida's (well, just over 2 miles northeast, actually) is the headquarters of *Connecticut Forest and Park Association*

A Maze-ing Babe

Every year Lyman Orchards sponsors a fund-raiser for the American Cancer Society in the form of a 4-acre corn maze. Every year the maze has a theme. In 2012 it was baseball, and it featured a truly amazing likeness of the New York Yankees and the Boston Red Sox. To help launch the season was a very special guest: Durham resident Linda Ruth Tosetti threw a strike to a high school softball player to officially open the maze. Why Tosetti? Well, her grandfather was the legendary Babe Ruth!

(16 Meriden Rd.; 860-346-2372; ctwoodlands.org). Commonly known as CFPA, this association of wonderful staff and a huge network of volunteers manages and maintains more than 800 miles of hiking trails throughout the state. With the creation of the Blue-Blazed Hiking Trail System in 1929, CFPA realized a long-term objective to protect land (both public and private) for public enjoyment. Since its first members organized in 1895, CFPA has helped secure more than 100 state parks and forests for the use and enjoyment of outdoor enthusiasts. As you travel throughout the state, you'll likely see CFPA's signposts and parking lots to access points to the blue trails. Trail maps can be found in CFPA's publications, with information also available on its website. The organization also hosts a variety of workshops throughout the year.

If shopping is more your style than hiking (or you simply want to do both!), be sure to visit **Perrotti's Country Barn & Christmas Shoppe** (288 Baileyville Rd.; 860-349-0082), where you'll find a large selection of gifts and collectibles. This shop is seriously packed full with such lines as Chamilia Beads, Jim Shore, Alex and Ani, Vera Bradley, and more. They also offer ice cream seasonally at the Caboose Ice Cream Stand, which is next door. Open Mon through Fri 10:30 a.m. to 6 p.m., Sat 10 a.m. to 6 p.m., and Sun noon to 6 p.m.

Middletown

Middletown was once a bustling seaport on the Connecticut River. It boasts many historic houses and a varied history. The **Middlesex County Historical Society** (151 Main St.; 860-346-0746; middlesexhistory.org) sponsors the

Middletown Heritage Trail, which begins at the Middletown Police Station (222 Main St.). Free brochures, which include a map of the trail, are available at the police department, at the society's offices, at Russell Library (123 Broad St.), and at the Middlesex County Chamber of Commerce (393 Main St.).

Being a college town, home to Wesleyan University, Middletown has no shortage of cool little places to eat. You can take your pick, but we suggest you don't leave Middletown without stopping at the *Middlesex Fruitery* (191 Main St.; 860-346-4372). This is an old-fashioned, family-run greengrocer with primo produce. Not only do the owners personally select your produce for you, they carry it out to your car. Open 8:30 a.m. to 5:30 p.m. Tues through Sat.

If you have little ones, don't pass up the chance to visit *Kidcity* (119 Washington St.; 860-347-0495; kidcitymuseum.com), where kids ages 1 to 8 will enter a world just their size. Toddlers can crawl through sea caves (and stay dry) on the lower level; the first floor offers a Space Age Roadtrip, a fishery, a farm, and a clipper ship for children a little older to explore. Every room has easily visible entrances and exits so you can relax while you let your children explore; you'll know where they are at all times. This place really is built for them. There is admission, and we highly recommend if you're going to be traveling the state anyway (otherwise, why did you buy this book?) that you purchase a membership to the museum. This will allow you entrance to other kid-friendly museums across Connecticut. It is a great bargain if you think you'll have time to visit then all (or revisit one multiple times). Open Sun through Tues 11 a.m. to 5 p.m., Wed through Sat 9 a.m. to 5 p.m.

Portland

Brownstone Exploration & Discovery Park (161 Brownstone Ave.; 866-860-0208; brownstonepark.com) is located in a former *Portland* brownstone quarry less than 30 minutes from Hartford, New Haven, and Waterbury. Here you'll find challenges for even the most hard-core adventurer in your group. They offer rock climbing up steep walls of brownstone, zip lining, cliff diving, rope swings, scuba diving, wakeboarding, kayaking, a play area for smaller kids to play and swim, and more. Some activities require an additional fee, and some are included with your admission. Visitors are required to wear a life jacket (provided) at all times. You can bring in your own food and beverages, and there is plenty of space to spread out for a picnic. You might even be able to snag one of the floating gazebos (extra charge), which are pretty cool. Open mid-May through Oct, weather permitting.

The owners recently purchased the former Powder Ridge Ski Area in Middlefield and have plans to turn it into an adventure park along the same lines as Brownstone. We look forward to seeing how they progress.

portlandtrivia

Portland supplied so much brownstone for Manhattan town houses that it was called the "city that changed the face of New York City."

East Haddam

East Haddam is the heart of the lower Connecticut River Valley's resort country and was once a mecca for New Yorkers seeking to avoid the crowding closer to the shore. The area is still liberally sprinkled with holiday camps, lodges, gift shops, antiques stores, and similar establishments.

East Haddam is the only town in the state to occupy both sides of the Connecticut River, and as you approach the eastern part of the township from across the river, you pass over the longest *swinging bridge* in New England. This uncommon bridge actually pivots sideways to open a path for passing boats. The first thing you see on the other side is a glorious three-story American gothic palace that looks like a wedding cake and dominates the East Haddam skyline. This symphony in gingerbread is the *Goodspeed Opera House* (33 N. Main St.; 860-873-8668; goodspeed.org). Founded by William Goodspeed more than a century ago, the Goodspeed is widely known as "the birthplace of the American musical," thanks to the number of Broadway hits that received their first tryouts there. The opera house has a fascinating history, including being used as a town garage for years before being saved by a community action group and being restored to its former glory. An extended summer season—Apr through Dec—of professional theater is still offered in this renovated structure. You can also enjoy the view from the Goodspeed's porch bar.

Right outside the entrance to the Goodspeed, you'll find the *Gelston House* (8 Main St.; 860-873-1411; gelstonhouse.com), a beautiful waterfront restaurant and lodging. The food is wonderful, and the rooms are gorgeous.

It's a perfect accompaniment to a show at the Goodspeed, and the two make for a wonderful weekend away. Apparently we aren't the only ones who think so. East Haddam old-timers whisper that the Gelston House, built in 1853, was once a hideout for rumrunners during Prohibition. The restaurant can get busy on show nights. Open Tues and Sun 11:30 a.m. to 9 p.m., Wed and Thurs 11:30 a.m. to 11 p.m., and Fri and Sat 11:30 a.m. to midnight.

While you're in East Haddam, stop by **St. Stephen's Church** (31 Main St.; 860-873-9547; ststeves.org) in the center of town. The church bell up in the belfry was cast for a Spanish monastery in AD 815 and is probably the oldest bell in the New World. Behind the church is the **Nathan Hale Schoolhouse** (29 Main St.; 860-873-3399; connecticutsar.org) a one-room establishment where Hale taught in 1773–1774. Originally called Union School, it was renamed for Hale after he became an acknowledged American hero. Today the schoolhouse is a museum containing Hale possessions and displays of artifacts relating to local history. The church and school are open May through Oct, Wed through Sun noon to 4 p.m., or by appointment. Admission.

goodspeedtrivia

Three timeless American musicals had their debuts at the Goodspeed Opera House: *Man of La Mancha, Annie,* and *Shenandoah.*

During World War I a militia unit was posted in the Goodspeed to guard the East Haddam swinging bridge against possible U-boat attacks.

On opening night, October 24, 1877, the premier production at the Goodspeed Opera House comprised a comedy, *Charles II,* and two farces, *Box and Cox* and *Turn Him Out.*

Historians don't agree on how the **Devil's Hopyard** (366 Hopyard Rd.; 860-873-8566) in East Haddam got its name, but they do agree that a lot of fascinating legends surround the 860-acre state park outside the town. The most lurid one has Satan himself playing in the house band while the locally renowned Black Witches of Haddam held sabbat in the area. According to this legend, Mr. Scratch would sit on a rock near the 60-foot cascade of Chapman Falls in the center of the park and play while his minions cavorted.

Nutmeggers' Yankee forebearers were kind of obsessed with Satan, and the sabbat origin certainly seems reasonable. Sadly, the origin of the park's strange name is probably more commonplace than legend admits. There are those who maintain that a local farmer and noted bootlegger named Dibble once cultivated a hopyard along Eight Mile River and brewed his harvest into a particularly potent moonshine. According to this version, the park's name began as Dibble's Hopyard, which later evolved into Devil's Hopyard.

Whatever the true origin of its name, there is no denying that this isolated, heavily forested, and reputedly haunted park is a truly spooky place at night. During daylight, though, Devil's Hopyard is a great picnic spot, and the big rocks around Chapman Falls are especially nice for spreading a blanket and whiling away a summer's afternoon. There are some picnic shelters scattered around the park, but most people just lay out a spread near the falls. The park is open from 8 a.m. until sunset.

The granite structure that is East Haddam's *Gillette Castle* (67 River Rd.; 860-526-2336) was built over a five-year period from 1914 to 1919 as the retirement home of the famous actor William Gillette, who designed the edifice, including its unique, hand-carved interior furnishings and appointments. Built on 122 acres, the 24-room mansion is now a museum, kept almost as it was when Gillette lived there. Among the actor's possessions on display is his collection of more than 100 scrapbooks filled with pictures of cats. Gillette's best-known stage role was as British detective Sherlock Holmes, and Gillette Castle also houses the largest collection of Holmesiana in the world, including a complete re-creation of Holmes's sitting room at 221B Baker Street.

Gillette specified in his will that the property not "fall into the hands of some blithering saphead who has no conception of where he is or with what he is surrounded," thus Gillette Castle is now owned by the State of

Chester–Hadlyme Ferry

A very cool way to visit Gillette Castle is to take the Chester–Hadlyme Ferry (Route 148; 860-443-3586) from across the Connecticut River in Chester. This is the second-oldest continuously operating ferry in the US (the Glastonbury–Rocky Hill Ferry is the oldest). It runs 7 a.m. to 6:45 p.m. Mon through Fri and 10:30 a.m. to 5 p.m. weekends between mid-Apr and mid-Nov. The ferry can accommodate up to 8 cars at a time. There's a minimal charge for this fun little ride.

Do You Hear What I Hear?

The small village of **Moodus** in East Haddam is the site of a curious phenomenon steeped in legend. At more or less regular intervals, loud noises like the voices of the damned can be heard throughout the town. These are the famous "Moodus Noises."

Native Americans said these noises were the voice of an evil spirit who lived on nearby Mount Tom. Early colonists believed the noises were the result of an ongoing battle between the Good Witches of East Haddam and the feared Black Witches of Haddam. According to this myth, when the battle between good and evil goes on too long, a benevolent spirit, Old Machemoodus (for whom Moodus is named) awakes and waves his sapphire wand, clearing away the evil witches and ending the battle. The Black Witches of Haddam then gather their powers once again, and the battle is rejoined, causing more Moodus Noises.

According to geologists, the true cause of the noises is the rubbing of tectonic plates against each other along a fault line, a phenomenon known to generate earthquakes. In fact, in 1791 Moodus was shaken by two quakes that were felt as far away as New York and Boston. In March 2011 the area was shaken again by a 1.3-magnitude earthquake. At first residents feared something had exploded, and firefighters and police searched for a cause before they were alerted that there had been a geological disturbance. Another quake is expected sometime during the next few centuries, and there have been predictions that someday Moodus will be swallowed up by the fault and disappear into the earth forever.

Connecticut. While there is ample parking, the facilities are generally modest, and the rustic beauty of this spot has been well preserved. The view down the Connecticut River from the castle's broad terraces is one of the best in the state. In late winter and early spring, before the facility opens for the season, you can stand on the main terrace in splendid isolation and watch eagles soar above the river.

In addition to his many other passions, Gillette was a train enthusiast. He had two small working trains that used to make loops around the castle grounds, but they long ago fell into disuse. One has since been refurbished and is now on display.

Gillette Castle is open from 10 a.m. to 5 p.m. (last tour leaves at 4:30 p.m.) from the Sat of Memorial Day weekend through Columbus Day. There is a modest admission fee for the castle tour, but none to picnic or walk the grounds, which are open year-round from 8 a.m. until sunset. A snack bar and gift shop are also located on the grounds.

Allegra Farm (Town Road; 860-537-8861; allegrafarm.com) on Route 82 calls itself a "living history museum." Home to the Horse Drawn Carriage and Sleigh Museum of New England, the farm is located on Lake Haward, where the owners work hard to keep the past alive. Horses and carriages from the farm have been featured in movies such as *Amistad, Time Machine, Kate and Leopold,* and Cuba Gooding Jr.'s independent film *Something Whispered,* as well as on TV in *Sex and the City,* of all things. The museum, located in a post-and-beam carriage house and livery stables, is chock-full of carriages, sleighs, coaches, and any other horse-drawn vehicle you can imagine. Once you've taken in the vehicles, go outdoors and check out the creatures that draw them. You can also see chickens, sheep, and a llama. Horse-drawn carriage rides, sleigh rides, or hayrides are available on reservation. All the horse-drawn rides provide refreshments that vary with the seasons, from iced mint tea to hot chocolate served by a campfire. In the spring and summer, carriages from Allegra Farm are a familiar sight carrying wedding parties throughout the Connecticut River Valley. The museum is open by appointment.

Lyme

Sankow's Beaver Brook Farm (139 Beaver Brook Rd.; 860-434-2843 or 800-501-WOOL; beaverbrookfarm.com) has been in the same family since 1917 and is a wonderful place to visit. The 175-acre property was originally a working dairy farm, but in the early '80s, owners Stan and Suzanne Sankow tried their hands at sheep farming. Successful at that for nearly 20 years, they then reintroduced cattle. Today the farm is home to more than 600 sheep and a dozen cows. They produce high-quality products, including incredibly fluffy and luxurious sheepskins (wonderful baby gifts); all-natural woolen clothing, such as vests, hats, and very cute sweaters finished with pewter farm-animal buttons; yarn; artisanal cheeses, yogurt, milk, and more—all made from the farm's own herds. If you're interested, they also offer fresh lamb meats and homemade white bean chili and lamb curry stew. If you're partial to making your own, you can take one of the cooking or knitting classes offered.

The farm is open daily from 9 a.m. to 4 p.m. Farm tours are available by reservation. You can also find this farm's products at various farm markets around the area. If you're in the area the weekend after Thanksgiving, check out Farm Day at Beaver Brook Farm for sheepshearing and spinning demonstrations, hayrides, and free samples of the farm's delicious products.

Old Lyme

The *Florence Griswold Museum* (96 Lyme St.; 860-434-5542; flogris.org) is housed in Florence Griswold's ship-captain father's 1841 house, which she turned into a boardinghouse and salon for painters back in the 19th century. The light is supposed to be particularly good in this part of the state, due to its proximity to large bodies of reflective water; the shore is very near, and the Lieutenant River runs behind the house. Anyway, a community of artists ended up boarding at the Griswold home, where they worked, played, and inspired one another to greater efforts.

The doors and woodwork throughout Florence Griswold's home came to be decorated with original paintings by the likes of Willard Metcalf, Henry Ward Ranger, and Childe Hassam. The vast Griswold collection, including the works of some 110 local artists, is on public display inside. The museum is open year-round from 10 a.m. to 5 p.m. Tues through Sat and 1 to 5 p.m. Sun. Admission.

Ferry Landing Park is home to the *Connecticut Department of Energy and Environmental Protection Marine Fisheries Headquarters and Boating Division* (333 Ferry Rd.; 860-434-8638 for boating and

---

Connecticut Art Trail

The word *impressionism* generally conjures the revolutionary work of French masters Monet, Renoir, and Degas, but Connecticut was where American impressionism began. From 1885 to 1930, American painters were drawn to Connecticut's picturesque landscape. They painted scenes of bucolic beauty and community life in a distinctive style characterized by vivid colors and broken brushstrokes. Connecticut is home to 9 museums, including the Florence Griswold Museum, that display the work of some of the artists who played leading roles in the American Impressionist movement. These museums, along with 5 other museums and historic sites, compose the *Connecticut Art Trail,* a self-guided tour of the diverse art collections within the state. For a complete list of the museums and more information about the trail, visit arttrail.org.

860-434-6043 for fisheries) and offers a way-cool boardwalk with the added allure of that universal kid (and adult) favorite, trains. This is a wonderful, out-of-the-way destination for parents and kids. (Don't be put off by the dead-end sign on Ferry Road. Just go all the way to the end, and turn into DEEP marine headquarters; the parking lot is beyond the main building.)

The boardwalk meanders along the river and ends at a marsh. At the marsh you'll find an elevated platform, ideal for bird-watching or just watching the river flow. Markers along the walk identify the different animals you might see. The fisherfolk who congregate along the river are more than willing to tell tales to anyone who stops to listen of the big one that got away.

The boardwalk also rambles under a railway bridge that gives you a very unusual view of speeding trains: underneath! The best time of year to visit is spring through fall. Trains cross the bridge mornings (about 9:30 a.m. to 1 p.m.) and afternoons (around 4 to 6:30 p.m.). The site offers free parking, is wheelchair accessible, and has well-maintained picnic tables and restroom facilities. The park closes at sunset.

East Lyme

If you are dedicated to sleuthing out the places that "only the locals know," take our suggestion by following their trail to **Flanders Fish Market and Restaurant** (22 Chesterfield Rd.; 860-739-8866 or 800-242-6055; flandersfish .com) on Route 161. It is a place you probably wouldn't find on your own, but once found, it becomes a regular on your "always-eat-here-when-at-the-shore" list. It's an unpretentious place with good food and friendly service. On the menu you'll find not only shore perennials, such as lobster bisque and oyster stew, but also the increasingly rare clear, broth-based clam chowder. Worth mentioning, too: their clam fritters, the hot lobster roll, and the blackened swordfish. The side dishes, sometimes forgotten in fish places, are especially good, including the Flanders fries and the sweet potatoes, either fried or baked. For dessert, try the crisp of the day. The restaurant knows not all kids like fish, so a peanut-butter-and-jelly sandwich and a milk shake are also on the menu. On nice days, it's fun to take your food outside and eat in the picnic area. Open 9 a.m. to 9 p.m. Sun through Thurs and 9 a.m. to 10 p.m. Fri and Sat.

If you liked your lobster so much you want to share it with the folks back home, Flanders Fish Market ships lobsters anywhere in the US. Lobster line: (800) 242-6055 (in Connecticut); (800) 638-8189 (nationwide). Open daily 9 a.m. to 9 p.m.

You don't have to be a book lover to spend many contented hours at the **Book Barn** (41 W. Main St.; 860-739-5715; bookbarnniantic.com) in the village of **Niantic.** To call this place a used bookstore is like calling the Grand Canyon a neighborhood park. The Book Barn is a compound of 6 buildings, each overflowing with volumes and, luckily, meticulously arranged by subject—so, for example, one building houses fiction and poetry, while another is devoted to science and history. There is also an area

OTHER ATTRACTIONS WORTH SEEING IN COAST & COUNTRY

Clinton Crossing
Premium Outlet Mall
Exit 63 off I-95
(860) 664-0700
An open-air shopping complex of 70 top-shelf stores.

Essex Saybrook Antiques Village
345 Middlesex Turnpike
Old Saybrook
(860) 388-0689

Mohegan Sun
1 Mohegan Sun Blvd.
Uncasville
(888) 226-7711
Casino, moderate-to-expensive restaurants, shops, cabaret, expensive high-rise hotel.

Richard D. Scofield Historic Lighting
90 Pond Meadow Rd.
Ivoryton
(860) 767-7032
Handmade reproductions.

Sunbeam Express
Captain John's Sport Fishing Center
381 Rope Ferry Rd.
Waterford
(860) 443-7259
sunbeamfleet.com
The lighthouse cruise is a 5-hour tour of 11 Long Island Sound lighthouses, including a narrated history of each. The 100-foot boat, which can accommodate 6 to 149 passengers, is also available for private charter and open party boat fishing.

Thankful Arnold House
14 Hayden Hill, off Route 154
Haddam
(860) 345-2400
haddamhistory.org
Unusual architectural features and gardens; 1795 house.

Wesleyan Potters
350 S. Main St.
Middletown
(860) 344-0039
Prestigious craft gallery.

dedicated exclusively to children's books. Best of all, the proprietors want you to stay as long as possible. Chairs, benches, and couches are strategically placed throughout the complex to entice you to linger. There are also picnic tables, beautiful gardens, and a play area, including a playhouse, for children. A dozen cats also live here and truly believe everyone works for them. There is a goat, too, that you can feed.

If all that doesn't convince you to make an afternoon of it, there's also free coffee, doughnuts, biscuits, and juice. Checkers and chessboards are set up for anyone who has the time and urge to play. Paperbacks cost $1, and hardcover novels run about $4 to $5. The Book Barn also purchases books; check the website for details.

The Book Barn's inventory grew so massive that the owners opened two new locations: the ***Book Barn Downtown*** (267 Main St.; 860-691-8078) and the ***Book Barn Midtown*** (291 Main St.; 860-691-3371) in downtown Niantic. We wonder where they'll go next! All stores are open daily 9 a.m. to 9 p.m.

A few doors down is the ***Niantic Cinema*** (279 Main St.; 860-739-6929; nianticcinema.com), considered by many to be the best independent movie theater in the area. The 5-screen theater shows first-run movies as well as independent films you won't find at your mall multiplex. Ticket prices are reasonable, and the popcorn is actually affordable.

Also nestled in the Niantic is the absolutely awesome ***Children's Museum of Southeastern Connecticut*** (409 Main St.; 860-691-1111; childrensmuseumsect.org). Frequently children's museums overflow with activities for kids over 5 but fall short for those younger than that, so this interactive educational center is a real discovery. The exhibits and activities are designed to appeal to, but never talk down to, kids and are engaging enough to capture the attention of adults, too.

Nursery Rhyme Land is a wonderful place for toddlers to explore, as is Kidsville, a kids-size town. The Discovery Room, best for kids 6 and up, brings the wonders of science to life. In one such activity youngsters get serious when they "play doctor" and bandage and splint up each other or Mom and Dad. Throughout the year, the museum features a number of exhibits, field trips, seminars, and musical performances of interest to kids, including a respected summer camp program that focuses on the environment, science, and the arts. Admission. Open 9:30 a.m. to 4:30 p.m. Tues through Sat; noon to 4 p.m. Sun. Open Mon during summer and school holidays. A picnic area is available. Admission; kids under 2, free.

Although Hammonasset State Park in Madison gets most of the press, **Rocky Neck State Park** (exit 72 off I-95 in Niantic) is another great location, especially for off-season picnics. If you like things historical, be sure to check out the pavilion, constructed as a Works Progress Administration project. For picnics, though, walk out to the end of the rocky point, where you have the waters of Long Island Sound on three sides. This is a beautiful and peaceful place to pitch a blanket and share a meal. Be sure to bring some stale bread or a couple of anchovy pizzas for the gulls; they seem to expect it. The park has a picnic area and a place to cook. Open daily from 8 a.m. to sunset. Parking fees apply in season.

Salem

Salem Valley Farms (20 Darling Rd.; 860-859-2980; salemvalleyfarms icecream.com) near the junction of Routes 11 and 85 in **Salem** is another great ice cream stop. "Rich" is one word for Salem Valley Farms' ice cream—rich and, well, eccentric. How else would you describe an establishment that peddles outrageous flavors like ginger and espresso fudge? Actually, the menu features plenty of familiar flavors as well as an ever-changing menu of innovative items. Open noon to 9 p.m. daily; shorter hours in cooler months; closed Jan and Feb.

Mohegan Country

Colchester

Located off Route 16, the 1872 **Comstock Bridge** (now honorably retired) is one of Connecticut's few remaining covered bridges. It is now used mainly by fishermen and folks just watching the river flow. The wheelchair-accessible area was designed by Peter Reneson, a polio victim who grew up in **Colchester.**

Lyman Trumbull, a US senator from Illinois, one of the founders of the Republican Party and co-author of the Thirteenth Amendment, was born and raised in Colchester in the home of his grandfather, historian Benjamin Trumbull, at 80 Broadway St. The house still stands today, but is private and not open to the public.

Lebanon

Jonathan Trumbull was the only colonial governor (1769–1784) to support the American War of Independence. He organized George Washington's supply line almost single-handedly, and it was largely thanks to Trumbull that Connecticut came to be called the "Supply State." Today at least three buildings in *Lebanon* are associated with the Trumbulls and the governor's historic efforts to support the Revolution. Two are located very near each other on W. Town Street (Route 87) on the green.

The *Jonathan Trumbull House* (169 W. Town St.; 860-642-7558; gov trumbullhousedar.org) was once the governor's home. It was built by Governor Trumbull's father between 1735 and 1740. Today it is furnished with period furniture and administered by the Daughters of the American Revolution. Also on this site is *Wadsworth Stable.* Originally located in Hartford, this stable was saved from demolition due largely to the efforts of Katherine Seymour Day, who raised enough funds to have it relocated. In 1954 the Daughters assumed ownership, dismantled the stable, and moved it to Lebanon. Today it serves as a museum and holds numerous antique wagons and farm implements. While we can't say George Washington slept there, we're pretty sure his horse did. Both museums are open mid-May through mid-Oct. The house can be toured 1 to 6 p.m. Fri, 10 a.m. to 5 p.m. Sat, and 11 a.m. to 5 p.m. Sun. The stable is open 10 a.m. to 5 p.m. Sat, and 11 a.m. to 5 p.m. Sun. Weather can be a factor, so as usual, please call first. Donations accepted.

The home of Dr. William Beaumont, the "father of physiology," is also located nearby. The *Beaumont home* (16 W. Town St.; 860-642-6579) is maintained by the Lebanon Historical Society and houses a display of surgical instruments. Open noon to 4 p.m. Sat mid-May through Columbus Day. Adult admission.

Blue Slope Country Museum

Tiny Franklin offers the Blue Slope Country Museum (138 Blue Hill Rd.; 860-642-6413; blueslope.com), where city slickers can get acquainted with farm implements and tools housed in a Pennsylvania Dutch–style Amish barn. The museum offers educational programs and demonstrations relative to the importance of farming in this country. Special events in Oct.

The third Trumbull property, the 1769 *Jonathan Trumbull Jr. House* (780 Trumbull Hwy.; 860-642-6100; lebanontownhall.org/trumbulljunior museum.htm), is a center-chimney farmhouse with 8 intricately carved corner fireplaces and a gorgeous original cherry staircase with a molded rail. Today it is furnished with both reproductions and period antiques. Open mid-May through Columbus Day, Sat and Sun, noon to 4 p.m. Adult admission.

Built in 1727 as the Trumbull Family Store, the *Revolutionary War Office* (149 W. Town St.; 860-873-3399; lebanontownhall.org/war-office.htm) was where the Council of Safety met to plan the logistical effort that kept Washington's army in the field during the Revolutionary War. Today the building is owned by the Sons of the American Revolution and is open noon to 4 p.m. Sat and Sun, Memorial Day through Labor Day. Donations accepted.

Norwich

Located at the confluence of the Yantic and Shetucket Rivers, *Norwich* was founded in the second half of the 17th century. By 1776 it was the second-largest city in Connecticut, and it was a major Patriot stronghold during the Revolutionary War. Among Norwich's sons who fought in that war was Benedict Arnold, the infamous American general who tried to turn West Point over to the British and who later burned New London. *Benedict Arnold's birthplace* (299 Washington St.) can still be seen today. Please be aware that although there is a plaque in front of the house explaining its significance, the home is privately owned and not open to the public. Please be respectful.

A block from Arnold's birthplace is the *Christopher Leffingwell House* (348 Washington St.; 860-889-9440; leffingwellhousemuseum.org), a unique restoration of 2 small saltbox houses joined together to form a single home. The oldest portion dates from 1675. In 1701 Ensign Thomas Leffingwell opened a tavern on the premises, and there his son entertained George Washington in 1776 when the general was on his way to Lebanon. Open Apr through Oct, Sat noon to 4 p.m. or by appointment. Admission.

There must be a dozen other historic buildings scattered along Washington and Town Streets, most within easy walking distance of one another. One with an interesting history is the *Samuel Huntington House* (34 E. Town St.). Samuel Huntington was Norwich's most prominent citizen after Benedict Arnold; he signed the Declaration of Independence and presided over the signing of the Articles of Confederation. There's also the ***Joseph Carpenter House*** (71 E. Town St.), which dates from the 1770s, when it was home to one of New England's most successful silversmiths. The homes are private and can be viewed only from the street.

The ***Slater Memorial Museum and Converse Art Gallery*** (108 Crescent St.; 860-887-2506; slatermuseum.org), on the campus of the Norwich Free Academy, doesn't have the romantic lure of some of Norwich's historical attractions, but it's well worth a visit, especially if you've never been able to get to the Louvre or any of the other great European sculpture galleries. This imposing 3-story Romanesque structure was built in 1888 to house a truly impressive collection of plaster casts of famous Greek, Roman, and Renaissance sculpture. The casts are still the main attraction, but in addition to that collection (one of the three finest in the US), the museum also has displays of antique American and European furniture, Native American artifacts, textiles, and various fine art, including one of the best collections of Hudson River School art in America. Open Sept through June, 9 a.m. to 4 p.m. Tues through Fri, 1 to 4 p.m. weekends. Open July and Aug, 1 to 4 p.m. Tues through Sun. Admission.

norwichtrivia

Yantic Falls is the site of *Indian Leap,* where it is reported that after the Battle of East Great Plains in 1643, the Mohegans pursued a band of fleeing Narragansetts into this gorge, and forced them to jump to their deaths.

Among the best places to visit in New England during the fall or any time of year, really, are our old, hallowed cemeteries. The headstone inscriptions tell us much about rich and poor families as well as entire social histories. Travelers with proper doses of curiosity can easily get lost in the past. ***Old Norwichtown Burial Ground*** (Old Cemetery Lane; 860-886-4683) off Town Street reveals a rich colonial history. Open every day until dusk. Brochures are available at the cemetery entrance for self-guided tours.

Montville

Early in the 17th century, a Pequot subchief named Uncas formed a new tribe, the Mohegans. During the Pequot Wars of 1638, Uncas and his people sided with the British, beginning a century of intimate involvement in the affairs of European settlers. The Mohegans and Pequots eventually united under Uncas's leadership, and they became a powerful force in southwestern Connecticut. The first major American novelist, James Fenimore Cooper, recounted part of their story in his 1826 sensation, *The Last of the Mohicans,* one of his famous Leatherstocking Tales.

Chief Uncas died in 1682. He is buried in the Indian Burial Grounds on Sachem Street in Norwich. President Andrew Jackson laid the cornerstone of Uncas's monument in 1833.

In 1931 John Tantaquidgeon, a direct descendant of Chief Uncas, founded the ***Tantaquidgeon Museum*** (1819 Norwich–New London Rd.; 860-848-0594) on Route 32 in the Uncasville section of ***Montville.*** Here the culture and history of the Mohegans and other New England Indians are presented in a series of displays featuring artifacts of stone, wood, and bone made by Indian craftsmen, living and dead. Artifacts from other tribes of the Southeast, Southwest, and Plains are housed in their own sections. The hours are sporadic, but it's usually open Apr through Oct, Wed through Sat, 10 a.m. to 4 p.m., depending on the availability of volunteers. It's advisable to call ahead. Donation requested.

Just 200 yards from the Tantaquidgeon Indian Museum is the ***Mohegan Congregational Church,*** an 1831 meetinghouse that is still in use. West of Mohegan Hill, off Raymond Hill Road, is ***Cochegan Rock,*** the site of secret meetings between Uncas and his counselors (and said to be the largest boulder in Connecticut). Farther north, near the village of Mohegan, is ***Fort Shantok State Park,*** which contains an old Indian fort and a Mohegan burial ground, among other points of interest.

Montville also offers an attraction that is sure to delight young explorers: ***The Dinosaur Place at Nature's Art*** (1650 Hartford–New London Turnpike; 860-443-4367; thedinosaurplace.com). Visitors enter the park by walking under a life-size brachiosaurus that stands over 40 feet tall. They will encounter several more prehistoric surprises while on their woodland exploration of 3 trails showcasing creatures that roamed the earth millions of years ago. There is also a picnic area, children's playground, and ice cream shop. Open daily mid-June through Labor Day, 10 a.m. to 5 p.m.; reduced hours before and after the peak season. Last ticket to the park is sold 1 hour before closing. Admission.

After you finish with the dinosaurs, stroll over to Nature's Art, an interactive science, nature, and shopping experience. Activities include digging for gems and crystals or panning for "gold," keeping all the treasures you find. Unearth a dinosaur skeleton, make a craft, or select a geode that is millions of years old and have it cut open. The fossil gallery features life-size dinosaur skeletons and minerals and crystals from around the world. There are also a cafe, gift shop, and fossil gallery.

The Eastern Shore

Ledyard

In **Ledyard,** on Route 214, you'll find the 11-acre property on which sits the **Ledyard Powered-Up–Powered-Down Sawmill** (Iron Street; 860-464-2575; ledyardsawmill.org), an unusual restored 1860 water-powered vertical sawmill. The park also has a working blacksmith shop, a restored gristmill with a 2-acre mill pond, an 1878 "Lane" shingle mill, ice-harvesting equipment, and a picnic area. The park staff includes a working blacksmith. The saw operates when water level is sufficient, usually Apr, May, and mid-Oct to Nov; open to the public Sat 1 to 4 p.m. during those times.

New London

At its founding in 1876, the original name of the **US Coast Guard Academy** (15 Mohegan Ave.; 860-444-8500; cga.edu) was the Revenue Cutter School of Instruction. Today visitors are welcomed year-round to tour the academy. Tours are free and self-guided. Full-dress reviews, held at Washington parade field, happen most Fridays at 4 p.m. in the spring and fall. USCG sweatshirts and other souvenirs are for sale at the gift shop. The campus is open daily 9 a.m. to 4:30 p.m. The museum on campus, which spans 200 years of American maritime service, is located in Waesche Hall and is free and open 9 a.m. to 4:30 p.m. Mon through Fri, 10 a.m. to 5 p.m. Sat, noon to 5 p.m. Sun. Walking maps are available at the museum. A valid photo ID is required to get on campus.

The academy is also home to the **US Coast Guard Band** (860-444-8466; uscg.mil/band), which offers some wonderful band concerts of patriotic and popular music. Their schedule can be found on the website or by calling.

When in port, the 3-masted training barque *Eagle* is open to visitors; be sure to check the online schedule. Pets must be on a leash and cameras are permitted. There are no picnic facilities at the academy, but you can spread a blanket at **Riverside Park,** next to the academy. Much of the parking is restricted or reserved; park at the visitor center or next to the museum.

Though often crowded to the point of distraction, downtown **New London** has so much going for it that it would be a shame to miss the experience if you are anywhere in the vicinity. We recommend a fall or spring walking tour, including the **Captain's Walk** and **Whale Oil Row** with its flanking of 1832 Greek revival houses built by the leading figures in the whaling industry, of which New London was the center in Connecticut. Between 1784 and 1907, the city was home port to 196 whaling vessels, over twice as many as ventured from all other Connecticut ports combined. The industry peaked in 1846 and died off rapidly thereafter, but Whale Oil Row still carries some of the aura of those days when Connecticut whale oil helped light the lamps of America.

newlondontrivia

The grinder sandwich supposedly was invented by Benny Capalbo in New London in 1926. Despite our proximity to the sub base at Groton, Nutmeggers stick with the handle "grinder."

Don't miss the **Antientist Burial Ground** (near Hempstead and Granite Streets), which holds the grave of Flora Hercules, "the wife of Hercules, 'Governor of the Negroes.'" Her epitaph offers evidence of African-American governors in Connecticut during her lifetime (1689–1749). Also of note is the **New London County Courthouse** (70 Hunting St.), built in 1784 and still in use. In late July New London hosts America's longest-running polka festival. Come prepared to eat and dance the day and night away. Admission. The festival is held at Ocean Beach Park from noon to midnight.

Energetic walkers may want to head all the way down to Bank Street to see the granite-walled 1833 **Custom House Maritime Museum** (150 Bank St.; 860-447-2501; nlmaritimesociety.org). Being the oldest operating custom house in America, this building has seen a lot of history, including the ability of a slave to choose his own freedom. Now a stop on Connecticut's Freedom Trail, this museum is well worth a visit. Be sure to check out the front doors, which were assembled from planks taken from the frigate USS *Constitution* (Old Ironsides). Open 1 to 5 p.m. Tues through Sun. Suggested donation.

British soldiers led by Benedict Arnold burned New London in 1781, and just about every structure in the city today postdates that episode. The exception is the 1678 **Joshua Hempsted House** (11 Hempsted St.; 860-443-7949), the home of a famous Connecticut diarist and now the oldest surviving house in New London. One of the interesting features of this home is that it is insulated with seaweed. The house is owned by Connecticut Landmarks and is the home to a collection of abolitionist papers, including a letter from 1843 by Mary Hempsted Bolles in which she bravely challenges her church's stance on slavery. Her father went on to establish a school in this building, which unbelievably for the time, several African-American children attended. Open 1 to 4 p.m. weekends May, June, Sept, and Oct; 1 to 4 p.m. Thurs through Sun, July and Aug; and by appointment. Admission.

The area surrounding the Hempsted House is also a stop on the Connecticut Freedom Trail due to the homes purchased by free African Americans in the 1840s. Known as the Hempstead Historic District, the area includes Shiloh Baptist Church on Garvin Street; both the building and the name of the street, named for leader Albert Garvin, are evidence of the strong community ties this group of people had in the area.

New London has another—literary—side that's every bit as fascinating as its seagoing heritage. Eugene O'Neill, arguably America's greatest playwright, spent part of his childhood in **Monte Cristo Cottage** (325 Pequot Ave.; 860-443-0051; theoneill.org/monte-cristo-cottage) in New London. Named for O'Neill's actor-father's best-known stage role, Monte Cristo Cottage is a pretty little gingerbread structure that looks like it should be filled with light and laughter. Alas, the years O'Neill and his brother Jamie spent there were more like one of the Grimms' darker fairy tales. Both father James and brother Jamie were heavy drinkers. O'Neill's mother, Ella, addicted to morphine from O'Neill's birth, battled her own demons throughout his childhood. She is said to haunt the tiny cottage.

The Tyrone family in *Long Day's Journey into Night* is a reflection and expression of the misery of O'Neill's summers at the cottage. The comedy *Ah! Wilderness,* also set in Monte Cristo, portrays a life that O'Neill never knew except as an outsider; he based his happy and slightly zany characters on the McGinleys, the family of a childhood friend.

The cottage where O'Neill's dark dreams were born is a conglomeration of small buildings, all wrapped up in the Victorian pseudogentility of gingerbread, wraparound verandas, and turrets.

Inside, especially on the second floor, the rooms are grim and claustrophobic. The first floor of the cottage is fully restored and furnished. In a room adjacent to the living room, a short multimedia show narrated by the late actress Geraldine Fitzgerald describes O'Neill's life in New London in the early 1900s. Open Memorial Day through Labor Day, noon to 4 p.m. Thurs through Sat, and 1 to 3 p.m. Sun. Admission.

The *Lyman Allyn Art Museum* (625 Williams St.; 860-443-2545; lyman allyn.org) has a wonderful room full of Indian artifacts and a collection of antique dollhouses and toys. In addition, the museum has collections of Egyptian, Roman, medieval, and Greek artifacts as well as various changing exhibits. The small museum shop is a real find, offering both antiques and reproductions. Also located on the museum grounds is the historic *Deshon-Allyn House,* a 19th-century mansion that was home to whaling captain Lyman Allyn. The museum has a noncirculating reference library of art and art history books available for use during museum hours. Open 10 a.m. to 5 p.m. Tues through Sat and 1 to 5 p.m. Sun; closed major holidays. Admission; kids under 12, free.

newlondontrivia

Huddled beneath the 8-lane Gold Star Bridge is Ye Olde Towne Mill (860-447-5250), the nation's oldest industrial power plant (1650).

Wheelchair accessible. Wheelchairs and ASL interpreter available by reservation. Be sure to check their website for deals, such as free admission on the first Sat of the month. Also, if you visit on your birthday, you get in free!

Ledge Lighthouse in New London Harbor is said to be haunted by a ghost named Ernie. Some believe Ernie was a light keeper who, depressed by marital problems, cut his own throat and then jumped off the structure. Some reports say the ghost is a tall, bearded man dressed in a slicker and rain hat. The prankster ghost has been known to untie boats, hide coffee cups and radios, and slam doors. The Ledge Lighthouse is atop a 65-foot, three-story square building in the water at the meeting of the Thames River, Fisher's Island Sound, and Long Island Sound in New London Harbor. It was abandoned in 1987, and the 11-room structure took a serious beating from the elements with no one there to maintain it. But once again, Nutmeggers jumped into action and the New London Ledge Lighthouse Foundation was formed to save the iconic landmark. Today, fully renovated, the lighthouse once again stands in glory, complete with an interpretive museum and small theater. Seasonal cruises to Ledge Lighthouse are offered by **Project Oceanology** (860-445-9007; oceanology.org/lighthouse.html) and leave from Avery Point.

New London's **Shaw Mansion** (11 Blinman St.; 860-443-1209; nlhistory .org) is the home of the New London Historical Society, as it has been since 1907. No, that's not a typo. The New London Historical Society was founded in 1870 and is the oldest historical organization in eastern Connecticut. It is very fitting that they call this incredible building home. Considered the cradle of the American navy, the Shaw Mansion was built in the 1750s by Captain Nathaniel Shaw and served as Connecticut's naval office during the Revolutionary War. Five generations of Captain Shaw's family lived here until it was turned over to the historical society. Today the mansion serves as a museum with an impressive collection of items. Open Wed through Fri 1 to 4 p.m. and Sat 10 a.m. to 4 p.m. during the summer.

Groton

Groton is the birthplace of the atomic submarine and the site of the nation's largest submarine base. This history is commemorated at the **USS Nautilus Memorial** on the US submarine base off Route 12. In addition to touring the world's first nuclear sub, you can spend hours in the 12,000-square-foot **Historic Ship Nautilus and Submarine Force Museum** (1 Crystal Lake Rd.; 860-343-0079; ussnautilus.org) adjacent to the sub base. The museum includes extensive exhibits tracing the history of America's submarine fleet and offers a pair of top-notch multimedia shows in two different theaters: one tracing the history of the submarine force and one dealing specifically with *Nautilus*. The museum is free and open Wed through Mon, 9 a.m. to 5 p.m. May through Oct; to 4 p.m. Nov through April. The museum closes the last week of Apr and first week of Nov for maintenance.

Groton's **Fort Griswold Battlefield State Park** (Park Avenue; 860-449-6877) commemorates the warfare of a different era. The park is the site of a 1781 massacre of American troops at the hands of a force of 800 British soldiers under the command of the traitor Benedict Arnold. At that time Yankee privateers based in New London were a thorn in the side of the British in New York, and Arnold came to burn the town, which he did, destroying 150 buildings. The part of his force that advanced up the east bank of the Thames suffered heavy casualties assaulting Fort Griswold, which was held by a force of 150 militia under the command of Colonel William Ledyard. When Ledyard finally surrendered, he was murdered with his own sword, and 80 of his men were slaughtered.

Many of Fort Griswold's old emplacements remain, and there are some interesting historical displays. The 134-foot monument tower provides a nice view of the coast. The park is open year-round. The museum and monument are open Memorial Day through Labor Day, 9 a.m. to 5 p.m. Wed through Sun. The fort is open sunrise until sunset daily.

In our experience, children can be finicky, hard-to-please creatures. Tell them you're taking an environmental cruise, and chances are you'll get yawns; hum the theme song from *Jaws* and mention sharks and they're in the car in a New York minute. For budding Cousteaus and their parents, **Project Oceanology** (1084 Shennecossett Rd.; 860-445-9007; oceanology .org) at UConn's Avery Point campus makes an interesting and educational day trip (don't forget to hint at the possibility of shark attacks). You'll cruise the waters off Groton to learn about the environment and marine life in ways you never could at an aquarium. The boats, *Enviro-Lab II* and *Enviro-Lab III,* are oceanographic research vessels staffed by marine research scientists and teachers who really communicate their love for the sea and give kids a chance to participate in lots of hands-on adventures, such as catching lobsters and taking and analyzing samples from the ocean using oceanographic sampling instruments. It's so engaging you can probably drop the shark patter about five minutes after boarding. Meanwhile, you can kick

They Sacrificed All

Two African-American soldiers fought at Fort Griswold, Jordan Freeman and Lambert Latham. A bronze plaque at the fort depicts Freeman's efforts there. Both men perished in the battle but are remembered with the others for their bravery and sacrifice. For this reason, Fort Griswold is a stop on the Connecticut Freedom Trail.

back and enjoy some beautiful ocean views, including a slice of the southeastern Connecticut coastline and some postcard-pretty lighthouses. Admission. A variety of cruises, including seal watches and lighthouse expeditions, run throughout the year but times and dates vary, so it's best to check the website or call. Cruises take 2½ hours; children younger than 6 are not allowed for safety reasons. Reservations are required.

grotontrivia

The first diesel-powered submarine was built in Groton in 1912.

If you're out with the kids (furred or otherwise) and need to burn off some energy, Groton has some great state parks. **Haley Farm State Park** (Haley Farm Lane; 860-444-7591) is a great place to explore. It has 200 acres filled with trails near Palmer Cove. There is a bike trail as well that winds its way along beautiful former farmland. Groton also has **Bluff Point State Park** (Depot Road; 860-444-7591), a coastal reserve that offers a boat launch, shell and saltwater fishing, and hiking. This place is also pet-friendly, and a wonderful way to spend a day.

One of the best places in the world to eat lobster is **Abbott's Lobster in the Rough** (117 Pearl St.; 860-536-7719; abbotts-lobster.com), down by the shipyards in Noank. You have your choice of eating indoors in the dining room or outdoors at picnic tables scattered around the lawn and pier. We highly recommend you take your food outdoors; on good days, you can see three states. The view of the sea and the passing trawlers and sailboats is worth it.

coast&country trivia

When you're in southeastern Connecticut, call the Thames River the Thamz (rhymes with James), not the Timz like the one running through London.

During the summer Abbott's serves thousands of pounds of lobster a day, so just assume they wrote the book on cooking crustaceans. Your lobsters come steamed fresh from the pot, the way nature intended, with butter, coleslaw, and chips on the side. Nothing fancy, but you came to Abbott's for lobster, and lobster is what you get. Try it the way connoisseurs do: Order a large lobster (2½ pounds or more, depending on your lobster obsession) to split and fixings for two dinners. That way, you'll get more lobster and less shell for your money. The lobster rolls at Abbott's are a lazy person's way to get around the cracking, picking, sucking, and lip-smacking that go with demolishing a whole lobster. Each lobster roll consists of a quarter pound of premium butter-soaked lobster on a toasted bun. Abbott's also serves a classic shore dinner with steamers, cooked shrimp, and clam chowder in addition to the lobster.

lobstertrivia

A lobster tidbit: It takes between five and seven years for a lobster to reach saleable weight. Want to pick the very freshest live lobster? Easy—just pick the friskiest one with its tail curled tightly under its body.

However you take your lobster, be prepared to wait. This is a very popular place. Open for weekends only, noon to 7 p.m. early May until Memorial Day, at which time they open noon to 9 p.m. daily until Labor Day.

Mystic

If you're planning a trip to Connecticut, you probably know as much as we do about **Mystic,** Mystic Seaport, and other Mystic attractions. After all, this is just about the most popular tourist destination in the state, and the folks at Mystic do a wonderful job of getting the word out about this attraction.

Mystic Seaport (75 Greenmanville Ave.; 860-572-0711; visitmysticseaport.com) is a grouping of some 60 buildings and 4 vessels from all over the New England coast that re-create life in an old Yankee seaport.

The admission is steep, but one ticket is good for two consecutive days. Open Apr through Oct, 9 a.m. to 5 p.m. daily; Nov through Mar, 10 a.m. to 4 p.m. daily.

mystictrivia

Mystic derives its name from the Pequot Native American word *mistuket.*

Mystic Drawbridge Ice Cream (2 Main St.; 860-572-7978; mystic drawbridgeicecream.com) is a cute ice cream parlor that locals claim has the best ice cream around. The Kona coffee flavor, made from Hawaiian coffee ground on the premises, and the Barbados buttered rum come highly recommended. It's open 10 a.m. to 11 p.m. during summer and 10 a.m. to 9 p.m. in winter. By the way, that cute drawbridge is called a *bascule* (French for "seesaw"), and you'll have plenty of opportunity to contemplate its rare beauty because car traffic along Main Street goes into gridlock when it's raised to allow boats to pass.

Mystic has its share of formal dining, but its more relaxed family places are appealing, too. Number one on most lists for travelers to Mystic is ***Mystic Pizza*** (56 W. Main St.; 860-536-3737; mysticpizza.com). Until the movie *Mystic Pizza* came out, this was just another small-town pizza parlor. Now it's a movie trivia–buff pilgrimage. Everyone wants to see where a young Julia Roberts served up pies—even though she was actually on a set in nearby Stonington Borough. Movie buffs will have a good time with all the movie memorabilia on the walls (and for sale) in the restaurant. Open daily 10 a.m. to 11 p.m. Closed major holidays. There is now a second location on Route 184 in North Stonington. Their pizzas are also available in the frozen food sections of most grocery stores.

You'll find the ***Sea Swirl*** (30 Williams Ave.; 860-536-3452; seaswirlof mystic.com) at the junction of Routes 1 and 27. When food pundits compile their "best of" lists, the Sea Swirl is a perennial on the Best Fried Clams list. Without a doubt, this tiny drive-in is the best place in Connecticut for fried whole-belly clams. The other fried seafood offerings are similarly stellar. Open daily Apr through Oct, 11 a.m. to 8 p.m.

Kitchen Little (36 Quarry Rd.; 860-536-2122; kitchenlittle.org) has been lauded in more travel guides and articles than you can shake a stick at. As you'd guess from the name, this is a small restaurant. In fact, the breakfasts are almost bigger than the restaurant itself. Size and fame conspire to draw crowds, so be prepared for a short wait. Eggs—any way, shape, or form—are big here, but you might prefer the french toast or ham-and-cheese-stuffed pancake sandwich. Lunch offerings are equally

mystictrivia

The ***Hoxie Scenic Overlook*** between exits 89 and 90 on the northbound side of I-95 offers a postcard view of Mystic Seaport. To the east you can see the seaport, home port to the *Charles W. Morgan* whaling ship, the *L. A. Dunton,* and the square-rigged *Joseph Conrad,* among others. The bluff on the right is where the Pequot Indian War was fought.

good and generous; prices are beyond reasonable. Open 6:30 a.m. to 2 p.m. weekdays for breakfast and lunch, and 6:30 a.m. to 1 p.m. weekends for breakfast only.

Stonington

Stonington is perched on a mile-long peninsula so narrow that you can stand on some cross streets and see the ocean on either side. Were it not for the town's protected harbor, it is unlikely that anyone would ever have chosen to build in such a confined space. That harbor, however, made Stonington a center of New England's whaling and sealing industries in the first half of the 19th century. It also helped make Stonington an important railroad terminus. In the early days of railroading, before rail bridges crossed the state's major rivers, Stonington was on the most direct route between Boston and New York, and 17 separate tracks once converged on the town. In those times, passengers arriving by rail from Boston had to board steamboats in Stonington Harbor for the trip to New York.

At the height of Stonington's fortunes, the town's two main streets were packed cheek by jowl with commercial buildings and the fancy homes of wealthy merchants. When whaling and sealing fell off, the railroad moved on, and Stonington, which lacked the real estate to expand into a bedroom community, was left frozen in the mid-19th century. Most of the beautiful federal and Greek revival homes are still there, only now they're B&Bs, restaurants, antiques stores, and crafts shops.

In 1820 Captain Nathaniel Palmer left from Stonington harbor and embarked on a sailing trip that resulted in the discovery of Antarctica. You can visit the *Captain Nathaniel B. Palmer House* (40 Palmer St.; 860-535-8445), which Captain Nat, as he was known, built with his brother, Alexander. Built in the late federal style, the home has 14 rooms and a cupola that looks out over the shipyard and lighthouse. The worn floorboards of the lookout tower are a testament to how often

stonington**trivia**

Stonington has the only active commercial fishing fleet left in Connecticut, and the town still holds a time-honored tradition called the *Blessing of the Fleet,* which includes a Mass, the laying of a wreath to honor those who have lost their lives at sea, and a parade of boats into the harbor.

worried family members paced the floors watching for sea captains return-ing from their trips. A restored outbuilding with an icehouse and workshop is located on the grounds, along with a genealogy library and a collection of oil portraits. This National Historic Landmark also has a permanent exhibit that traces the Palmer family's role in the state's maritime history. Changing exhibitions relate to Palmer, Stonington, and maritime history. The home is bordered by water on three sides, and the property has been naturalisti-cally landscaped. Visitors are encouraged to stroll the grounds and bring a picnic lunch. The Palmer house is open May through Oct, 1 to 5 p.m. Thurs through Sun. Admission.

Cannon Square, toward the south end of Market Street, marks the site where the Stonington militia successfully fought off the British in August 1814. It and the surrounding streets are the center of Stonington's historic district.

Stroll up Main Street from the square (away from the point) and admire the architecture of the 1827 **Old Customs House** and the elegant 1780 **Captain Amos Palmer House,** both worth more than a passing glance, although privately owned. In fact, James MacNeill Whistler, who painted *Whistler's Mother,* spent part of his boyhood in this house.

Down at the end of Water Street is an especially popular local land-mark, the **Old Lighthouse Museum** (7 Water St.; 860-535-1440). It was constructed in 1823 but was moved to its present location in 1840 to protect it from erosion. It is now a museum housing 6 rooms of exhibits, whaling and nautical displays, a collection of pre-1835 pottery made locally, an ice-harvesting exhibit, and the popular lighthouse display, featuring a fourth-order Fresnel lens and photography of the lighthouses of Long Island Sound. There is also a children's room with an antique dollhouse. If you care to climb the stone steps to the top of the lighthouse, you'll be rewarded with a stunning view of Long Island Sound, including Fisher's Island. If you're at the museum around day's end, linger awhile to see a spectacular sunset over Stonington Point. Open weekends 1 to 5 p.m. during Apr, then 10 a.m. to 5 p.m. Thurs through Mon, May through Oct.

The **Mashantucket Pequot Museum and Research Center** (110 Pequot Trail; 860-396-6800; pequotmuseum.org) on the Mashantucket Pequot Reservation in Mashantucket is without a doubt one of the most beautiful, stunning, and moving museums in all of Connecticut.

ANNUAL EVENTS IN COAST & COUNTRY

FEBRUARY–MARCH

Eagle Watch Cruises
Essex
(860) 662-0577
What more spectacular way to see America's national symbol than with a cruise along the Connecticut River? Bring binoculars, dress warmly, and prepare to be dazzled.

MAY

Lobster Days
Mystic Seaport
75 Greenmanville Ave.
Mystic
(860) 572-0711
mysticseaport.org/lobsterdays
Outdoor lobster bake on the banks of the Mystic River. Lobster as you like it, along with all the family entertainment Mystic does so well, such as sea chanteys, demonstrations, entertainment, and food.

JUNE

Antique & Classic Boat Rendezvous
Along the Museum of America and the Sea's waterfront
Mystic
(860) 572-5302
mysticseaport.org
Features antique vessels built before 1965.

JULY

Annual Guilford Craft Expo
Guilford Town Green
(203) 453-5947
guilfordartcenter.org
One of Connecticut's oldest and finest outdoor juried shows.

July 4th Extravaganza
Marina at American Wharf
Norwich
(860) 886-6363
americanwharf.com
Family fun and lots of children's activities; huge fireworks display.

OpSail
New London City Pier
opsail2012ct.com
Parade of tall ships; vendors at various city venues.

Mashantucket Pequots invested $135 million of the monies earned from the nearby Foxwoods Casino into building this state-of-the-art museum and research center. The museum brings to life the story and history of the Mashantucket Pequot people, a history spanning 20,000 years, from the last ice age to today, and that of other Native American tribal nations.

AUGUST

Annual Podunk Bluegrass Music Festival

Dodd Stadium
14 Stoff Ave.
Norwich
(860) 887-7962
podunkbluegrass.net
Brings some of the best bluegrass to the state.

OCTOBER

Chowder Days

Mystic Seaport
75 Greenmanville Rd.
Mystic
(860) 572-0711
mysticseaport.org
Peruse several different chowder vendors and taste assorted gourmet sandwiches and delectable desserts.

NOVEMBER

Artistry

Guilford Art Center
411 Church St.
Guilford
(203) 453-5947
This holiday sale features innovative and unusual crafts from more than 500 of the country's leading artists.

Harvest Celebration at Mashantucket Pequot Museum

110 Pequot Trail
Mashantucket
(800) 411-9671
pequotmuseum.org
Two-day celebration of the harvest with food and fun events.

DECEMBER

Christmas at Mystic Seaport

Mystic Seaport
75 Greenmanville Ave.
Mystic
(860) 572-5315
visitmysticseaport.org
You'll swear you've been transported back to the 1800s as Mystic goes all out to make the holidays of yesteryear come alive. Don't miss the evening Lantern Light Tours (by reservation only).

The life of woodland Native Americans is portrayed in stunning detail with dazzling multisensory dioramas and exhibits. Based on years of scholarly research and the works of Native American artisans, re-creations of life in a 16th-century Pequot village, a 17th-century Pequot fort, and an 18th-century farmstead were created. You can hunt caribou along simulated glacial crevasses—complete with howling winds and the sounds of creaking ice. When you visit the village, you'll hear the sounds of children playing and women working and smell the smoke of many campfires. The detail of each diorama is magnificent, especially the life-size, hand-painted Indian figures, cast from living Native Americans. In a specially designed theater, you can watch a 30-minute film called *The Witness,* which recounts the 1637 massacre of 600 Pequots at the Mystic fort.

Don't miss the 185-foot stone-and-glass observation tower, which gives you a sweeping view of the area. In fall this is one of the best places in the state to take in the brilliant reds and golds of a New England autumn. It's best to visit the tower before going through the museum. Somehow seeing the sweep of the Pequot homeland makes the exhibits and dioramas all the more meaningful.

The museum is open Wed through Sat 9 a.m. to 5 p.m. (last admission at 4 p.m.). Closed major holidays. Admission.

North Stonington

On Route 2 in *North Stonington* is the *John Randall House* (41 Norwich–Westerly Rd.). This is a house with a history. The Randall family's original clapboard building dates to 1685, with additions made in 1720 and 1790. The house is a landmark on the National Register of Historic Places as well as a stop on the Connecticut Freedom Trail. In its history it has been a home, a restaurant, and an inn. Sadly, today the building sits empty. While it was a restaurant called Randall's Ordinary, diners would be served by waiters in

Follow the Vine

Connecticut has many vineyards open for tours and tastings. In fact, it's one of the fastest-growing wine regions in the US. The number of wineries has doubled since the previous publication of this guide. While we have listed some of the wineries, we could not include them all, but you can check them out on the *Connecticut Wine Trail* (74 Chester Maine Rd., North Stonington; 860-535-0202; ctwine.com), a tour that takes you through some of the state's most picturesque and historic towns. The tour, which is marked by blue signs throughout the state, will take you a few weekends to complete.

period costumes while their dinners were cooked over open-hearth fires. Of note inside were the heavy shutters that were hung for protection from Indian attacks during the colonial period and a trapdoor used to conceal escaped slaves when the inn was a station on the Underground Railroad in the 1830s. We're not sure of any future plans for the property, but we hope that once again community action will save this historic landmark.

Griswold

Griswold native Isaac Glasko owned a blacksmith shop in the center of what is now the Glasgo section of town. He changed the way of farming and carpentry when he figured out how to harness waterpower to run a trip-hammer. He also specialized in making whaling implements, for which he held several patents. Fishermen all over New England used his harpoons, spades, lances, and knives. Even though he was of Native American and African-American descent, he was well respected throughout the community. His daughter attended Prudence Crandall's academy in Canterbury. Isaac Glasko is remembered well, and many places in town bear his name, including the village where his shop once stood.

What do you do with an acre of sunflowers? Well, they're pretty, sure, but they don't have much use except for feeding the cows. The owners at **Buttonwood Farm** (473 Shetucket Turnpike; 860-376-4081; sunflowers forwishes.com) had another idea. They started the Sunflowers for Wishes fund-raiser to benefit the Connecticut chapter of the Make a Wish Foundation. The following year, they planted 10 acres that produced approximately 300,000 blooms. They sold those for $5 a bundle, and 100 percent of the $500,000 they raised went to the foundation. Now they are up to 14 acres. The event usually runs the third week of July, 10 a.m. to dusk. All bouquets are on a first come, first served basis. When they're gone, they're gone.

The farm also offers homemade ice cream and other products and events Mar through Oct. Hours vary depending on the time of year. Check their website for details.

Places to Stay in Coast & Country

MADISON

Madison Beach Hotel
94 W. Wharf Rd.
(203) 245-1404
madisonbeachhotel.com
Moderate
Beautiful gray-shingled beach resort/hotel; prices include breakfast.

Tidewater Inn
949 Boston Post Rd.
(203) 245-8457
thetidewater.com
Moderate to expensive
A former stagecoach stop offering 9 guest rooms. Off-season rates are more reasonable.

MYSTIC

Hilton Mystic
20 Cookan Blvd.
(860) 572-0731
hiltonmystic.com
Moderate to expensive
Best bet for lodging with children; close to the aquarium, the seaport, and Old Mystick Village. Open year-round.

House of 1833 B&B
72 N. Stonington Rd.
(860) 536-6325 or (800) FOR-1833
houseof1833.com
Moderate to expensive
An elegant and romantic Greek revival mansion.

OLD LYME

Old Lyme Inn
85 Lyme St.
(203) 434-2600.
oldlymeinn.com
Expensive
Thirteen rooms, all with private baths.

OLD SAYBROOK

Deacon Timothy Pratt B&B
325 Main St.
(860) 395-1229
pratthouse.net
Moderate
Located next to James Gallery and Soda Fountain, this beautiful B&B has 9 rooms and is open year-round.

PRESTON

B&B at Roseledge Herb Farm
418 Rte. 164
(860) 892-4739
roseledge.com
Moderate
A 1720 B&B with canopy-topped high featherbeds.

Places to Eat in Coast & Country

COLCHESTER

NuNu's Bistro
45 Hayward Ave.
(860) 537-6299
nunusbistro.com
Moderate to expensive
Charming bistro located in a cute Victorian carriage house offering traditional Sicilian and American cuisine. BYOB.

GROTON

Paul's Pasta Shop
223 Thames S.
(860) 445-5276
paulspastashop.com
Inexpensive
You can take away prepared food or buy your own pasta and sauce.

MIDDLETOWN

It's Only Natural
386 Main St.
(860) 346-9210
Inexpensive
Award-winning natural food.

Udupi Bhaven
749 Saybrook Rd.
(860) 346-3355
Inexpensive
Authentic Indian cuisine that is purely vegetarian.

MYSTIC

Captain Daniel Packer Inne Restaurant & Pub
32 Water St.
(860) 536-3555
danielpacker.com
Moderate to expensive
Located in a 250-year-old inn; several menus to choose from; children's menu available.

NIANTIC

Niantic Diner
26 W. Main St.
(860) 739-2975
Inexpensive
Pleasantly informal.

OLD LYME

Hallmark Ice Cream
113 Shore Rd.
(203) 434-1998
Inexpensive to moderate
Hallmark Ice Cream is a great place to stop on your way home from the beach for an ice cream. With window service and outdoor seating, you don't have to worry about brushing all that sand off your feet! If you're hungry for more than ice cream, they also serve a variety of seafood next door at Hallmark Diner.

OLD SAYBROOK

Al Forno
1654 Boston Post Rd.
(860) 399-2346
alforno.net
Moderate to expensive
Fine Italian cuisine and pizzas.

Dock & Dine
Saybrook Point
(860) 388-4665
Moderate
Where the Connecticut River meets Long Island Sound.

Pat's Kountry Kitchen
70 Mill Rock Rd. East
(860) 388-4784
Moderate to expensive
Definitely try the clam hash.

WESTBROOK

Cafe Routier
1353 Boston Post Rd.
(860) 399-8700
caferoutier.com
Expensive
One of the best French bistros in the state.

THE QUIET CORNER

East of Hartford is an area the state's tourism promoters have nicknamed "the Quiet Corner." Bounded on the north by Massachusetts and on the east by Rhode Island, the Quiet Corner encompasses the lightly populated, slightly bucolic uplands of Tolland and Windham Counties. It is an area of peace and tranquility that has escaped both the bulldozers of the state's developers and the attention of the chic set. In truth the Quiet Corner has such an air of serenity that in many places you can easily imagine that this is the way all of Connecticut looked 350 years ago. Fertile farmland abounds, and herb and flower gardens are among the region's most popular attractions. There are country inns that wouldn't be out of place in France. With some exceptions, the antiques here are neither quite as antique nor nearly as pricey as those sold in the trendier stores across the state in Litchfield County. And if other regions have more to offer the casual traveler, for the patient, the Quiet Corner has its own rewards.

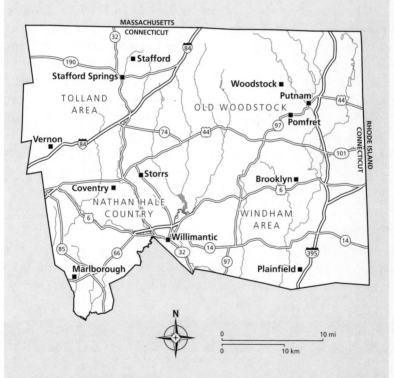

Nathan Hale Country

Marlborough

Seeing a small cluster of picturesque shops around a pond in **Marlborough** means you've reached the **Shoppes at Marlborough Barn** (45 N. Main St.; 860-295-1114; marlboroughbarnantiques.com) Actually, it's several barns and outbuildings. This is the place to shop for country furniture, crystal, antiques, knits, quilts, ironware, stoneware, collectibles, and more; many works are by local artisans. There's always something to pique your interest in the beautifully decorated room settings. Open Fri through Sat, 10 a.m. to 5 p.m., until 7 p.m. Thurs; Sun 11 a.m. to 4 p.m.

Take a break from shopping with breakfast, lunch, or dinner at **Sadler's Ordinary** (61 N. Main St.; 860-295-0006; eatatsadlers.com), a low-ceilinged old tavern. If you come in winter, ask to sit near the fireplace, and savor such New England dishes as chicken potpie and salmon cakes. You will be equally pleased with the bread baskets, full of sweet quick breads and warm-from-the-oven sunflower bread, crunchy with sunflower seeds. For dessert, try the old-fashioned creamy tapioca pudding covered with freshly whipped cream, or cream cheese–pecan pie. Or grab a quick snack in the bakery in front of the restaurant, then settle down at one of the picnic tables to rest your feet and relax. Open Mon through Thurs 11 a.m. to 8 p.m., Fri 11 a.m. to 9 p.m., Sat 8 a.m. to 9 p.m., Sun 8 a.m. to 7 p.m.

Hebron

Hebron is a small town along Route 66 with not a lot going on. But one of its claims to fame is **Eagle Rock,** on the border with Marlborough. This is another example of Connecticut's roadside rock art. This rock had previous

AUTHOR'S FAVORITES

Antiquing in the Northwest

Memory Lane Countryside Antique Center

Prudence Crandall House Museum

University of Connecticut, Storrs

Willington Pizza House

lives as a frog, a box turtle, and others, but it became an eagle in 1989 thanks to the talents of graduating RHAM High School student Jason Sawyer. Others now maintain the majestic bird, adding their initials and dates to its side.

Did you know that it takes 40 gallons of sweet sap from the sugar maple tree to make one gallon of maple syrup? Maple syrup comes in grades, with Fancy being the lightest in color and the most delicate. As you move from Grade A Medium Amber to Grade B, the syrup's color gets darker and the flavor stronger. Real maple fanciers might want to check out the ***Annual Hebron Maple Festival,*** usually held the second weekend in March. It's a good place to enjoy sugar on snow, a taffy-like candy made by pouring boiling hot maple syrup on clean snow. Visit hebronmaplefest.com.

Andover

Once in ***Andover,*** you will come across the ***Hurst Farm*** (746 East St.; 860-646-6536). If your kids have never seen livestock up close and personal, then we suggest a visit. The farm boasts 45 gardens, hayrides, and a country store. You'll also find lots of standard farm critters, such as cows, goats, and lambs, as well as some of those exotic chickens with the punk-rocker hairdos. Big people will probably find more than enough to interest them at the food shop with James Hurst's own salsas, jams, and dried-herb blends, and lots of "only in Connecticut" food products. In the fall there are pick-your-own pumpkin and dig-your-own chrysanthemum patches. Call ahead for hours and information about special events, such as the hayrides.

Coventry

You can easily miss the turn onto Silver Street from US 44 in ***Coventry.*** But, hard as it is to find, ***Caprilands*** (534 Silver St.; 860-742-7244; caprilands .com) was for many people the crossroads of the world. Visitors would flock from all corners of the earth to the 50-acre herb farm, and the guest book was as likely to contain the names of visitors from distant New Zealand as from nearby Hartford.

Part of the lure of Caprilands was its famous mistress. Adelma Grenier Simmons, the farm's owner and grande dame of American herbalists, was famous for her lectures on herbs and for her herb-spangled lunches, which varied with the season. The eccentric Adelma, who died in 1997 at the age of 94, often dressed in swirling cloaks, odd hats, and exotic jewelry and liked to describe herself as the "Agatha Christie of the herb world." Simmons bequeathed her entire estate to a nonprofit educational institute with the hope that her beloved farm would be used to further research and education of the herbs and plants she so loved. As the transition continues, only the gardens are open to the public, but updates are often posted on Caprilands' Facebook page, so check back for further developments.

Near Caprilands, at the junction of US 44 and Route 31 North, is **Memory Lane Countryside Antique Center** (2224 Boston Turnpike; 860-742-0346; memory-lanes.com). Gail and Gene Dickson's multidealer shop consists of a house, a large barn, and several sheds full of antiques. Two dozen dealers have items on display here, so a wide variety of styles and tastes are represented. The large, airy barn is mostly furniture, organized into a dozen or so separate displays, including some of the better 19th-century oak furniture in the area. The house also contains some quality furniture and a raft of smaller items: jewelry, glassware, tools, and the like. One whole room is given over to some of the best estate, antique, and plain old costume jewelry in the state, most of it very reasonably priced. Don't leave

A Day in the Country

The Bolton watershed area is actually a collection of wilderness areas in the Bolton Notch and Valley Falls area, including Bolton Notch Park, Valley Falls Park, Freja Park, and the Shenipsit Trail. You'll find several marked trails through the woods, perfect for hiking, and streams just right for a little canine swim. Be careful on the trails, however, as the marking isn't quite ready for prime time. Autumn seems to be the best time to see the area in all its glory, but we like late spring walks. Remember, whatever you carry into Connecticut state parks, you must carry out, including trash and garbage. The Bolton watershed area is located off exit 5 from I-384. Take a left at the exit to the commuter parking lot at the junction of Routes 6 and 44, and park in the commuter lot. Enter the watershed area just south of the parking lot. The area is open during daylight hours.

In recent years there's been heated debate around the state over whether dogs should be allowed off their leashes in public parks. This dogfight is far from settled, so if your canine companion comes along, throw a leash in the backseat, just in case. Then, when you get to the park, check the leash policy, which will surely be posted at the park entrance.

without saying "hey" to the kitties who preside over the premises. Open 10 a.m. to 5 p.m. Wed through Sun.

Next door to Memory Lane is **Memories Too Antique Center** (860-742-2865; memory-lanes.com) another antiques cooperative worth a gander. This store is owned by AnnMarie Rizza, but the two shops don't consider themselves competitors, just good neighbors.

Nathan Hale is Connecticut's official state hero, and there are Nutmeggers who feel about him kind of the way Tennesseans feel about Elvis. Hale (Yale class of 1773) was a fervent patriot who left his position as a local schoolmaster to join the rebellion against the British as soon as word arrived of the doings up at Lexington and Concord. He fought with the Continental army through most of 1776. In September of that year, he slipped into New York to gather information on British strength and deployments. After being caught (possibly as a result of being betrayed by a cousin), Hale was hanged by the British for spying. He was just 21. Our history books always reported his last words as "I only regret that I have but one life to lose for my country." However, the recently revealed diaries of British captain Frederick MacKenzie, who witnessed Hale's execution, report young Nathan's final remarks as, "It is the duty of every good officer to obey any orders given him by his commander in chief."

The **Nathan Hale Homestead** (2299 South St.; 860-742-6917) was once Hale's home, which is sufficient to make it some sort of landmark. Hale himself might not recognize the house in which he grew up: It was rebuilt the year he died in the then-fashionable Georgian style. He'd probably recognize the surroundings, though. The house sits in the middle of the 1,219-acre **Nathan Hale State Forest,** a wooded setting not too dissimilar from the surroundings of Hale's boyhood 300-acre farm. Today the farmhouse holds a collection of colonial antiques, including many of the personal possessions used by two generations of Hales. The homestead is the site of an encampment and muster in July, a corn maze the first week in Aug, the annual Nathan Hale Day celebration in Sept, and a regional farmers' market on Sun 11 a.m. to 2 p.m., June through Oct. The homestead is open in May, Sat and Sun noon to 4 p.m.; June through Sept, Wed through Sat noon to 4 p.m., and Sun 11 a.m. to 4 p.m.; Oct, Sat noon to 4 p.m., Sun 11 a.m. to 4 p.m. Admission.

By the way, while the nearby ***Nathan Hale Cemetery*** (Lake Street) in Coventry is a nice enough old graveyard—there's even a very impressive marker for the great man—he isn't buried there. After they hanged him, the British dumped his remains in an unmarked grave that now lies somewhere under 66th Street and 3rd Avenue in Manhattan.

Mansfield & Storrs

Connecticut tourists almost never have the campus of the ***University of Connecticut at Storrs*** on their itinerary, but they should. The UConn campus is home to more than students; it also houses attractions that leave many more heavily promoted facilities in the dust.

The ***Connecticut State Museum of Natural History and Connecticut Archaeology Center*** (2019 Hillside Rd.; 806-486-4460; mnh.uconn .edu) has more than 2 million holdings. Displayed on a rotating basis, the collections provide fascinating insights into Native American cultures, birds of prey, sharks, minerals, even honey bees. Open 10 a.m. to 4 p.m. Mon through Fri. Admission is free; donations accepted.

Movies Under the Stars

Like other states, Connecticut has a proud history as the one-time home of many drive-in movie theaters. There were at least 30 of them during the peak years of the 1950s. But, as has happened in the rest of the country, the drive-ins have gone dark town by town, leaving just two survivors. They're worth the trip.

The **Pleasant Valley Drive-in** (47 River Rd.; 860-379-6102; driveinmovie.com) in Barkhamstead is a vintage site that feels almost like the year it was built: 1947. You will be treated to bonus cartoons and get a chance to feast on hot dogs, fries, and pizza at the concession stand. The movies start at dusk, Apr through Oct (Thurs to Sun during spring and fall).

The state's other perennial is the **Mansfield Drive-in** (228 Stafford Rd.; 860-423-4441) in Mansfield Center. Going strong since 1954, it has 3 screens, all with double features. Open Apr through Oct, weekends only during spring and fall.

Regardless of which drive-in you choose, plan on arriving early. On some nights they're packed.

Great Scoops at UConn

With all the attention showered on UConn's famed basketball program, it's easy to forget that the school is also widely known for its excellent agriculture department. An offshoot of that department's activity is the **UConn Dairy Bar** (3636 Hill Rd. Extension; 860-486-2634; dairybar.uconn.edu), which has been around since the 1930s and has been scooping up fountain treats at the current location since the early 1950s. Every day about 25 flavors of frozen treats are on the menu, with old favorites such as chocolate, vanilla, strawberry, and coffee. Specialty flavors such as Jonathan Supreme (named for the school's mascot), which is peanut butter–swirled vanilla with chocolate-covered peanuts, show up from time to time. According to more than one pistachio ice cream fanatic, the Dairy Bar is one of the few places in Connecticut that still churns up his favorite flavor with real pistachios, instead of green-dyed almonds. Servings are colossal. Be sure to check the website for hours and days of operation.

Also on campus is the ***Ballard Institute and Museum of Puppetry*** (6 Bourn Place; 860-486-4605; bimp.uconn.edu), a collection of more than 2,000 puppets. More than half the puppets were created by Frank Ballard, puppetry wizard and professor emeritus of dramatic arts. Puppets and puppet lore dominate here. Some of the puppets are beautiful and charming; others are dark and disturbing; all are exquisite. Open noon to 5 p.m. Fri through Sun from Mar to Dec. Admission by donation.

Chaplin

A short distance from the busy UConn campus at Storrs, the Natchaug River rumbles through a shallow gorge and pours over a small waterfall into a clear pool at the center of a secluded, sun-dappled clearing. Winding over, under, and around the tumbled boulders on either shore are a handful of gentle walking trails. This is ***Diana's Pool,*** and it is a secret picnic ground used mainly by local fisherfolk and UConn students.

Diana's Pool isn't easy to find, but it's worth the effort. Take US 6 and look for signs directing you to South Chaplin or Sherman Corners. Turn right onto Diana's Pool Road. This is a dead end, but about 100 feet up the road there's an unmarked parking area on the left (look for a NO SWIMMING sign). From there walk about 100 feet down the trail; it branches a couple times, and if you're not sure which branch to follow, walk toward the sound of the water. At the end of the trail you'll find yourself in a sylvan glade so perfect, you'll expect to see dryads and fauns frolicking. If you want to picnic, you'll have to do without picnic tables, but the sun-warmed rocks above the pool are a great place to spread a blanket and watch the play of sunlight and shadow on the water. Diana's Pool is relaxing at almost any time of the year. Cool autumn temperatures kill off the mosquito population and the fall foliage is in full color. Be sure to wear boots or high-top sneakers for walking and rock climbing.

Tolland Area

Willington

Like Union, the town of **Willington,** south of Stafford Springs, is one of those places most travelers pass by unknowingly. Don't, especially if you're hungry. You don't want to miss having a meal at **Willington Pizza House** (25 River Rd.; 860-429-7433; willingtonpizza.com) on Route 32. It's a little slice of heaven, with its small-town setting and decor running to carousel horses. Don't be fooled, though—the pizza selection is definitely big-city sophisticated. There's a broad selection of pies and toppings, including some low-fat pies for people watching their cholesterol. But the reason most people make the pilgrimage to Willington is the delicious Red Potato Pizza. This was the pie that gained nationwide attention on the CBS Morning News. Although pizza pros in New Haven would disown it, the crunchy crust, garlicky roasted potatoes, and sour cream topping make for a rich and different pie that needs to be judged (repeatedly) on its own merits. You're always liable to come across picky pizza-pie mavens who claim that the only way to eat a Red Potato Pizza is with a side dish of iced caviar for topping each yummy slice. We also recommend the Chipotle Chicken Pizza, made with homemade chipotle sauce of tomatoes, red onions, green peppers, and lots of cheese and garlic. Yum. Open daily at 11 a.m. There's now another location, **Willington Pizza Too** (11 Phelps Way; 860-429-9030).

Tolland

The lights are on, but nobody's home at the **Daniel Benton Homestead** (154 Metcalf Rd.; 860-870-9599; tollandhistorical.org/daniel-benton-homestead). A ghostly figure in a military uniform seems to appear at the front door. Foot-steps echo through the east wing and then gradually trail off into silence. Occasionally the whole house shakes without making a sound.

A spokesman for the Tolland Historical Society, which acquired the Benton Homestead in the late 1960s, enigmatically notes that an old house plagued by a flying squirrel "can produce a lot of noise" but refrains from speculating on the subject of the supernatural. The society prefers to concen-trate on the house's unusual architectural details, original paneling, and period furnishings, and the fact that it was the ancestral home of former US senator William Benton and used to house Hessian prisoners during the Revolution.

Area ghost watchers, on the other hand, have an abiding interest in the place and eagerly place the blame for certain strange goings-on at the homestead squarely on the shoulders of one Elisha Benton. In 1777 patriot Benton contracted smallpox while being held in a British prisoner-of-war camp. Sent home to Tolland to die, he was nursed by his 17-year-old sweet-heart, Jemina Barrows. A little more than a month after Benton died in this house, Jemina succumbed to the same disease. Their graves lie 48 feet apart on the west lawn of the homestead.

During the years since this incident, the Benton Homestead is said to have played host to various ghostly activities. A member of the household staff claimed to have seen a weeping apparition in a white dress; a guest once reported having heard inconsolable sobbing at midnight; a common story has a uniformed figure wandering the house with arms outstretched as if pleading. The Benton Homestead is open Sun 1 to 4 p.m., May through Oct. Donation appreciated.

Two other antique buildings in *Tolland* have a less lurid past. In colo-nial times the *Hicks-Stearns Museum* (42 Tolland Green; 860-875-7552) was first a tavern, then a private home. It was later made over in the Victo-rian style, a form that it retains today. The building now houses a collection of Victoriana, including faux bamboo furniture and a collection of children's toys. The museum also sponsors a summer concert series, a Victorian Christ-mas open house, and a Victorian fall evening walking tour. The house is open Sun 1 to 4 p.m., mid-Apr through early Dec, only by appointment. Donation appreciated.

The 1856 *Old Tolland Jail Museum* (860-870-9599) on the green at the junction of Routes 74 and 195 housed prisoners until 1968. Today the intimidating iron-and-stone structure houses the Tolland Historical Society's collection of antique manufactured goods, farm implements, furniture, and Indian artifacts. The museum is open mid-May through mid-Oct, 1 to 4 p.m. Sun or by appointment.

Vernon

As a rule, Nutmeggers understand deli about as well as New Yorkers understand chowder. Which is to say that neither understands the other very much at all. The pleasant exception is ***Rein's Deli-Restaurant*** (435 Hartford Turnpike; 860-875-1344; reinsdeli.com) on Route 30 in ***Vernon.*** This is a large, noisy place, with brisk service and small tables that would be right at home in Gotham. The only reminders that you're still in Connecticut are the signs making witty references to New Yorkish things and places (with the restrooms naturally located in Flushing).

But never mind the decor. What counts is the authentic deli food you wouldn't be surprised to find at Manhattan's famed Carnegie. The half-sour pickles are crisp and briny. The firm, fat chips arrive smoking hot. The turkey, pastrami, and corned beef are eminently respectable; same for the combo sandwiches. And the Reubens rival the ones you get at the Manhattan deli from which that sandwich gets its name. If your taste doesn't run to deli meats and sandwiches, don't worry. The menu here is huge, and everything on it seems to be available all day. No matter when you stop by, you can get anything from blintzes to bagels, to lox and eggs, to a full dinner, to a diet plate. And all of it has that special deli touch. If you've ever

Connecticut Freedom Trail

Still-life artist Charles Ethan Porter lived in Vernon in the 1850s. He owned a home at 17 Spruce St., which is still there and is on the Freedom Trail but is privately owned and not open to the public. He attended art school and traveled abroad before returning to Vernon and becoming an art teacher and civil rights advocate. His work declined in the early 1900s, and Porter passed away in 1923 at the age of 76. He is buried in his family's plot in ***Grove Hill Cemetery*** (22 Cemetery Ave.), not far from where he lived. Follow the main drive of the cemetery, turn right at the fourth paved path, and look for the family plot on the right.

,wondered why New Yorkers rave about deli, here's your chance to find out without traveling to New York. Open daily 7 a.m. to midnight.

Stafford Springs

Continuing north and east, you'll come to **Stafford Springs.** Once upon a time, the springs drew crowds to take their healthful waters. Today the remnants of life in a former Victorian spa–cum–mill town can still be seen in many of the beautiful Queen Anne and gothic revival houses that crowd the town's hilly streets. Stafford Springs is also home to a raceway and a perfectly wonderful little enthusiasts' museum called **Gasoline Alley Automotive Museum** (58 Buckley Hwy.; 860-684-2678) on Route 190.

In the collectors' lexicon, we're not sure what comes after "car nut," but whatever the word is, Don Passardi fits it to a T. He collects everything connected with the car industry, from vintage gasoline pumps and oil cans to restored autos, such as a 1946 Ford Sportsman, one of only 743 manufactured. In danger of being squeezed out of his living quarters by his "collection," Don did what any sensible person in the throes of passionate collecting would do: He built a 4,800-square-foot building next to his house and christened it the Gasoline Alley Automotive Museum. Admission to the museum is by appointment only.

Union

North of Stafford, hard by the Massachusetts line, is Connecticut's smallest town, the diminutive settlement of **Union** (population 620). Most travelers pass it by, but for bibliophiles, it's a standard stop en route to Massachusetts. For here resides one of the state's unique eateries, the **Traveler Restaurant** (1257 Buckley Hwy.; 860-684-4920) on Route 86 (I-84, exit 74). The Traveler is first and foremost a place for good, home-style cooking. Full-tilt-boogie turkey dinners and turkey potpies at very moderate prices are the specialties here, and the Traveler reputedly serves 12 tons of the big bird a year. What we like, though, is one special little twist.

Not only can you order a decent meal here, but customers are invited to pick out 3 books from the shelves lining the walls, read while eating, and then take them home. That's right: Buy a meal, get a book. Children are well treated, and the supply of kids' books is great. The owners estimate they give away 1,000 to 2,000 books . . . a week. Open 7 a.m. to 8 p.m.

Mon through Thurs and Sun; 7 a.m. to 9 p.m. Fri and Sat. The Traveler does breakfast, lunch, and dinner. Breakfast is served until 11 a.m., but omelets and lighter fare are available all day.

Eastford

Buell's Orchard (108 Crystal Pond Rd.; 860-974-1150; buellsorchard.com) in nearby ***Eastford*** is a century-old farm stand par excellence. Starting in June with strawberries, the stand sells fresh produce throughout the growing season. August brings fresh peaches. Apples appear during the fall and can last well into the winter, depending on the size of the apple crop. The stand also sells cider, Vermont cheese, and pumpkins. The caramel apples are made with a special caramel sauce into which are dipped "firm late apples." We guarantee that they are among the best you've ever tasted. The season for caramel apples starts about Labor Day and ends around Halloween.

Gentlemen, Start Your Engines

If the death of car-racing legend Dale Earnhardt in 2001 taught us anything, it's that you don't have to live in the Heartland or south of the Mason-Dixon Line to care a lot about NASCAR racing; it's a hugely popular spectator sport nationwide. Here in Connecticut it also offers a welcome alternative to all the scenic vistas, quaint shops, historic homes, and nautical lore. In addition to Lime Rock, the racetrack that attracts the biggest names both on the track and in the stands, three other cozy, family-friendly NASCAR tracks in Connecticut offer weekly schedules of qualifying rounds, featured races, and special events:

Stafford Motor Speedway
55 West St.
Stafford Springs
(860) 684-2783
Racing every Fri on paved, semi-banked half-mile oval track, Apr through Sept.

Thompson International Speedway
203 E. Thompson Rd.
Thompson
(860) 923-2280
Racing on ⅝-mile banked oval track. Thurs evening, Apr through Oct.

Waterford Speedbowl
1080 Hartford Turnpike
Waterford
(860) 442-1585
Sat evening races.

On Columbus Day weekend, the Buells celebrate the harvest with an open house that includes hayrides and free cider and doughnuts. Open 8 a.m. to 5 p.m. Mon through Sat, 1 to 5 p.m. Sun. Hours are known to change with the season, though, so be sure to check.

Now that you've stocked up on yummy apples, cheese, and other goodies, you need a good place to have a picnic. Why not follow in the footsteps of tons of people and eat with the Frog. Yep, we're talking about another one of those great roadside pieces of rock art, only this one is probably the oldest in Connecticut and isn't exactly on the road anymore. The brainchild of Thomas Thurber, a legislator in the 1880s who used to pass this rock every day, **Frog Rock** was on the side of the original Route 44. The story is that Thurber used to see it and envision a frog, so one day he stopped and painted it the way he saw it. It's been a frog ever since. Because it was along a heavily traveled road, it became a popular place for travelers to stop and picnic. When the new Route 44 was built, it no longer followed the same path and Frog Rock faded into the background. In 1997 a group of Thurber's descendants gave Frog Rock a fresh coat of paint and included a memorial to their ancestor. It's still a great place for a picnic, albeit a little hard to find. It's on the northeast side of Route 44 in Eastford; watch for the shoulder of the road, where you'll see a guardrail and a small gravel pull-off. Frog Rock is about 50 feet down the remains of old Route 44. There are still a few picnic tables in the area.

Old Woodstock

Pomfret

Christ Church (521 Pomfret St.; 860-928-7026; christchurchpomfret.org) on Route 169 in ***Pomfret*** is definitely not the traditional white New England church with pointed steeple. Instead, this is a stone-and-brick building with a certain Byzantine influence. The interior, decorated in what one might call "high Victorian camp," makes an ideal backdrop for 6 extraordinary stained-glass windows, designed by famed Arts and Crafts designer Louis Comfort Tiffany early in his career and installed in the church in 1882.

Tiffany, a native of nearby Killingly, created the windows before moving to New York City, and all but one is an original Tiffany design. It is believed that Tiffany copied the Saint George window from an original

Venetian design. Interestingly, the dedications and inscriptions in all 6 windows are rendered in lead, not in the more common paint, and the glass used is chunkier and more faceted than later Tiffany efforts. The themes here aren't normal to Tiffany, either. Instead of the common Tiffany floral and pastoral compositions, these items feature religious subjects. Besides Saint George, there are two crosses, one with a stylized peacock, of all things. There's also a window depicting the Parable of the Wise and Foolish Virgins and one depicting the Parable of the Talents, with the inscription, "Well done, my good and faithful servant." Finally, there is a rose window depicting Ezekiel and the wheel. Visit about an hour before sunset to get the full effect through the rose window. Ask at the church office for a tour. Make sure you take a good look at the church's interior. It's a haven for gorgeous Arts and Crafts wood carving and tile work.

Route 169 weaves south from Woodstock through Pomfret, Brooklyn, and Canterbury and has been officially dubbed one of the 10 most

I Scream . . .

You didn't think they keep all those cows just for pretty, did you? The Quiet Corner is home to some of the most sinful homemade ice cream in the state. Besides UConn's Dairy Bar, here are some more super scoopers to check out.

D. Fish Family Dairy Farm (20 Dimock Ln.; 860-646-9745; fishfamilyfarm.com) is off Route 85 in Bolton. Here's your chance to show the kids each step in the ice cream–making process, starting with petting the calves. Well, okay, that's not really an official step, but how can you not pet a calf? Milking occurs twice each day (6 to 8 a.m. and 4 to 6 p.m.). Bottling is more or less constant. Ice cream–making happens Mon. All of these activities are open for viewing. Of course, the big treat is sampling the ice cream. The dairy store at the farm sells milk; very rich, very creamy ice cream; fresh organic produce; and locally made jams and jellies. Pony rides and other special events are offered from time to time. The dairy store is open 8 a.m. to 6 p.m. Mon through Sat. Ice cream is scooped noon to 6 p.m.

We-Lik-It (728 Hampton Rd.; 860-974-1095; welikit.com) on Route 97 in Pomfret's village of Abington is nestled in a 19th-century cider mill, complete with farm critters and the occasional movie star. Paul Newman, whose Hole in the Wall Camp for terminally ill children is just down the road, used to be spotted indulging in We-Lik-It's ultra-rich frozen confections. Open Apr through Oct, 11 a.m. to 8 p.m. Mon through Thurs; 11 a.m. to 9 p.m. Fri through Sun.

outstanding scenic byways in the US. This section of the book wouldn't be complete without making adequate reference to Pomfret's favorite hangout, the **Vanilla Bean Cafe** (450 Deerfield Rd.; 860-928-1562; thevanillabean cafe.com). Housed in a renovated 19th-century barn, this is one irresistible place for lunch, dinner, or a midafternoon cup of cocoa. The soups here are fabulous—nothing fancy, just deliciously prepared simple blends. The tomato Florentine paired with a salad is ideal for summertime weather. When winter comes, go for a warmer-upper, such as cheese-topped chili with beef or a vegetarian alternative. Their sea-bass cakes will erase memories of school-cafeteria fish cakes. The turkey sandwiches taste like the best of part of Thanksgiving dinner: day-after leftovers. They also offer a host of gluten-free options. The Vanilla Bean is run by Barry and Brian Jessurun, and chances are, you'll run into them when you visit. Unless you wind up being too full for dessert, the homemade ice cream really hits the spot after a chili lunch. In the evenings patrons are often treated to entertaining poetry readings, folk concerts, and poetry slams. (The UConn campus at Storrs is close by, so creative talents abound.) Open from 7 a.m. to 3 p.m. Mon and Tues, until 8 p.m. Wed and Thurs, until 9 p.m. Fri, 8 a.m. to 9 p.m. Sat, and 8 a.m. to 8 p.m. Sun.

Called by *Travel + Leisure* magazine "a Caprilands for the '90s," **Martha's Herbary** (589 Pomfret St.; 860-928-0009; marthasherbary.com) on Route 169 at the junction of US 44 and Route 97 is a sweet-smelling treasure

Won't Fade Away

The *Bara-Heck Settlement* at the junction of US 44 and Route 97 in Pomfret is another of those abandoned villages that just won't go away. Founded by two Welsh families in 1780 and abandoned in 1890, stories persist that somewhere in time, the town still lives.

Visitors to this abandoned spot have reported hearing the sweet silver laughter of children, as well as cows mooing, dogs barking, mothers calling children in from play, and wagon wheels creaking along unpaved tracks. The sounds reportedly appear most prevalent near the town's old cemetery and some of the cellar holes. Some visitors have also reported seeing the ghosts of a bearded man and a small child. The property is now privately owned and not open to the public.

snuggled in the carriage house and servants' quarters of an 18th-century house. The gift shop is packed to the rafters with potpourri, soaps, essential oils, cooking herbs, and lotions. Cooking demonstrations and classes take place in the kitchen in the back. Outside, the gardens overflow with perennials, heirloom vegetables (vegetables grown from old strains of the plant, many dating back to colonial times), edible flowers, fish ponds, a sunken garden, and row upon row of herbs. Classes are offered throughout the year on a variety of topics, but reservations are required. The shop is open Tues through Sat 10 a.m. to 5 p.m., Sun noon to 5 p.m.

The *Brayton Grist Mill & Marcy Blacksmith Shop Museum* (147 Wolf Den Dr.) on US 44, at the entrance to Mashamoquet Brook State Park, showcases two establishments that in 1857 made an agreement to jointly support a dam and flume on Mashamoquet Brook.

The four-story Brayton Grist Mill is a reminder of long-ago days when every town on a river or creek had a water-powered mill to shell corn and grind grain. The gristmill on Mashamoquet Brook was operated by William Brayton from 1890 until his death in 1928. The equipment on display includes the turbine, the millstone, and a corn sheller patented in 1888.

woodstock&
pomfrettrivia

During the mid- to late 19th century, Woodstock and Pomfret were dubbed "inland Newports" due to their popularity with the rich and ostentatious, who trained up from New York or down from Boston to build lavish summer "cottages" in the Quiet Corner.

The Marcy Blacksmiths also plied their trade in a shop along Mashamoquet Brook; in fact, the area became known as Marcy Hollow. In 1830 Orin Marcy of Pomfret opened the shop, which used a water-powered bellows and trip-hammer. The next two generations of Marcys prospered, perfecting their craft. Darius, Orin's son, won first prize for his horseshoes at the Chicago World's Fair in 1893. A number of antique tools are displayed at the blacksmith shop; some are farrier's tools, and others are wheelwright's tools. Several tools are specially made and stamped "O. Marcy." The museum doesn't have a telephone, but it is open 2 to 5 p.m. weekends, May through Sept. Admission is free.

Ashford

Continuing west along US 44, you'll wind up in the quaint community of **Ashford,** home to a wonderfully thrifty, only-in-New England version of recycling: a library in the old town dump! It's a metaphor for the regional motto, "Use it up. Wear it out. Make it do or do without." Which makes this "library" at the **Ashford Transfer Station** such a practical idea. It happened this way: A few years back, folks began remarking that a lot of perfectly good books were being sent to the dump, so the people down at the town's **Babcock Public Library** put their heads together to come up with a way to get some more mileage from these castoffs. What they came up with was an "annex" of the library at a central location—the, er, dump—where people could drop off or pick up used books free of charge.

So the Ashford Transfer Station, where residents take their recyclables and trash, gained a plywood shed with simple plank shelving. Now, when residents drop off their recyclables, more often than not they stop by the "annex" to browse the shelves and pick up a couple novels. The arrangements are simple. Books are divided into broad categories such as "mysteries," "westerns," or "romance," with titles running the gamut from those of Stephen King and Tom Clancy to books of philosophy and children's books; drop off what you've read and take as many other books as you want. People from outside of Ashford—such as you—are welcome to use the library, but trash services are for Ashford residents only. The transfer station "library" (232 Upton Rd.; 860-429-3409) is open 2 to 8 p.m. Wed, 8 a.m. to 4 p.m. Sat, and 10 a.m. to 4 p.m. Sun.

Woodstock

Merchant and publisher Henry Chandler Bowen had two great obsessions: roses and the Fourth of July. He indulged both at his summer residence in the center of **Woodstock,** in the northeastern corner of Connecticut. There, in 1846, he built himself a board-and-batten-sided, gingerbread-encrusted gothic revival palace. Outside he planted a rose garden, and inside he upholstered much of the furniture in pink. The house itself he painted a fashionably subdued light lavender, but it was later repainted pink with green shutters and dark green and red trim, reminiscent of the flowers that Bowen loved. He named this classic Victorian "painted lady" **Roseland**

Cottage (556 Rte. 169; 860-928-4074; historicnewengland.org) but today most folks in Woodstock just call it "the pink house."

It was at Roseland, during the latter half of the 19th century, that Bowen held the most extravagant series of Fourth of July celebrations that America had ever seen. On the day before each celebration, prominent guests from all over the country would arrive by train in neighboring Putnam, whence they would be transported by carriage to Woodstock for an evening reception that featured (what else?) pink lemonade. The next day a huge American flag would be displayed on one side of the house. The guests would then parade down Route 169 to Roseland Park, where they would amuse the public and each other with exchanges of high-flying rhetoric until it was time to return to Roseland for further diversions of a nonalcoholic nature.(Bowen was a temperance man.) What makes all of this so remarkable is that no fewer than four US presidents—Benjamin Harrison, Ulysses S. Grant, Rutherford B. Hayes, and William McKinley—participated in these shenanigans; two

gloriousfalldrive

In the Quiet Corner, there's no prettier fall drive than Route 169 North. Start at the intersection of Rocky Holly Road in Lisbon and head off to Woodstock and points north.

No Clothes, No Kidding

Solair Recreation League (65 Ide Perrin Rd., Woodstock; 860-928-9174; solairrl .com) is what our mothers in their most shocked voices used to call a "nudist camp."

It's been around since the '30s and offers 300 acres of wooded solitude. Amenities include a lake, rental cabins, pool, tennis and volleyball courts, and a social hall.

Visitors are welcome provided you make reservations in advance. If you're interested in learning more, the office welcomes visitors daily but suggests you come in on a weekend between 10 a.m. and 2 p.m. to meet with a staff member who can show you around. You'll find the Solair Recreation League off English Neighborhood Road in Woodstock. Before dropping in, call for directions, hours, more information, and reservations. Open from mid-Apr through early Nov.

of them—Harrison and Grant—while in office, the others while they were congressmen.

Today Roseland Cottage and its grounds and outbuildings are maintained by Historic New England and are open to the public. Everything is much as it was in the glory days. The rose garden is still there, along with an 1850s maze of boxwood hedges, and so is most of the original gothic revival furniture. The famous flag is displayed in its traditional location each Fourth of July. Even the bowling alley out in the barn, thought to be the oldest such facility in a private residence in America, is still as it was. One can almost imagine Ulysses Grant—who seems to have coped well at Roseland despite the fact that he was most definitely not a temperance man—bowling his famous strike there during his July 4 visit.

Roseland Cottage is open 11 a.m. to 5 p.m. (last tour at 4 p.m.) Wed through Sun, June through mid-Oct. Admission.

The **Christmas Barn** (832 Rte. 169; 860-928-7652; thechristmasbarnon line.com) is more than just a red barn full of Christmas paraphernalia. The year-round display of Christmas decorations upstairs is balanced by displays of country furniture, crafts, lace curtains, curios, collectibles, quilts, craft supplies, and Victoriana suitable for all seasons. Besides, owners Joe and Kris Reynolds are that rare breed of people who seem able to keep the Christmas spirit alive all year. Open June through Dec, 10 a.m. to 5 p.m. Tues through Sat, noon to 5 p.m. Sun.

When you venture off the beaten path in Connecticut, one of the first things you'll notice is the labyrinth of stone walls that snake across the landscape. Some were built with the precision of Egyptian pyramids; others look like day-care projects. Whatever the level of construction skill, the origin of these natural building blocks is yet another reminder of the limitless power of Mother Nature. Glaciers that inched their way across the region close to 20,000 years ago scraped the earth as they went, carrying tons of rocks and boulders with them. Farmers had to remove this debris so they could till the soil and plant their crops. The mortarless stone walls you see throughout the area were originally built to make use of the rocks that had been liberally deposited everywhere and to mark field boundaries. Today they serve as elegant property accents, adorning many of the state's most opulent homesteads. These days craftsmen who have mastered the ancient art of stonewall construction are well compensated.

Putnam

Woodbury may boast Connecticut's "Antique Avenue," but in **Putnam** you've got a whole Windham County town full of antiques shops. Okay, some carry merchandise that's somewhere just above "tag-sale stuff" on the antiques food chain, but most are chockablock with high-quality, well-maintained furnishings, collectibles, and jewelry.

When its main industries quite literally went south, the community and its citizens could have held a pity party and thrown in the towel. Instead, they transformed Putnam into one of the hottest antiques shopping districts in New England. Now more than 400 dealers do business here; most are scattered throughout the Main Street area in a former mill, the old courthouse, and an 1880s Victorian department store.

OTHER ATTRACTIONS WORTH SEEING IN THE QUIET CORNER

Connecticut Audubon Society Center
218 Day Rd.
Pomfret
(860) 928-4948
ctaudubon.org

Eastern Connecticut Flea Market
Mansfield Drive-in
228 Stafford Rd. (junction of Routes 31 and 32)
Mansfield
(860) 456-2578
Eastern Connecticut's largest weekly outdoor flea market.

Goodwin Conservation Center
Goodwin State Forest
23 Potter Rd. (Route 6)
Hampton
(860) 455-9534

Special Joys Antique Doll and Toy Shop
41 N. River Rd.
Coventry
(860) 742-6359
Also a cozy bed-and-breakfast.

Theatre of Northeastern Connecticut at the Bradley Playhouse
30 Front St.
Putnam
(860) 928-7887

Wright's Mill Farm
63 Creasey Rd. (Route 6)
Canterbury
(860) 774-1455
wrightsmillfarm.com
Sports facilities, hiking trails, ponds, 5 antique water-powered mill sites; horse, carriage, and wagon rides; hayrides.

The anchor attraction is the four-story ***Antiques Marketplace*** (109 Main St.; 860-928-0442; antiquesmarketplace.com) in what used to be the C. D. Bugbee Department Store. Jerry Cohen, a transplanted Californian, accomplished the changeover. Head up to the second floor's Mission Oak Shop, stocked with authentic Gustav Stickley furniture, reproduced circa-1910 Van Erp lamps, and Arts and Crafts–style pottery from Woodstock, New York. The place isn't just for big stuff, though. There's lots of good collectible jewelry, china, and glassware, plus vintage Christmas ornaments. The entire antiques district is open from 10 a.m. to 5 p.m. daily.

Arts and Framing (112 Main St.; 860-963-0105; artsandframingputnam .com) is the place to visit for antique mirrors and frames, custom hand-gilding, and glass as well as some antique furniture and accessories.

Jeremiah's (26 Front St.; 860-928-6978) is a large, multidealer shop, with an ever-changing display of estate jewelry, china, and glass, in addition to Victorian and country-primitive furniture.

If all that walking has left you a tad peckish, central Putnam offers a modest selection of handy eateries for lunch and light noshing. A recommendable luncheon choice, with homemade soups and a selection of artful sandwiches, is the ***Courthouse Bar & Grille*** (121 Main St.; 860-963-0074; courthousebarandgrille.com). Open Sun through Wed 11:30 a.m. to 9:30 p.m.; Thurs 11:30 a.m. to 10 p.m.; Fri and Sat 11:30 a.m. to 11 p.m.

If you tend more toward a snack, try ***Mrs. Bridges Pantry*** (292 Rte. 169; 860-963-7040; mrsbridgespantry.com), featuring food, teas, and British gifts. You'll also find such "Brit stuff" as tea cozies, lemon curd, and imported cards. One of the owners is a cat fancier, so cute kitties abound. You can order a mini-luncheon consisting of scones, a "cuppa," or a complete teatime meal with sandwiches and desserts. Their low-fat ginger scones and ginger-peach iced tea make for a refreshing pick-me-up after a long afternoon of serious antiquing. The tearoom is open 10 a.m. to 6 p.m. daily except Tues.

Windham Area

Killingly

You know you've found ***Zip's Dining Car*** (Route 101; 860-774-6335; zipsdiner.com) when you see the neon sign that towers over the building advertising with commendable brevity: EAT. Located at the junction of Routes 101 and 12 (exit 93 off I-395) in the Dayville section of **Killingly,** Zip's is an original O'Mahoney diner, built in 1954.

The diner is actually a New England invention. Its progenitor, the lunch wagon, was invented by Walter Scott in 1872 in Providence, Rhode Island. More improvements followed, and in 1906 the Worcester Lunch Car Company was born. It soon was the primary popularizer of the Art Deco, neon-crowned, nickel-alloy (later stainless-steel) structure that we now associate with the American diner.

Zip's is one of the last of the original stainless-steel diners still in operation and is especially notable for its pristine condition. The quilted and beveled stainless steel and the blue-accented chrome just gleam. This is a family-run restaurant that has been in the same family for three generations.

Zip's menu is diner classic, featuring freshly prepared food, most of it made from scratch. The roast turkey with all the trimmings and the Yankee pot roast are both big dinner favorites. For lunch hoist a huge Zip burger (an especially good cheeseburger on a bulky roll) or a turkey club (made with freshly roasted turkey); these examples of the sandwich-making art are as well executed as you will find anywhere. But what Zip's is really famous for are its desserts, especially its homemade puddings and custards and the strawberry shortcake made with a flaky biscuit—all topped with real whipped cream, beaten with a wire whisk. It takes something special to stand out in this crowd, but the one dish that manages to do so is the Grape-Nuts pudding, a house specialty. Open daily 6 a.m. to 9 p.m.

Head south from Zip's on Route 12 and you'll hit **Logee's Green-house** (141 North St.; 860-774-8038; logees.com). With the revival of all things Victorian, violets have never been more popular, and the best place to see and buy violets is Logee's. The business has been a family operation since 1893, so when it comes to plants, they speak gospel truth. The 8 greenhouses have the feel of Victorian conservatories with their displays of orchids, jasmine, ferns, and a dazzling variety of begonias. Logee's publishes a mail-order catalog that's available at a small charge. Logee's is open daily 10 a.m. to 5 p.m., with longer hours (to 6 p.m.) Apr through Memorial Day and shorter hours (to 4:30 p.m.) Nov through Feb.

Plainfield

If you're into fishing, consider putting **Plainfield** on your itinerary. The modern **Quinebaug Valley Trout Hatchery** (Trout Hatchery Road; 860-564-7542) in the township's Central Village is one of the largest hatcheries in the East, producing 280,000 pounds of trout annually. The operation is open to the public year-round, and visitors can view the hatchery through a big glass wall. The state allows restricted fishing in the nearby waters weekends from Mar through Memorial Day.

Keep driving west from the Plainfield area on Route 14A until you're almost in Rhode Island. There, in the hamlet of **Oneco** (where Route 14A is known as Pond Road), you'll find something called **River Bend Campground** (41 Pond St.; 860-564-3440; riverbendcamp.com), which offers the Lucky Strike Mine and Gemstone Panning Sluice. While you won't exactly find the treasure of the Sierra Madres here, children can don miners' hats and delve into an aboveground man-made mine in search of gemstones, fossils, or shells, or try their luck panning the sluice. Open 9 a.m. to 5 p.m. daily, early Apr through mid-Oct. Admission.

quietcorner**trivia**

The tiny settlement of **Sterling** near Plainfield in the Quiet Corner is named for a doctor who reneged on his promise to build the village a library if they named the town after him. Guess it was too much trouble to change the town's name yet again to Piker.

Is **Moosup** (pronounced MOOSE-up) Connecticut's most patriotic town? Come visit this village in the town of Plainfield on the Sunday closest to August 14 (V-J Day, the day Japan surrendered) and find out. It always warms our hearts to see our veterans honored. The whole town turns out for its "Victory over Japan" parade—sadly, the last of its kind in the country. You'll see flags, brightly costumed marching bands, and baton twirlers, but the day really is for the vets. You'll probably have to brush away a tear or two as you watch these brave men, some wearing chestfuls of beribboned medals, walking in the parade or lining the sidewalks. The marchers parade from N. Main Street to Prospect Street. The parade starts at 1:01 p.m. (the time Japan surrendered) and lasts until around 3:30 p.m. The parade is free; come early and bring your own lawn chairs. Call (860) 564-8005.

Canterbury

In 1832, at the request of the community, Prudence Crandall opened an academy on the Canterbury Green to educate the daughters of local wealthy families. The school flourished until the following fall, when Crandall admitted Sarah Harris, a 20-year-old African-American woman. Outraged parents withdrew their daughters, forcing the school to close. But Crandall reopened it as a school for the education of "young ladies and little misses of color." The state responded by passing the "Black Law," which made it illegal for Crandall to run her school. Crandall was arrested and spent one night in jail. She was taken to court, but the case was dismissed for lack of evidence. Despite her legal victory, the school closed after it was attacked by a mob. Although Crandall's school was open for less than two years, it stands as a powerful symbol in the fight for racial equality and civil justice.

The 1805 building in *Canterbury* where Miss Crandall's academy was housed is preserved as the *Prudence Crandall House Museum* (1 S. Canterbury Rd.; 860-546-7800), a site for both permanent and changing exhibits on the history of black Americans in pre–Civil War Connecticut. There are also exhibits dealing with the life of Prudence Crandall and the development of Canterbury. The museum has a gift shop and a research library. Open May to Nov, 10 a.m. to 4 p.m. Wed through Sun.

Brooklyn

Mention the *Golden Lamb Buttery* (499 Wolf Den Rd.; 860-774-4423; the goldenlamb.com) in a roomful of Connecticut foodies, and chances are that the initial reverent silence will shortly be followed by exclamations of "Isn't it just the best?" This woodsy eatery off Route 169 may just be the most romantic restaurant in the state.

Original owners Virginia "Jimmie" and Bob Booth (cook and host, respectively) certainly knew how to set a scene, and now granddaughter Katie carries on the tradition. During the warmer months, cocktails are served on the veranda of the antique- and treasure-filled barn. During northeastern Connecticut's chilly weather, dinner is served next to a roaring fireplace. This place is truly a Connecticut gem. Be sure to make time to stroll the grounds and explore the rich history that abounds at this family-owned barn.

Dinner starts with soup, always seasoned with fresh herbs from the garden and always a knockout. There's usually a choice of several entrees. Duck is a perennial, but lamb and beef are common, and there's almost always some kind of fish or seafood. Veggies, lots of them, are served family-style with the meal; marinated mushrooms always seem to be on the menu, and other vegetables ebb and flow with the output from the farm's garden. Everything is fresh, and it's all cooked without salt or preservatives. The desserts here are endearingly homey, especially the cakes.

Dinner is prix fixe and is served at 7 p.m. Fri and Sat; there's one seating only, and you must have a reservation. Tues through Sat the restaurant also serves lunch from noon to 2:30 p.m. (without the stage dressing, but still

ANNUAL EVENTS IN THE QUIET CORNER

AUGUST

Brooklyn Fair
Route 169 and Fairgrounds Road
(860) 774-7568 or (860) 779-0012
The oldest continuously active agricultural fair in the US. A real old-fashioned fair with oxen and horse pulls, home-and-garden exhibits, livestock displays, entertainment, and carnival attractions.

SEPTEMBER

Hebron Harvest Fair
Hebron Lion's Fairgrounds
347 Gilead St. (Route 85)
(860) 228-0892
hebronharvestfair.org
Large agricultural fair with livestock shows, midway, entertainment, and crafts.

Woodstock Fair
Routes 169 and 171
(860) 928-3246
woodstockfair.com
Connecticut's second-oldest agricultural fair complete with livestock shows, food-and-garden contests, midway, entertainment, and petting zoo. Labor Day weekend.

OCTOBER

Walking Weekend
Northeast Quiet Corner
(860) 774-3300
Historic, cultural, natural history, and scenic guided walks through 25 towns in Connecticut's northeast corner.

NOVEMBER

Connecticut Children's Book Fair
University of Connecticut
bookfair.uconn.edu
Book talks with authors and characters.

quite wonderful). Dinner seatings are booked months in advance; lunch is easier to get into. The restaurant is closed Jan through Apr.

Creamery Brook Road in bucolic Brooklyn is bordered by the usual Quiet Corner collection of quaint stone walls and verdant pastures. That's as expected. What's completely unexpected is the herd of shaggy bison. After all, Connecticut isn't exactly known for being where the buffalo roam— except that they do now. Austin and Deborah Tanner started out buying one bison for their dairy farm and ended up with a small, shaggy herd of American bison on their ***Creamery Brook Bison Farm*** (19 Purvis Rd.; 860-779-0837; creamerybrookbison.net).

The Tanners offer a 40-minute tour of their working farm, including a visit and petting session with their enormous but gentle bison. Farm tours also include trying your hand at churning butter or ice cream. The Tanners and their employees will happily teach you about the healthful qualities of lean, red bison meat, and you can purchase various cuts of bison meat and souvenirs at the farm store. The Tanners suggest bison burgers are a good way to start. Tours are held July through Sept at 1:30 p.m. Sat. Also, visitors can partake of buffalo burgers on the grill and take wagon rides. Admission.

The ***Brooklyn Town Hall*** (4 Wolf Den Rd.) was built in 1820 as the Windham County Courthouse. It was here in 1833 that Prudence Crandall was tried for violating the "Black Law" by running a school for African-American students in nearby Canterbury. Taking a stand against discrimination, Crandall pleaded not guilty and refused to post bail. She defiantly spent a night in a cell in the basement of the courthouse, but she wasn't alone. Mary Benson, daughter of prominent abolitionist George Benson, volunteered to stay with her. The next day, George Benson and Rev. Samuel May paid the bond for her release. Benson and May were staunch supporters of Crandall. In fact, when Crandall first envisioned opening the school, Reverend May spoke for her at a Canterbury town meeting since at that time it was not considered appropriate for women to do so. Benson allowed her to remain at his house during her two-day trial.

You can still see the ***Benson family home*** (60 Pomfret Rd.), where Reverend May officiated the 1834 wedding between George Benson's daughter Helen and William Lloyd Garrison, the publisher of *The Liberator* of Boston. You can also see the ***Unitarian Meeting House*** (7 Hartford Rd.), the first church of its denomination in the state, where May served as the first pastor starting in 1822. *May's home* (73 Pomfret Rd.) still stands as well. All these places are on the Freedom Trail. While you can visit the town hall and meetinghouse, please respect the privacy of the owners of the Pomfret Road homes, which are not open to the public.

Windham & Willimantic

Willimantic ("Willi" to locals), a village in Windham, is home to the largest thread mill in America and is sometimes called the "Thread City." So where else would you locate a museum dedicated to the history of the textile industry? The *Windham Textile and History Museum* (411 Main St.; 860-456-2178; millmuseum.org) occupies two 1877 buildings inside the mill complex of the old Willimantic Linen Company on Main Street. Dugan Mill is a two-story brick building housing a factory setting re-creating conditions of a century ago. There's a fully equipped shop floor with a spinning frame, carding machine, loom, and 1880s cast-iron proof printer. Overlooking the shop is an 1890-vintage overseer's office.

The museum's three-story main building houses a re-creation of the company store that once occupied the site; it's now set up as a gift shop. The museum also offers re-creations of a 19th-century mill owner's mansion

Independence Day, Willi-Style

On July 4, Willimantic, like most towns in New England, celebrates Independence Day with a patriotic parade. Nothing very off-the-beaten-path about that, except Willimantic's parade is a *Boombox Parade.* That's right, thousands of marchers all bopping along, boom boxes held high, all tuned into the town's radio station, WILI-AM. The radio station obliges by playing stirring patriotic marches and music. Anyone can join in as long you obey a few simple rules: wear red, white, and blue; tune your box to WILI; and be prepared to have a heck of a good time and not take anything too seriously. Aside from those few simple rules, your costume is limited only by your imagination (and good taste). Marchers costumed as George and Martha Washington, rocket ships, snowmen, and frogs (Windham is nearby) are regular participants. No preregistration is necessary. Participants usually assemble in downtown Willimantic, and the area is well marked with signs. The Willimantic Recreation Department can usually answer questions about this year's parade. Call (860) 465-3046.

and a mill worker's home. The Dunham Hall Library, on the third floor, contains a one-of-a-kind collection of books, photographs, and manuscripts, including a collection of old textile industry pattern books. Open Fri, Sat, and Sun 10 a.m. to 4 p.m. Guided tours Sun at 2 p.m., self-guided at other times. Admission. The museum sponsors special events throughout the year.

The sleepy village of **Windham** isn't well known these days. Two centuries back, however, the **Windham Frog Pond** was famous throughout England and her colonies. During the long hot summer of 1754, war and drought endangered Windham. As that summer drew to a close, ponds and streams across Connecticut were almost dry, a catastrophe for an agricultural community. That year, though, Windhamites had other worries. With the French and Indian War in full swing, they could expect especially ferocious Indian raids at the end of summer. One hot night, worried residents heard an uproar coming from a marshy pond outside the village. It sounded, they thought, like the chanting of hundreds of Indians working themselves up to an attack. Some even thought they heard someone utter the words "Colonel Dyer and Elderkin, too." Dyer and Elderkin were the community's leaders.

All night long the sound continued as the town marshaled its defenses. In the last hour before dawn, the noise rose to a crescendo before dying out at first light. Their nerves drawn taut as bowstrings, the desperate colonists prepared to fend off the expected attack. But it never came. After a while, a scouting party crept through a swamp to the pond from whence the startling noises had come. There, they found not the expected French and Indians, but thousands of dying bullfrogs choking in the shallow waters of the pond. No one could explain what had happened, but it was a wonder and no mistake. Some speculated that the nightlong noises were the sounds of the frogs fighting for territory in the restricted waters, but it was only speculation.

The Frog War story eventually became well known in Europe, so much so that it was made into a popular operetta that brought notoriety, if not fame, to the small town of Windham. In honor of the frogs, the town renamed the site Frog Pond. Windham Frog Pond can be seen today about a mile east of Windham Center on the Scotland Road (Route 14); the pond is on your left as you cross Indian Hollow Brook.

A few years ago, Windham announced that it was adopting a new town seal. The winning entry featured—you guessed it—a frog.

To that end, the town has another frog attraction: ***Frog Bridge*** just outside of downtown Willimantic. Completed in 2000, this bridge cost the city $13 million. On this bridge are four 11-foot frogs atop spools of thread. The bridge crosses the Willimantic River and connects Routes 66 and 32.

When Frog Bridge was constructed, it replaced the original bridge downstream, which still stood but was deemed inadequate for the increasing traffic in the area. So what to do with the old bridge? The Garden Club of Windham decided to create a Garden on the Bridge and secured funds to do so. Today the town and the club work together to maintain the old bridge and new gardens where you'll find beautiful colored pavers, stone planters filled with flowers, and many perennial shrubs and flowers. You can visit the club's website (gardenclubofwindham.org) and print out a brochure about the bridge.

Located in a former 1909 post office building, ***Willimantic Brew Pub*** (967 Main St.; 860-423-6777; willibrew.com) is just a cool place to visit. The pub is located in what used to be the customer lobby, the postmaster's office is now a private dining room, and their 7-barrel brewery can be seen from the former-work-room-turned-dining-room. Their 100-plus item menu is even post office themed, and the food is delicious. They brew a variety of hand-crafted beers every month and keep more on tap from all over New England. They host fun events throughout the year, including theme parties, beer tastings, and movie nights. There's just no reason not to visit. Open Tues through Thurs and Sun 11:30 a.m. to 1 a.m., Fri and Sat 11:30 a.m. to 2 a.m., Mon 4 p.m. to 1 a.m.

Places to Stay in the Quiet Corner

COVENTRY

Daniel Rust House B&B
2011 Main St.
(860) 742-0032
thedanielrusthouse.com
Moderate to expensive
Located in a lovingly restored pre-Revolutionary homestead on 2 acres of land.

POMFRET

Feather Hill Bed & Breakfast
151 Mashomoquet Rd.
(866) 963-0522
featherhillbedandbreakfast.com
Moderate
Country inn located in the Quinebaug and Shetucket River valley.

WOODSTOCK

Elias Child House Bed & Breakfast
50 Perrin Rd.
(860) 974-9836
eliaschildhouse.com
Moderate
A quaint B&B situated on 47 acres; all guest rooms have private baths

Inn at Woodstock Hill
94 Plaine Hill Rd.
(860) 928-0528
woodstockhill.com
Moderate to expensive
Twenty-one guest rooms, 8 with working gas fireplaces. Fine dinners.

Places to Eat in the Quiet Corner

PUTNAM

Bella's Bistro
83 Main St.
(860) 928-7343
bellasbistromarket.com
Moderate to expensive
New American and Italian cuisine; gluten-free, vegetarian, and vegan dishes available.

85 Main
85 Main St.
(860) 928-1660
85main.com
Moderate to expensive
New American fusion cuisine, including a full sushi menu.

Stomping Ground
132 Main St.
(860) 928-7900
the-stomping-ground.com
Moderate
Pub grub and live music; craft beer.

STORRS

Yukon Jack's Hilltop Grill
497 Middle Turnpike (Route 44)
(860) 455-4626
yukonjacksgrill.com
Moderate
Great family dining near UConn at Storrs; steak, subs, pizza.

WILLIMANTIC

Nita's
28 North St.
(860) 423-0062
Inexpensive
Best breakfast in town! Wonderful Polish food.

Index

About the Author

Cindi D. Pietrzyk is a freelance writer and editor based in Connecticut, where she has lived since she was four years old. She is the author of several books, including Globe Pequot's *Short Nature Walks in Connecticut* and *Boston's Freedom Trail.* She and her family enjoy exploring the back roads and small towns of their state as well as the cities with all the culture they offer. Check out *Connecticut Off the Beaten Path* on Facebook and be sure to let her know about the hidden treasures you have found.